Outpacing the Competition

Patent-Based Business Strategy

Outpacing the Competition

Patent-Based Business Strategy

Robert L. Cantrell
Landon IP, Inc.

WILEY

John Wiley & Sons, Inc.

Library of Congress Cataloging-in-Publication Data:

Cantrell, Robert L.
   Outpacing the competition: patent-based business strategy/Robert Cantrell.
      p.   cm.
   Includes bibliographical references and index.
   ISBN 978-0-470-39085-6 (cloth)
  1.   Strategic planning. 2. Patent practice. 3. Competition.
  I. Title.
  HD30.28.C362 2009
  658.4'012–dc22

                             2008045555

Printed in the United States of America
10 9 8 7 6 5 4 3 2 1

Contents

Foreword

This latest book from Robert Cantrell and Landon IP is an attempt to further the understanding of the strategic use and nonuse of patents to achieve a larger business purpose. Having edited our previous book from Landon IP, I know how hard it can be to say something meaningful and to say it succinctly. The treatise *Outpacing the Competition: Patent-Based Business Strategy* is no exception.

Robert Cantrell, who leads our patent consulting operation, has worked hard throughout his career to raise the awareness of the business value of patents while providing tools and heuristics for assessing your IP strategies and that of your competitors. He has often worked at the edge of the industry where few people understand or appreciate what is seemingly esoteric. Fortunately, he has transformed and related many of these concepts over time, and applied them in our consulting practice. He has made "the difficult" more mundane and useful to organizations and individuals worldwide.

As context for the book, Landon IP is the largest patent search and IP analytics company in the United States. As of 2009, the company employs 185 full-time professionals across a wide range of technological disciplines. A large and growing amount of our revenues is the result of analyzing patent and technological information for businesses and law firms, and providing them with strategic options. We research patent portfolios in both emerging and developed technologies, and we help companies predict the behavior of their competitors with respect to their intellectual property. The company also teaches scientists, engineers, and business managers how to conduct patent analysis, maximize the value of their intellectual property holdings, and understand where future technological and business opportunities may exist.

To this extent, Robert Cantrell is a unique figure in the intellectual property field. He is one of the few practitioners who are relentlessly focused on improving the tools and techniques for making good intellectual property decisions. This is no easy task, as few individuals in the business world truly understand the strategic value of patents or patenting. Still fewer individuals have tools at their disposal to put this endeavor into successful practice.

It is our sincere hope that you will benefit from this treatise on patent strategy for business purposes. We expect that this book will generate significant thought and research, along with increased understanding and proliferation of patent-based business strategies. Robert and I would love to hear from you as you read or apply the principles and approaches espoused in the book.

Thank you for taking an interest in this important work.

David Hunt, CEO
Landon IP, Inc.
Alexandria, Virginia USA
January 1, 2009

Preface

T his book, *Outpacing the Competition*, is about business strategy. I have written it, however, from the perspective of one component of business strategy: patent strategy. Patents are one of the primary tools that research and development-based companies use to establish and maintain their brands in the marketplace. Patents provide a window of opportunity for companies to enforce the exclusivity of their inventions before competitors have the opportunity to copy their ideas. If companies take advantage of this opportunity, they will have established their brands for the patented technology by the time competitors can enter the marketplace, and can use those brands as platforms to fund and launch their next generation of patented inventions. Still, despite this leading role of patents in business strategy, in addition to their various other valuable roles in innovation and collaboration, patents and patent strategy are practically absent from leading business strategy texts. This book intends to address that absence by providing a business strategy text where patents are up front and center, and then explore some new territory in strategy that has so far been little discussed in business circles.

This book, although it is centered on patents, combines business strategy with legal strategy and classical strategy (political, military, and

survival strategies associated with the human condition) to create a comprehensive picture of all aspects of a company's power to advance its
products and services into the marketplace. This reflects the nature of
patents as documents on one hand concerned with the minutiae of individual inventions and on the other hand often the drivers of multibillion
dollar flows of economic value from the sale of products, services, and
companies. Patents are macro and micro simultaneously. The flow of
fortunes can depend on the interpretation of just a few words within a
patent's claims.

Further, an underlying theme of this book is the race of decision
cycles that determines business tempo. Companies use tempo to succeed
in highly contested but valuable fields by proficiently executing strategy
at a pace faster or slower than competitors can cope. The competitive
dynamics of business are currently as tough as they have ever been, and
will likely grow tougher as more and increasingly capable companies
enter the marketplace from the diverse global economy. Using tempo to
outpace the competition is an important way to address this challenge.

To illustrate the ideas presented in this book, I draw from many
sources both inside and outside the business world. This approach is in
keeping with an insight I gained some time ago when I was in the Army.
That insight is that new ideas and change originate at the borders. In
the Army, borders typically meant where countries and cultures came
together. In this book, borders mean the linkages in thought between
different professional disciplines, different functional entities within organizations, and in some cases, different sciences. My own career has very
much resided at the borders of many professional disciplines as a provider
of products or services that solve problems. Throughout most of my
career, I have been paid to create, sell, and implement solutions. I believe
I have succeeded here by stepping into the shoes of my customers, learning how they perform their jobs and then helping them to perform their
jobs. Nothing allows you to solve problems better than experiencing and
developing your solutions from the point of view of your customers.

I have had a unique opportunity to work with some of the best-
performing people in many professional disciplines. These include top
lawyers in the legal profession, top business people in the professions
of business, top military professionals from all service branches, and top
scientists in research and development professions. I have also worked

with top intellectual property managers who tend to have at their root one or more of the aforementioned four professions, and whose job entails helping people from all backgrounds to benefit from the patent field and intellectual property as a whole. Intellectual property managers also work at and cross the borders between professions and can readily be both identifiers and creators of new ideas and change.

My own entry into the intellectual property field started by accident at a crossroad between careers. In October of 1993, I made what I thought would be a short career pit stop out of the financial industry. I found a sales position at a patent information company, Derwent Information, where I planned to work until I sought a full time MBA that following September. The move to Derwent Information provided me with the unanticipated benefit of having free access to the Derwent World Patents Index (DWPI). The DWPI was the main product that I sold to Derwent Information customers.

The DWPI is a proprietary and indexed collection of several million global patent abstracts that, in the 1990s, only the largest companies could afford to use on a regular basis. Having free access to this database meant that I could run statistical experiments on the data within the DWPI that would have been cost-prohibitive for Derwent Information customers to perform. These experiments greatly accelerated my learning curve as a new entrant into the intellectual property industry. By February of 1994, I gave my first patents and competitive intelligence presentation to Becton Dickenson in New Jersey. That presentation attracted most of the company's legal counsel at that office. Within two months, I gave the same talk to three other major companies. Recognizing an opportunity, I arranged to seek my MBA at night and stayed in the patent information industry.

My time in the patent information industry has offered many challenges. Overall, it has been an exciting and rewarding 15 years during which I have had the opportunity to meet and work with many great people and to travel around the world. In my field, I have worked with people in all the major positions associated with patent strategy. These include CEOs, heads of research and development, corporate counsel, outside counsel, intellectual property managers, individual inventors, all manner of consultants, competitive intelligence professionals, licensing executives, accountants, investment bankers, corporate librarians, patent searchers, patent analysts, patent agents, patent liaisons, and salespeople.

I learned a number of things along the way. One is the limited utility of knowledge as a business tool unless that knowledge draws people to important solutions to their problems. A second is the high utility of one area of professional knowledge—the fundamentals of strategy—in creating the insight needed to understand problems, see opportunities, and find sought-after solutions. A third, which stemmed from the previous two, was a complete disassociation from binary thinking of black and white, good or bad, competitor or facilitator, in that almost every event, organization, and person ultimately is a little of both.

These three insights would come into play when the time came to write this book. First, patents, as quantified knowledge, provide their greatest value to the extent that they solve real problems and therefore draw people and resources to their owners and implementers. Second, patents, by affording their owners the right to enforce exclusivity on inventions, provide a tool from which to execute fundamentals of strategy as they apply to business. Third, patent strategy occurs in a world shaded in gray where patent positions are rarely either totally competitive or cooperative in regards to other patent owners, and where any patent owned by any entity may serve as a tool to advance your own business, if you properly manage the conditions that can make that so.

In 2005, after a short hiatus from the intellectual property field and into the defense and healthcare world, I met Dave Hunt, CEO of Landon IP, Inc. Landon IP, Inc. at its core, is a patent search and information company that is often tapped upon to do much more for its customers in order to identify research and development opportunities and prepare for patent litigation. Dave needed someone who could address these more involved projects for Landon IP, Inc. Our work complemented each other. Landon IP, Inc. offered an unparalleled pool of technology experts from which to draw in order to create project teams to turn ideas into results.

My work for Dave has been various, and has ranged from the highly strategic, such as pioneering Landon IP's entry into Japan, to the highly tactical, such as market development and lead generation. Along the way, I have had the opportunity to give patent strategy courses and run innovation workshops for some of the best and the brightest people in the business. Dave has been gracious in allowing me the time and opportunity to prepare this book. This book has been a long-term personal goal since I became acquainted with this industry.

Much of the material in this book has been refined over the last three years at Landon IP, Inc. through seminars and workshops we have given at customer sites and through patent strategy courses I taught at Patent Resources Group. All of this material has been used in practice by Landon IP, its customers, or both, and in fact stems from solutions devised for real world problems. The material has been developed specifically for patent strategy based upon fifteen years of working with people at over one hundred major corporate intellectual property centers worldwide. These intellectual property centers have shown us both the best and worst practices of practitioners of the intellectual property arts and sciences, and their consequences to business. One of the universal signs of success that we saw was the capacity of winning patenting organizations to outpace their competitors from many different angles so that they, not their competitors, have the greatest influence on the market situation. That led to the title of this book.

As a last note to readers regarding the many case examples in this book, because many of the case examples have a legal component, there are always confidential details about the intended strategy of the participants that I or any other outsider could not access. So these cases are observations based upon the information available to me at the time of writing. In any real life event, there is always what apparently happened and what really happened, and often only the insiders will ever know the latter. I learned about this in real time from a question on my last MBA final exam. The question asked why the ROLM telecommunications merger with IBM failed. Since I worked at ROLM during that time when IBM sold ROLM to Siemens, I knew a lot about what really happened, down to the influence of personalities and personal agendas in the situation. I answered the question as such, and proceeded to have the entire answer marked wrong by the professor, at least until I had the opportunity to explain. So if you are an insider on any case example that appears in this book, I would love to hear more that you can disclose about what really happened if it is appreciably different from the presented interpretation shown here for future updates of this book.

Acknowledgments

I have been making notes on topics that would appear in this book since my time with the 101st Airborne Division starting in 1987. I had the good fortune to become acquainted with the intellectual property industry shortly afterward because it allowed me to draw on and develop a diverse range of skills, from classical strategy up to the latest in innovation sciences. To list everyone who has influenced my work on this book, therefore, would take many pages. I would, however, like to offer special thanks to Dave Hunt, the CEO of Landon IP, Inc., who afforded me the time and the platform from which to write this book. Dave has a strong sense of how to run a business, and he has grown Landon IP, Inc. from a company of 9 people to a company of nearly 200 during the past 10 years. He has shown the courage in business to try new ideas and the willingness and skill to make the adjustments needed to see those ideas succeed.

I would also like to offer a special thanks to Marshall Phelps, Corporate Vice President, IP Policy and Strategy at Microsoft, and Brad Olson, Counsel at Dickstein Shapiro, who I asked early on to peer review the first draft of the final manuscript. They did two things that were very helpful. To start, their business and legal advice was first rate and key to my efforts to tighten and refine the messages in this book. Second, their phenomenally fast turnaround with their reviews provided me with a critical window of opportunity to research their suggestions and put them into the book.

In addition, I would like to thank José Jimenez, Jeff Hovis, Paul Gardner, Mark Connolly, Tony Handel, Ed Kahn, and my father Robert Cantrell all of whom provided me with great insight and advice on important matters in the text of this particular manuscript. José Jimenez is the Chief Intellectual Property Counsel at AMS Research Corporation who reviewed the manuscript and provided insight both on where I could tighten the manuscript and where I made important points that I could further emphasize. Jeff Hovis, the Managing Principal at Product Genesis, reviewed the main body of the text. Jeff both offered important new advice and confirmation regarding important refinements suggested by earlier readers. Paul Gardner is the Academic Director of Patent Resources Group and Mark Connolly is the Global Director—Patents & Intellectual Property at DuPont. Both reviewed the Orientation section of this book, which is a patent primer for business people suggested for inclusion by Marshall Phelps. Tony Handel, Partner and patent litigator for Thomson Hines, and Ed Kahn, consultant on the business side of intellectual property, have both participated with me in giving patent strategy courses through Patent Resources Group and have both influenced this material directly. My father, Robert Cantrell, is a retired IBM executive on the sales and marketing side who also has extensive experience in international operations with Siemens. He read this material from the perspective of someone with absolutely no background in patents so that I could clarify anything that might not make sense to people outside the industry.

I would like also to thank my colleagues at Landon IP, Inc. and Patent Resources Group, with a special note of appreciation to Jeremy Hargis, as well as to Debi Dandridge and Susan Mathis. Jeremy Hargis is a Patent Search Trainer at Landon IP, Inc. who worked in intellectual property management for the automotive industry. He conducted a deep and contributory editing to the first draft of this book based on his day-to-day experiences in industry. This was no small task, which he performed over several months between his primary duties. Debi Dandridge and Susan Mathis from Patent Resources Group also made several reviews of the text for editing purposes leading up to each of the Patent Resources Group courses, in which earlier drafts of this text were used as course material. I would also like to offer my thanks to the many customers and colleagues with whom I have worked on matters outside this book, several of whom because of their corporate policy cannot be named here but who certainly influenced the material inside.

I would last like to offer my gratitude to the late Col. John Boyd, Air Force fighter pilot, and later classical strategist, who I have never met but who I feel I know and whose ideas have also greatly influenced this work. A colleague of mine, Richard Taylor, from Taylor Rodgers, introduced me to John Boyd's work when he saw a commonality between Boyd's papers and my first book, *Understanding Sun Tzu on the Art of War*. Boyd's work, his own published intellectual property, accelerated my work going forward and allowed me to complete this book expeditiously. We have all been students of the work of Sun Tzu, a famous Chinese classical strategist from 2,500 years ago, whose teachings and wisdom have stood the test of time.

About the Author

Robert Cantrell is a strategist who has contributed ideas and observations to a wide range of professions that include intellectual property, the focus of this book, as well as military, innovation, sales, and the biological sciences. He heads the intellectual property consulting effort at Landon IP, Inc., one of the largest privately held patent search, analysis, and consulting firms in the United States. Robert holds a BA in Biology and Military Science from Duke University and an MBA from Edinburgh Business School, UK. He served as an infantry officer for the 101st Airborne Division of the United States Army. Robert has an extensive business development background that includes employment at IBM/ROLM, Dean Witter, Derwent Information, and Manning & Napier. Robert is currently a member of the Intellectual Property Owners association and the Licensing Executive Society. He is a previous member of the Society of Competitive Intelligence Professionals, and spent two years on the board of the United Professional Sales Association. Robert lives in Alexandria Virginia. His favorite hobby is shark photography.

Orientation

Patents are a key driver of business growth for companies that rely on research and development to create the products and services they sell. They provide an incentive to innovate by affording the means to secure and advance inventions in contested technological fields. As such, they are at the center of a discussion on business strategy that will follow. Before we begin with this discussion, however, there are a few things you should know about patents. Even if you are already familiar with patents, your review of this material will help to align our orientation on the subject.

The Grant

To start, you should know that a patent is the grant of the right to exclude others from making, using, or selling the claimed invention for the life of the patent within the jurisdiction of the granting patent office. A granted patent is most often sought by people applying for a patent either because they plan to enforce the exclusivity of their claimed invention or because they want to maintain their freedom of operation by preventing a competitor from obtaining a patent on that same invention first. For the latter, simply applying for the patent can prevent a competitor from obtaining a similar patent by establishing that invention in the public domain as prior art (an already existing invention). In order to make the former purpose useful, the patent owner needs to be willing to enforce this granted right to exclusivity, or present to the world of potential infringers a credible expectation that patent enforcement will occur if they do not otherwise establish suitable arrangements with that owner. Having the patent itself, and the willingness to enforce the right to exclusivity it grants, however, does not guarantee that its owner will actually succeed when enforcing that right, or even have the capacity to enforce that right if challenged by an infringer of the patent's claims.

At any time during the life of a patent, a second party may, by accident or design, infringe on the claims covered by the patent. The term "infringe" means that another party has made, used, or sold an invention claimed within the patent in violation of the patent owner's rights. This infringement in itself is a matter on which two parties may disagree, provided that the patent owner even discovers the infringement. A disagreement can arise about whether the invention of the alleged infringer actually infringes on the patent claims or whether the patent owner should have the rights to the patent claims as granted.

Since the claims of a patent are open to interpretation, ultimately by a court of law, the granted patent really offers its owner only a right to exclude, based on the presumption that the claims of that patent can be enforced. Furthermore, both the owner of the patent and potential infringers may assess the probability of successful enforcement on the part of the patent owner differently. That difference in assessment is one of the factors that leads to patent disputes, because it necessarily means that the relative value of the predicted outcome of a patent challenge for each party will not be the same. If both parties view their chances of winning as high, regardless of the ultimate truth of the matter, the risk of conflict is correspondingly higher than it might be if opposing sides had more accurate views of their relative positions.

The actual value associated with the probability of successful patent enforcement to two or more involved parties will generally be reconciled monetarily at the time of a transaction, settlement, or court judgment involving the patent. At any other time in a patent's life, its present value is based on the probability that it can successfully be enforced, and that will further vary considerably depending on the capacity of owners or licensors to enforce the patent and commercially exploit the invention it describes. Whether this probability is closer or further away from the value desired at the time of a transaction, settlement, or court verdict may very well depend on the relative skills of the negotiating teams involved. The patent owner will also receive value indirectly from any infringements on inventions that did not occur because a potential infringer respected the patent claims and the patent owner did not actually have to enforce them or even know about the threat. The sum value of the patent will further depend on the following:

- The quality and coverage of the patent itself
- The quality and coverage of other patents and associated intellectual property within the patent's sphere of influence
- The quality of the legal counsel charged to enforce the patent
- The way the patented invention is used in the market
- The resources available and employed to support any enforcement effort
- The quality of all aspects of the opposition
- The particular court (and jury, if any)
- The enforceability of patent laws within the jurisdiction covered by the patent

In short, anyone involved with patents has a lot of variables to consider and uncertainties to address to make those patents both valuable and useful.

With all variables and uncertainties considered, the stakes in any challenges to a patent's claims are often high, and the process to enforce them is often both expensive and risky. Enforcement is also not a one-sided matter, since a given patent owner may have the same propensity to challenge the claims of a competitor's patents as that competitor may have to challenge the claims of that patent owner's patents. In fact, the measure of a patent owner's capacity to both challenge and defend patents is often the key determinant in whether that patent owner can maximize the value of patents in the market and mitigate or avoid the harmful effects of patent disputes.

Because patent enforcement is both expensive and risky, you, as someone involved with patent strategy, will generally prefer strategies that encourage competitors to respect your patent claims without actually challenging them, since that means you can focus your efforts on advancing the business and not on patent litigation. An exception to this tendency is found within a few businesses or departments of businesses designed and funded specifically to challenge patents. With the majority in mind first, the reason that enforcing patents is both expensive and risky and generally a distraction is that the process can play out as a business equivalent of war, albeit and fortunately fought with money and careers instead of actual lives. Wars are often expensive, even for the winners. That patent disputes can play out as the business equivalent of war relates to the fact that the practice of law itself, of which patents are a part, has its origins in history as a means to resolve disputes by some method other than the sword. But that enforcement is often only one step removed from more physical and often even more costly means of creating a resolution.

Patent law, like law in general, exists to create order in the affairs of people and organizations covered by those laws so that people comply with rules they might otherwise ignore in the absence of potential consequences for breaking those laws. These consequences can be significant in that they may decide the flow of millions to billions of dollars. Any organization that might deliberately or accidentally infringe on another's patent claims or that might decide whether to undertake the enforcement of a patent's claims, needs to be concerned about all manner of potential consequences in order to balance the risk of infringement and enforcement with the potential reward. These consequences also should be weighed against any imbalances of risk that may occur between the involved parties. Regardless of whether you are challenging or defending a patent position, you will generally prefer to bear less risk than your opponent.

Patents, as legal documents, provide a tool to establish some order regarding the ownership and use of inventions that the owner would like to see enforced, namely to prevent the unauthorized making, use, or sale of the inventions described within a patent's claims by parties that have not properly obtained the right to make, use, or sell those inventions. The owner of an invention invests in patents specifically because patents help that owner to mitigate the pressures of nonexclusive competition, meaning that the owner can, through the successful enforcement of the patents, exclude people from making, using, or selling claimed inventions or require people to pay premiums, royalties, or some other form of remuneration that they might not otherwise pay to make, use, or sell the inventions in the absence of the patents.

In exchange for the rights granted by a patent for a period extending up to 20 years after the filing of a patent application, the patent carries with it an explicit agreement within the jurisdiction of the patent-granting authority that the owner will disclose the details of an invention within the patent application and associated documents for the benefit of the public. From this disclosure, society as a whole can study the invention and use it to spur new creative efforts for the future. Because of this agreement, the primary value of a competitor's patent to you can be the knowledge it gives you without your needing to recreate that knowledge yourself. That knowledge could help you to determine your own research and development direction, or you might access it more directly through a vehicle such as a patent license or through the purchase of a product or service that uses the invention.

The key to understanding any given patent is to understand the scope of the invention claimed by that patent, the jurisdiction (country or countries) that the patent covers, and the length of time remaining before the patent expires. These are also the three elements around which many patent disputes revolve. Patent counsel, depending on its role to support the plaintiff or the defendant in a case, may argue about the scope of a patent's claims and whether or not any infringement on those claims has actually occurred. Patent counsel may also argue about the validity or invalidity of the patent claims themselves. Patent counsel will take into account the jurisdiction covered by the patent and also the jurisdiction of the court that hears a patent case, since the probability of successful patent enforcement will differ from place to place. With that difference in mind, jurisdiction has two sides to it, given that a patent can afford the right to exclude a competitor from making an invention in a given patent jurisdiction and can also afford the right to exclude products for sale or use in a given patent jurisdiction, even if they are legally made outside the jurisdiction covered by the patent. This last point is important to understand when you talk through where to seek patent protection with your patent counsel. You do not necessarily need complete global patent protection to achieve the level of global patent protection that you require on a given invention.

Regarding patent expirations, while the life of a patent can be extended under certain conditions, this is an exception to the rules. Such exceptions, which can, for example, be granted to restore time lost from a patent term while a drug awaited regulatory approval, can also be at the center of patent disputes. Naturally, in this example, the interests of the pharmaceutical companies to extend patents in whole or part is usually opposite to the interests of generic drug manufacturers that want to put generic drugs onto the market as soon as possible. In any case and in all industries, considering all aspects of disputes, patent expiration is an important determinant of the value of proceeding with an enforcement or challenge effort, because it determines how long the benefits of having a patent can last. The cost to the business of that enforcement or challenge effort would need to be covered within the remaining life of the patent, keeping in mind that cost can go beyond money to include other factors, such as the reputation of the business in the minds of potential customers. The length of time remaining until a patent expires is also a factor in determining the value and nature of licenses and remuneration resulting from a patent dispute.

Jurisdictions and Costs

Further to understanding patents, you should also know that a single given invention might have several patents behind it from several different patent authorities. For example, it might have a U.S. patent through the U.S. Patent Office, a Japanese patent through the Japan Patent Office, and a European patent covering a collection of European countries through the European Patent Office. Patenting in many patent authorities affords you the opportunity to enforce invention exclusivity within all the jurisdictions covered by the granted patents. This comes, however, with an attendant higher cost to gain and maintain those patents than if you filed for a patent in just one authority. Furthermore, each patent authority has its own variation on patent laws, meaning that just because you succeed at enforcing exclusivity in one jurisdiction you will not necessarily succeed at enforcing exclusivity in another. The scope of claims and the date of expiration for patents on the same underlying invention from different authorities may vary for the same reason. As a rule, you will seek patents in the countries that are major markets for the business and will consider also seeking patents in countries that are major manufacturers when such patents make sense for your strategy considering the potential value of the invention and the expected enforceability of the patent in each jurisdiction.

The monetary costs associated with patenting also differ by patent authority. In the United States, $10,000 to $25,000 is a common figure for the cost to obtain a patent, inclusive of filing fees and the use of a patent attorney, although as noted to the author, in some industries that figure can fall into the $25,000 to $50,000 range per patent. Other patent authorities have similar costs, meaning that if you file for patents in Japan and Europe, you might add another $15,000 to $20,000 or more each to your total. These costs are variable and depend mostly on the technology and its complexity, the patent authority, the number of claims sought, and the cost of retained legal counsel.

Additionally, each patent authority will have a schedule of patent maintenance fees that also differ by patent authority and by the number of claims in the patent. Added up, to obtain and maintain global patent protection for an invention can cost more than $100,000 over the life of the family of patents that protect it. ("Patent family" is used herein to refer to the collection of patents from multiple patent authorities directed to the same invention.) For any given invention, therefore, it is important to appreciate these costs in order to determine whether having the right to enforce the exclusivity of a claimed invention is worth the cost in each sought-after jurisdiction.

When determining the cost and potential benefit, also keep in mind that the cost to actually enforce patent exclusivity can completely eclipse the cost of gaining and maintaining the patent itself if you cannot otherwise establish an amicable settlement or mutually beneficial license to end a dispute. An analysis presented by one prominent law firm headquartered in the United States stated that, at the time this book was being written, for cases with more than $25 million at stake, the average cost of patent litigation is $3.2 million through the end of discovery and $5.2 million through trial.[1] All these determinations on cost are made all the more difficult, because typically you have no guarantee that an invention will have real or continued value in the future, or whether the patent or patents behind it will ultimately stand up in court.

People accept the costs of patent litigation because the stakes involved are so high and the uncertainty of patent coverage and enforceability leaves open a possibility of succeeding through proper legal maneuvering even in less than perfect cases. This latter point is important to understand, because if all parties knew the exact rights the patents in a dispute afforded, they would know the outcome of any legal contest in advance and could respond to that outcome without the expense of the litigation.

Uncertainties

Managing the costs associated with patenting and enforcing patents is one of the key balancing acts that patent strategists need to perform. If, as someone involved with patent strategy, you spend too little on any or all things associated with patent protection, you can make your supported organization vulnerable to competitors. If you spend too much, you can overly tax other important efforts that your business intends to pursue and again make your organization vulnerable to competitors, albeit in a different way. You also need to balance your actions against who your competition is. As a small start-up, you cannot generally expect to go head-to-head against Microsoft, Hewlett-Packard (HP), Merck, or any other patent powerhouse in a patent arms race if they choose to invest in your line of research and development. In contrast, if you are a patent powerhouse, you have the collective patents of all the start-ups and all the other major and minor players to consider. So no matter who you are, you need both efficiency and creativity to get the most out of the resources you have and to deal with uncertainties inherent in the process of leveraging patents.

Leading the list of uncertainties, and to reemphasize the point about uncertainty, you simply cannot guarantee that a given patent will work as a tool to enforce the exclusivity of an invention until that patent is actually used to enforce the exclusivity of that invention. That uncertainty underpins a number of decisions the patent strategist needs to make. So while making those decisions, the adept patent strategist will often leverage this uncertainty as an advantage since it also affects competitors. For example, the threat that you, as a patent owner, can enforce exclusivity on an invention often has more power than the act of actually enforcing that exclusivity, given that once challenged, your competitor could find a way to defeat your patent claims, eliminate your threat, and cause you to spend a small fortune in legal fees during the process. Oftentimes, you might posture with the threat that you will enforce exclusivity so that your competitor will determine that, even given the best possible outcome of a patent challenge, the risk and expense to challenge your patent position is too high a risk to take. So this management of uncertainty is at the heart of succeeding with your primary purpose behind investing in a patent—the right to enforce exclusivity on claimed inventions, without needing to use the patent in an actual court of law. The proactive use of uncertainty is therefore essential in keeping the costs of patenting and patent enforcement manageable.

Due to the uncertainty and expense of patent enforcement, any decision you make to enforce a patent should be a well considered decision. Patent claims may be interpreted differently by a court from what the patentee intended. Claim interpretation will depend on how well the patent was drafted, the relevant prior art (technology that was in the public domain prior to the invention), the comparative skills of those attorneys and other professionals supporting or opposing your position, and the makeup of the particular court. Despite the precise requirements of patent drafting itself, superior patent drafting is an art form the success of which is difficult to prove until tested, and enforcement of claimed inventions, itself another art form, involves any number of variables that could weigh in on the success or failure of the effort.

Patent Claims

Central to drafting an enforceable patent are the claims. Most patents have several claims, some of which are independent of other claims and some of which are dependent on (build on) preceding claims within the patent. Their interpretation is further influenced by patent specifications and drawings. Each patent claim is directed to a specific invention or aspect of an invention that the patent covers. So if we can, for illustration purposes, clean the slate of all past and present inventions and allow you to draft the patent for the first wheel, you would first draft a claim that covers the major embodiment of the wheel itself. This would be an independent claim that broadly describes the core wheel. Subsequent claims within the same patent that are dependent on the claim for the wheel might include additional embodiments of the total invention that makes the wheel useful, such as the axle, itself a type of wheel, or spokes.

Given this invention of the wheel, the job of your patent prosecution attorney (the attorney responsible for obtaining granted patents from a patent office) is to draft patent claims that allow you to enforce exclusivity on the wheel. If drafted thoughtfully, these claims will cover not only your primary intended use of that wheel, but ideally will cover ample uses outside the scope of that original intent so that your patent could also, for example, become a vehicle to license the wheel invention for other uses or set up new businesses using the wheel concept. You also want your patent prosecution attorney to draft claims that do not knowingly leave unguarded important technical elements that make your invention of the wheel useful. A wheel has limited application without an axle, which means that along with being able to enforce exclusivity on the wheel, you want to either be able to enforce exclusivity on the axle or at least have the freedom to use axles as you require.

This last point on freedom to use, often expressed in legal terms as "freedom of operation," is an important nuance to understand in patent strategy, because the other side of enforcing exclusivity for your patents is to seek a position where a competitor cannot enforce exclusivity against you. Sometimes just having the freedom to make, use, or sell an invention without restriction is the single most important (or a more important) requirement in your patent strategy for a given invention than having the right to exclude other people from using that given invention. You do not need a patent to establish the freedom to make, use, or sell an invention, because just publishing the specifics of an invention in an appropriate journal, or using an invention within a product, can prevent a competitor that does not otherwise have invention or filing priority from obtaining a patent on that same invention. (Priority is defined as an earlier claim to the invention; in the United States, priority is determined by who was first to invent, and in most of the rest of the world priority is determined by who filed a patent application first.)

Regarding the patent claims themselves, it is desirable to have claims of broad, intermediate, and narrow scope in order to maximize patent protection. Keeping with our illustration, a broad claim might cover the entire wheel, whereas an intermediate or narrow claim might cover some part of that wheel, such as the axle. This, too, is a matter of perspective since, considering all the potential inventions that could be components of an axle, a patent on an axle would be considered quite broad in relationship to those components. Seminal inventions in a given industry often allow for the broadest possible scope of patent claims, as per our example with the first wheel. If you in theory had invented the first wheel ever, your claims might cover just about every application of a wheel imaginable for which you could enforce those claims over the life of the wheel patent. Over time, once your wheel patent expired, you might still obtain new patents that include wheels, but on a narrower scope. For example, your patent might claim as an invention installed wheels on a suitcase so people can roll the suitcase instead of carrying it. Whereas such an invention might have infringed on a granted patent that claimed the wheel itself, it would do so only if that wheel patent had not yet expired or if you had not already obtained a license to the wheel suitable for your purpose with the suitcase.

As your patent application on wheeled suitcases progresses through the patent office, you might ultimately obtain a patent claiming wheeled suitcases at the same time another inventor claimed the use of wheels to create a conveyer belt. While the conveyer belt can also be used to move suitcases without needing someone to carry them, it would not violate a claim directed to a wheeled suitcase as an invention. But considering all possible competition, in general, your claims should be broader about what constitutes a wheeled suitcase rather than narrower, so that your patent litigation attorneys can argue broadly about what constitutes wheels on a suitcase. You do not want your broad claims to restrict the scope of your patent to some specific configuration of, say, two wheels, which might allow someone else to claim in another patent the attachment of a third wheel to a suitcase that would allow a person to roll a bag while it stands up on its own. Bottom line here: The claims are the central part of a patent that determine the invention, in whole or part, for which you have the right to enforce exclusivity. They are also the part that an opponent will most likely seek to challenge. Adequately broad and enforceable claims are desirable, as are intermediate and narrow claims. These factors, relative to your own invention and the current state of the art in technology, should be a part of your discussion with patent counsel.

Eighteen Months of Secrecy

The patent system has one uncertainty inherent in its design that arises from the patent application process itself. During the examination of a patent by most patent offices, the patent application remains secret for a period of 18 months. After that time, the patent offices publish those patent applications, regardless of whether they ultimately grant the patent itself. (The United States used to be an exception to this rule, and is still an exception in the sense that the U.S. Patent Office does not mandatorily publish after 18 months those patent applications filed only in the United States.) As someone involved with patent strategy, this 18-month window of secrecy can prove to be highly important for a number of reasons.

On the positive side of the 18 months of secrecy, it can create uncertainty for competitors about whether you have pending patents on inventions they would like to use or patent themselves. Competitors always run the risk that if they make, use, or sell a new invention, they might find out later that you have a priority patent application on the same invention, which might ultimately become a granted patent. This would leave those competitors in the position of infringing on your patent, along with the potential consequences for doing so. You can stoke any fears they may have about the potential consequences of infringing on the claims described within your potentially pending patent applications through the selective publication of invention disclosures and scientific papers. If at least some of the time you have pending patents behind your invention disclosures and scientific papers, any invention you disclose in any way, even those for which you have not sought patent protection, would still represent a potential infringement threat to competitors until after they wait 18 months to see whether corresponding patent applications appear. This dynamic will become important at the end of this book when we discuss a high-tempo patent strategy that leverages psychological means to protect inventions.

On the negative side, the 18-month window during which patent applications remain secret also creates uncertainty for you regarding potential competitive patent claims that could, in the future, affect decisions you need to make right now. Because the surest defense against patent infringement is to not infringe, reviewing the prior art before making a patent-related decision can make a lot of sense, except that this 18 months of secrecy means that no matter how careful you are, you always run the risk that you might be too late to obtain a patent of your own on an invention, or that you might infringe on patent claims that you did not and could not know about at the time. Due to the potential cost of the latter and often unavoidable mistakes, it is always important to have contingency plans in place should you run into an infringement situation that could include predetermined cross-licensing arrangements with competitors working on similar technologies. The risk of not doing so is high, because knowingly infringing on a competitor's patents can be more costly than accidentally infringing on a competitor's patents once you realize that an infringement has occurred. Treble damages come up frequently in U.S. courts for willful infringement, which is a term for knowingly infringing on a competitor's patents.

Requirements to Obtain Patents

The last part of our orientation addresses the requirements to obtain a patent. The first requirement is to have an invention that meets the given patent authority's legal definition of novelty. As with other aspects of patenting, this definition of novelty can differ by patent authority. U.S. patent law, unlike the patent law of the rest of the world, permits an applicant to obtain a valid patent so long as the patent application is filed within one year of the first publication, disclosure, or sale of the invention. In many other patent authorities, such as in Europe, even a disclosure of an invention to a potential business partner without proper nondisclosure documentation in place could cause an immediate forfeiture of the right to seek a patent within that authority. As explained to the author by a member of the European Patent Office, if you theoretically invented the first balsa wood glider and decided to test fly it in a park where other people could see it, then you would lose novelty for that invention since your test would be considered a public disclosure.

It is therefore important to discuss any invention disclosure with patent counsel in order not to lose the opportunity to obtain patents in patent authorities where you would like to seek patent protection.

A second requirement is usefulness. Usefulness means that the invention should afford some benefit to the person or persons who employ it. Usefulness also has different interpretations in different patent authorities, with some having a higher bar for usefulness in and apart from industry than others. In other words, different patent offices may view differently the usefulness of a given invention that is operative only a small percentage of the time under specific conditions. It is important to appreciate just what is considered useful by a given patent authority and to support that argument in your patent application documentation.

A further requirement to obtain a patent in the United States is that the invention be an unobvious variation of that which is in the prior art. Other countries outside the United States have a similar requirement couched in terms of demanding that technology for which you seek patent protection incorporate an "inventive step" rather than be "unobvious." For example, if you theoretically patented a headlight on a car, then a patent examiner might reject a patent for a headlight on a motorcycle by a competitor as being obvious (or lacking an inventive step) in view of your prior car headlight patent. It is important here, however, to understand that even if a patent examiner decides your claims on an invention pass the obviousness test, the court may not agree with that decision if someone challenges your patent in the future, nor should you ever assume that you cannot challenge any aspect of a competitor's patent if you have the evidence and skills on hand to support that challenge. Obviousness, as one of the points to challenge a patent claim, is also something to consider when drafting patent claims, since ideally you and your patent attorneys will have the insight to describe obvious applications of an invention such as, in the example, a headlight on vehicles other than the claimed car so that such an obviousness case would not become an issue.

Continuing with requirements to obtain a patent, since each patent authority has its differences, it is prudent to draft claims, supporting text, and drawings of the invention in accord with the requirements of each respective authority in which you seek patent protection. Sometimes that can include translating the patent application into the language of each authority. In addition, the drafted patent should include details of ownership and follow the guidelines of each patent authority as to who all the contributing inventors are. Any failure to prepare documents properly could lead to either a failure to obtain a patent on the invention or to a failure in enforceability if you have left open a legal detail for a challenger to exploit. Any failure to draft proper patent applications on the part of your competitor can also open opportunities for you.

Conclusion

We have presented some basic facts about patenting and patent strategy that you should know. You should further consult proper patent counsel to put patent strategy into practice, if you yourself are not qualified patent counsel. That patent counsel can fill you in on the details of your particular inventions and cases so that you execute the legal fundamentals well. That stated, although a patent strategist should always consider the strategic advice given by patent counsel supporting the situation, the final say on the who, what, why, when, where, and how of patent strategy rests with top business officers. That is not to imply that the patent strategist cannot also be patent counsel, a top officer in the business, or both. As this discussion of patent strategy develops, it will show that ultimately, whoever that person may be, important decisions involving patents should come from the person or persons responsible for the overall success of the business. These important decisions lead us now to the broader discussion of patent strategy and its role in the strategy of business.

Chapter 1

Introduction

I n today's technology-driven markets, most companies compete through ideas and relationships. Their most important assets are their intellectual property, knowledge, and people. Patents, as the most quantifiable of intellectual property assets, are the cornerstone of a new type of business strategy that, while practiced, has not been adequately described. This book intends to provide that description and to take the mystery out of patent strategy for business management.

When compared to marketing or financial strategy, patent strategy in business has barely been touched on as a professional discipline. Because of this, patent strategy presents a significant opportunity to gain a competitive advantage. Whereas an opportunity for financial arbitrage can have a lifespan of seconds before astute financial strategists notice and act, opportunities for arbitrage on the value of patentable ideas can remain open to discovery for years. An astute patent strategist can expect to find and create value far in excess of the investment required to capture that value, if for no other reason than that the patent field is less understood than other areas of business. In the patent field, all the treasures have not already been discovered; they may yet be hidden in the patent files of a company or more likely, in the minds of brilliant researchers waiting for the right connection of ideas and support.

Treasures in the patent world are both buried and emergent. This book focuses on the emergent treasures: the creation and acquisition of valuable inventions from bright people. This is in keeping with the fact that the vast majority of wealth generated by patents is gained from the patents used in a company's core business. Much has been discussed in professional circles about licensing non-core assets buried in the patent portfolio, and tangential value here should not be overlooked, but the fact remains that the primary value is emergent and in the business core.

With that in mind, we bring a thought from classical strategy into the present. Marcus Aurelius, a Roman emperor who reigned from 161 to 180 A.D., stated that "The secret of all victory lies in the organization of the non-obvious." Many historians consider Marcus Aurelius to be the last of the "five good emperors of Rome," and his philosophy for success on the battlefield still holds true to this day.[1] His statement pertains to military conflict, but it carries with it a universal truth that pertains to patent strategy: If you can understand and organize important people, ideas, and tools that your competitors cannot, then you can reach levels of success your competitors cannot hope to achieve.

This book will show you ways to organize and use non-obvious advantages from the point of view of patent strategy. To do so, it will introduce three key learning points as follows:

1. *The definition of patent strategy.* The first key to strategy, patent and otherwise, is to understand what strategy is. Strategy is a solution that takes you from a current situation to a new situation. As a solution, strategy addresses the necessary existence of options, uncertainty, and obstacles. It provides a way to take action even in the face of absolute unknowns so that you can produce a positive result within the constraints of your operation, even if it is not exactly the result you had conceived when your action began. Patent strategy is a component of business strategy that deals with the options, uncertainty, and obstacles involved in the creation, use, and defense of technical ideas. It addresses how to cost-effectively build and manage patent portfolios from which to advance and defend the business

in a research and development environment that is inherently unpredictable. This book discusses patent strategy in context with business strategy, of which it is part and parcel, along with the components of classical strategy from which all strategies are derived.

2. *The decision cycle.* Patent strategy is composed of decision cycles that include three phases:

   a. Assess—understand the situation
   b. Decide—choose a course of action
   c. Act—execute the decision

   In the face of many unknowns, an organization that can proficiently move through these decision cycles more quickly than its competitors can develop significant strategic advantages over its competitors in its ability to shape the competitive environment, respond to unpredicted opportunities and threats, and otherwise outpace the competition.

   Decision cycles are not one-pass-through events. They are continuous cycles of *assess, decide,* and *act,* whereupon each action leads to new assessments, new decisions, and new actions, the complexity of which increases proportionally to the ambiguity of the objective. In a research and development environment, where the output of creative investment is unpredictable, the ambiguity is often high. You cannot reliably forecast important products and services that people have not yet invented and the market has not yet seen.

   In patent strategy, proficiently moving through decision cycles involves proficiently creating or obtaining inventions, advancing those inventions into the market, and defending those inventions from competitors however the market ultimately develops. It also involves creating the orientation in the mind of decision makers that patents can serve as important tools from which to gain competitive advantage. The main body of this book uses the decision cycle as the primary guideline for how an organization should plan patent strategy and organize its intellectual property (IP) department.

3. *The interplay between interaction and isolation.* Patent strategy is an interplay between interaction and isolation.[2] The patent itself is a tool that fosters both interaction and isolation. For example, the patent provides a definable asset from which to arrange licenses, a form of

interaction, and it provides a tool with which to exclude competitors from making, using, or selling an invention in a marketplace, a form of isolation. This interplay provides the primary four rules from which you can build even the most complex and nuanced patent strategies. The rules are simple, but mastering the rules takes practice, experience, and a willingness to refine that practice throughout an entire career.

Although this book is about the business side of patent strategy, it is not specifically just about patents. Instead, it covers all aspects of business strategy in which patents play a part—namely, the creation, use, and defense of technical ideas. To try to explain patent strategy outside the context of business strategy would be like trying to explain the written word without showing its greater utility in sentences, paragraphs, and books. A single enforceable patent, like a single word, can have power; that power, however, is minor compared to the power available when that patent works in concert with other enforceable patents and all the other sources of power that people can use to advance and defend an invention in the marketplace. Furthermore, it is also important to understand that this is a book about what to do in patent strategy, not necessarily how to do it. Although it shows many examples of how to enact a patent strategy, if this was merely a "how to" book, it would not be about strategy. Each stratagem is a unique creation of the human mind that, while using common ideas, addresses situations that are never exactly alike.

Strategy Defined

Before we discuss patent strategy, we need to define specifically what we mean by "strategy." Strategy is a solution that takes you from your current situation "A" to a new situation "B." Strategy is nothing more than that, yet that simple definition still confounds people in practice. People often do not make proper assessments of their current situation "A," leading them to take actions they might not have taken if they had a better understanding of that situation. "B" can prove even more difficult to grasp than "A," since life, in patent strategy and otherwise, is filled with randomness that does not abide by a reliable plot line. You might know what you would like "B" to be, but in practice you will need to take defined action to get close enough to where a more ambiguous but satisfactory "B" is in order to take advantage of the outcome that actually develops. This becomes a balance between defining "B" so narrowly that you cannot hit it, or defining "B" so broadly that succeeding depends almost entirely on good fortune. So, bottom line: Strategy is a type of solution that, in the end, will work as planned or provide an unexpected result; in either case, it should not have so constrained a definition of success within it that the strategist cannot take the best advantage of both outcomes.

To succeed at strategy, you need to know how to make:

1. An accurate assessment of your current situation "A."
2. An accurate and realistic conception of your desired new situation "B" that is narrow enough to be useful but broad enough to account for unknowns.
3. A correct decision on how to get from "A" to "B" that adjusts for uncertainties that become known.
4. A way to measure your progress or any lack thereof.

Uncertainty is where strategy, as a solution, starts to differ from, say, a technical solution or a mathematical solution. The dynamic nature of strategy complicates your task of finding a successful solution because you cannot necessarily test out uncertainties. You have to address active and often intelligent opposition from people who do not want you to succeed, and who may not themselves know how they will react to you until you take action. You also must contend with the fact that, outside the artificial world of games perhaps, time in strategy does not stop. You are continually executing a strategy that takes you to a new situation "B" in the sense that even doing nothing takes you somewhere. You will go to a new situation "B" even if you do not know what "B" is and cannot articulate your strategy to get there. A ship with wind in its sail will go somewhere. A good strategist needs to get a handle on the situation he or she faces in order to arrive at a desirable destination through something other than the mere vagaries of the wind, while realizing, like ancient seafarers, that the outcome of any given journey to find new land, no matter how well planned, depends on the land that is actually there, not the land that the strategist would like to be there.

Results

To go where you want to go, you need to focus on the results of your actions. Any strategy will create predicted and unpredicted results, both beneficial and harmful. Your capacity to create a beneficial result that is preferably also your predicted result will depend on your understanding of your current situation "A," your desired situation "B," and the pros and cons of your chosen method of getting from "A" to "B." One of the hallmarks of intelligence in strategy is the strategist's capacity to make accurate predictions about potential outcomes most of the time. Your accuracy when making such predictions, as well as your capacity to act quickly and decisively on unexpected results, will depend on your having a solid grasp of "A," "B," and how you plan to get to "B." On the latter point, you should seek to craft a decision on how to get to "B" from the foundation of the past experiences that got you to your present situation "A." Your past experiences, along with the value you have retained from those experiences, provide the base from which you can move forward. Your patents themselves literally encapsulate value captured from your past.

With your desired results in mind, your strategic prowess is anchored on your capacity to:

1. Achieve your predicted and useful results
2. Recognize and exploit your unpredicted useful results
3. Mitigate or avoid your predicted harmful results
4. Mitigate or avoid unpredicted harmful results

In the development of the pharmaceutical compound *sildenafil* that became the commercial pharmaceutical Viagra®, Pfizer researchers achieved a predicted and useful result of increasing blood flow to the heart to treat heart conditions. The compound *sildenafil* was only a marginal improvement over existing treatments, and so while useful, the predicted result had little commercial value. An unpredicted result, however, allowed the same compound to be used for treating male erectile dysfunction. Pfizer patented the method of use and successfully exploited it.[3] So while we need to know our desired new situation, "B," we also need to pay attention to the unpredicted useful results that might offer us an even better outcome than expected.

In contrast to Viagra®, which had useful unpredicted results, the powerful painkiller Vioxx® showed evidence of producing harmful and unpredicted results. During its development, Merck researchers predicted that Vioxx® would produce manageable harmful side effects, such as abdominal pain, dizziness, and fatigue. They considered these side effects to be acceptable when weighed against the significantly improved capacity of Vioxx® to relieve pain. The market agreed and made the drug a commercial success. Things changed, however, when an unpredicted and harmful rise in heart attack and stroke appeared among some patients using Vioxx.®[4] To add to this, Merck's handling of the unpredicted harm, while not necessarily the case in reality, appeared to be the actions of a company more concerned about defending a line of profitability than the well-being of its customers.[5] Merck was sued under the accusation that its management had deliberately covered up test results that would have led to an earlier withdrawal of Vioxx® from the market. Unpredicted harmful results arose, and although Merck was forced to abandon its originally conceived and desired result "B," addressing the harmful results was a necessary and ultimately unavoidable step to improve Merck's long-term strategic performance.

Reasons for Unpredicted Results

Our present situation "A" is, more often than not, different from the way we predicted it would be. Although not necessarily to their detriment, most people spend most of their lives working on their alternative plans. For many companies, this tendency is the same. Consider that wireless telephony was barely conceivable and certainly not predictable when Nokia, the wireless telephony company, was founded around paper and power products in 1865.[6] Pursuant to our analysis of present situations, Robert K. Merton, a Columbia University sociologist and National Medal of Science winner, provides a framework for why we achieve unpredicted results from our strategies in his paper, "The Unanticipated Consequences of Purposive Social Action." Robert K. Merton's paper was published by the *American Sociological Review* in 1936.[7] It highlights several key reasons why conceived and executed strategies create unpredicted results. Exhibit 1.1 shows Merton's five reasons for unpredicted results.

The first reason for unpredicted results is ignorance, both because of what is not known that could be known and what cannot be known. An example of the former, ignorance of what is not known that could be

Ignorance	What is known What cannot be known
Error	Inappropriate course of action Missed elements
Immediacy Bias	Emotional drive Individual rationality
Basic Values	Wrong priorities Inappropriate beliefs
Consequences of Predicting	Bias toward the expected Interactivity by others to change the predicted

Developed from Robert K. Merton "The Unanticipated Consequences of Purposive Social Action."

Exhibit 1.1   Reasons for Unpredicted Results

known, occurred at a well-recognized automotive company. An internal assessment at that company showed that more than 50% of the new ideas its researchers put forward as new inventions already existed in the prior art. Moreover, 70% of that prior art was created by someone within the home company. This implied that its researchers, by being ignorant of the prior art, wasted a lot of time reinventing prior art, much of which their company already owned, instead of creating something truly new. While accounting for the fact that researchers may need to rework old problems to fully conceptualize new solutions, the possibility that more than 50% of the company's research and development time and resources was spent reinventing known ideas and inventions meant that the organization was losing considerable potential value simply by being ignorant of what it and others already knew. Aside from individual inventions, it also meant that the organization was less focused on researching less explored possibilities than if it had better appreciated where other organizations had already been.

You should make an effort, therefore, to reduce ignorance of what can and should be known. The unknowable already makes strategy challenging enough without that added burden. In patent strategy, this means searching and reviewing the prior art. Patent information is becoming more, not less, transparent with the increased accessibility and performance of patent databases from commercial and government sources. You can search, or have someone search for you, the prior art used by patent offices worldwide, and this is the best first way to understand a situation in patent strategy. After all, part of the trade-off you or anyone else makes when filing for a patent is to share knowledge in exchange for the right to exclude others from making, using, or selling the described invention for a period of time. Your competitor's "loss," (i.e., the trade-off made by publishing invention details in order to apply for a patent), should be your gain in leveraging the inherent knowledge described.

To reliably make good decisions, in patent strategy and otherwise, requires a full understanding of a situation. Not repeating mistakes requires knowledge of what those past mistakes were or building on the successes of other people that obviate your need to find solutions for yourself. Although you can find instances where successful people acted on an opportunity only because they did not know the improbability of that success, and although the expression "ignorance is bliss" has developed into a positive cliché in the English language, ignorance should not be considered an asset.

The Prior Art Search

The prior art search is a search of any information source that could show that a conceived invention already exists and at best would not be patentable, or at worst would infringe an already existing patent claim. Information sources can include patents, patent applications, research papers, conference proceedings, product manuals—in short, anything that both adequately describes the invention and for which someone could document the time or origin of the source. A large percentage of prior art searches is focused on patents and patent applications from one or more of the United States of America, the European Union, or Japan; most of the commercially important patents will appear in at least one of these authorities. Typically, these prior art searches take a day to perform. In litigation situations, where

(Continued)

the first line of defense is to invalidate the plaintiff's patents, a prior art search becomes an invalidity search whereby the defendant may "scour the earth" for prior art that could, for example, be hidden in an otherwise forgotten research paper at a Russian university written in the Cyrillic alphabet. Such invalidity searches can take quite a bit of detective work, including interviewing sources who may know where to find more obscure prior art references.

Complicating the issue of ignorance in patent strategy, some companies work under an institutionalized form of "ignorance is bliss," or plausible deniability, in an attempt to avoid treble damage awards if found to have willfully infringed another organization's patents. They deliberately do not perform prior art searches. They often take this course when they assess the risk of infringement as high because of the crowded nature of the field, and then address inevitable infringements as they occur, often with other patents in their portfolio as intended bargaining chips. In so doing, however, they run the risk of reinventing existing inventions and incurring the costs and the lost productivity associated with that. Unless your work is truly at the cutting edge of new technology, reinventing costs caused by an ignorance of the prior art can exceed the savings produced by possibly avoiding treble damages for willful patent infringement. This is particularly true considering that a review of the prior art, as a part of reducing ignorance, can in itself help you to avoid a charge of patent infringement in the first place. Each situation is different and should be considered on its own merits as opposed to a blanket policy.

Fail-Safe

A fail-safe strategy is a strategy that will produce a definitive outcome at some trigger point, no matter what your opposition does after activating that trigger. For example, in a properly secured house, once a thief triggers the house alarm, the police will show up to investigate, regardless of what the thief does next. A fail-safe strategy that some organizations employ to defend against potential treble damages in a patent infringement lawsuit is a policy of not looking at patent claims belonging to competitors so that the court, as the provider of the definitive outcome, cannot declare an infringement as willful. The idea is that you cannot willfully infringe on a patent claim you did not know was there, even if you knew that it could be there.

Many successful organizations continue as a general policy to avoid searching for prior art or reading patent claims, and this continuity of practice serves as evidence that the strategy works for them. There is certainly an argument, particularly at the very cutting edge of technology, that a prior art search cannot reveal the most likely source of patent infringement in the first place. Since it takes 18 months for most patent offices to publish filed patent applications, a prior invention that might prove to be the basis of a future patent infringement lawsuit by a competitor could simply be unavailable for review at the time you need to decide whether to proceed with your own invention. Then, once your invention is well into development or use within an actual product, there would be a further disincentive to look back at the prior art. This is because the only outcome a prior art search would likely induce is the discontinuation of the product so that you do not infringe, the need to obtain a license from the less-than-favorable negotiation stance of having already invested in the invention, or the creation of the situation where a patent infringement will now be willful if the holder of that patent decides to sue.

Anyone considering whether to conduct a prior art search could see all this as entirely negative, particularly if competitors show themselves to be less than vigilant in policing their own patents and therefore less likely to sue. After all, they might not notice an infringement anyway, or even if they did, they might not enforce their position. Also, since the reinvention risk diminishes at the cutting edge of technology, the commercial argument to conduct prior art searches in order to reduce reinvention costs also carries less weight in newer lines of research and development.

(Continued)

In actual practice, the question of whether to conduct a prior art search and read existing patent claims before investing in a course of action is really not a black-and-white issue. Organizations take many actions that both raise and lower the actual need for a prior art search or at least change the arguments for or against a prior art search in each situation. In an environment where competitors actively enforce their patents, the need for a prior art search rises, since it affords the opportunity to deal with a likely threat early and perhaps on better terms than otherwise.

In an environment with extensive cross-licensing or patent pools, the need for prior art searching can diminish; as organizations become more closely integrated technically and therefore economically, they will have less incentive to sue each other even when an infringement occurs. As a note, this is a common principle in strategy that explains outside the patent field, among other things, why the now integrated economies of Europe make the wars of the previous centuries, as a means to solve grievances, highly improbable. Following the same principle, a patent infringement lawsuit, which is patent strategy's equivalent to war, becomes less likely when two or more organizations have a lot to lose from any ill will that such an infringement lawsuit could cause. However, even in the case of patent pools, and sometimes because of them, since they afford the possibility to sue multiple organizations for the same offense, there is always the outlier issue that can prove highly problematic if missed in a prior art search.

So in the end, the decisions about whether to conduct a prior art search and who, if anyone, should read patent claims, really do not lend themselves to a policy. It is a judgment call for the situation. The author does maintain, however, that given the overall strategic advantage of knowing what is out there versus not knowing, that any decision *not* to conduct a prior art search in any given circumstance should be accompanied by a very good reason for not doing so.

Even if you can reduce ignorance concerning a decision, error remains a factor in strategy. Error happens when an organization or individual takes an inappropriate action or executes an appropriate action poorly. It is the second of Merton's reasons for unexpected results. Error can occur as a direct result of ignorance or misapplication of skills. It can also occur when personal and emotional elements of decision making take precedence over logic and common sense. The demise of the original Ford Taurus model, which had been the best-selling sedan in the United States, provides an example.

Consumers, the ultimate deciders of the success of a product or service, liked the early Taurus designs because they offered a contemporary look on a reliable and affordable platform. Ford, in an attempt to keep the Taurus on the cutting edge of design—its competitors had imitated original elements of style that had made the Taurus popular—decided to do a complete redesign of the car's interior and exterior. Their implementation of that decision ultimately created a car consumers did not like—the third-generation Taurus, model years 1996 thru 1999. Ford executives accepted a design that consumers did not accept. The executives' predicted result did not match the actual result produced by consumers, and that error essentially killed the product line for the following decade.[8]

Similarly, the effort taken to pursue an error in patent strategy—for example, to invent and patent around the wrong technical standard—can leave you worse off than if you had done nothing. How does such an error occur? Decision makers may not know which standard will succeed, either because the market has truly not defined the standard (this being a de facto standard such as Adobe PDF), or the court has not defined the standard (this being a de jure standard, such as Wi-Fi developed by IEEE). In this case, they take a gamble, and sometimes that gamble is necessary. In fact, when a strong enough player does make a commitment, it can influence the deciding parties of the standard, whether they are the market or a governing body.[9] Consider the uncertainty that occurred between the HD-DVD and Blu-Ray standards of high-definition television display as an example of a market-defined (de facto) standard. It was difficult to know which standard would win, and therefore difficult to determine which way to use limited resources in research and development. This was a classic "horns of a dilemma" problem in that splitting resources to focus on both could lead to inadequate resources being used to support either. Less forgivable, however, would be to gamble unnecessarily when available but not studied or appreciated trends do favor one standard over the other, or worse, simply because the company has a greater stake in the chosen standard than consumers have.

Third on Merton's list, immediacy bias, builds on the propensity for people to err based on emotional decision making. Company leaders who have a lot invested in a course of action may desire to see that course of action through, even though the facts clearly indicate that their original desired result is not attainable or no longer desirable. The emotion of desiring to complete the task can easily overwhelm the logic of abandoning it. United Technologies continued, with the encouragement of the Pentagon, to research and develop a new Crusader mobile tracked artillery weapon system well into 2002. This lumbering heavy-weapon system was designed to address a Soviet land threat that had ended 10 years earlier. To its credit, United Technologies created a new and desirable result "B" that used intellectual property created from Crusader system research and development when it designed a lighter and more mobile artillery unit suitable for current conditions.[10] Personal attachment to the original goal, both within the product maker and the product consumer, appeared to be a major reason behind delaying a new course that United Technologies could have taken much earlier.

Basic values inherent in people and organizations, number four on Merton's list, can also cause unpredicted results. In *The Innovator's Dilemma*, Clayton Christensen describes a scenario in which IBM executives bet on the continued dominance of mainframe computers while IBM's competitors developed disruptive smaller computers.[11] Related to IBM's choice to bet on mainframes, in the early 1990s, ROLM, a telecommunications subsidiary of IBM, focused only on linking PBX telephone systems to mainframe computers, the IBM core product, to create seamless call center systems. At the same time, competitors AT&T and Northern Telecom focused on linking their phone systems to LANs composed of personal computers, a disruptive technology from the point of view of IBM's mainframe business.[12] As a result, intellectual property developed at AT&T and Northern Telecom proved much more relevant for future office environments dominated by personal computers than that originally developed by IBM. Furthermore, while the intent of linking ROLM PBX telephony equipment to IBM mainframes was to grow ROLM's market share, its market share declined instead.

The consequences of predicting results, the last reason covered in this discussion, can also cause unpredicted results, since the prediction itself, whether spoken or shown by the actions of the predictor, will bias other people's actions. Your prediction of the future itself changes how people react to a situation and therefore can change the result that might otherwise have occurred. To illustrate, the prediction that open-source computer operating systems will eventually dominate the market will drive a body of people to focus their attention on open source computer operating systems, thus making that prediction true—a self-fulfilling prophesy, if you will. On the other hand, the same prediction could redouble efforts of companies such as Microsoft that have a high stake in proprietary software to alter the situation and make the prediction wrong. In any case, the prediction itself changes the environment and therefore the viability of the prediction. In the absence of an appropriate strategy, people with enough power could literally make your predictions wrong no matter what you do. All they have to do is change the situation.

The creation of patents is a purposive consequence of research and development initiatives, an insightful legal department, and supportive management. It is a prediction or a gamble by those who filed for those patents that they will have value when and if they are issued. The relevance of those patents for the future will generally correlate with the company's strategy as a whole, although the one does not necessarily precede the other. Rather they emerge together from all aspects of innovation, advancement, and security efforts. Not all patentable inventions develop from the predicted outcomes and intended plans of research and development initiatives, which themselves have a sloppy back end. You cannot always know for certain what will come out of an effort. An unpredicted but useful invention could substantially influence the fortunes of a company if its leaders are adept enough to recognize and leverage the opportunity. Thus, successful purposive action often requires flexibility to get the best out of what actually happens.

So, bottom line: Strategy is a solution for how to get from "A" to "B," but it is a special type of solution because it addresses active and often intelligent opposition from outside sources as well as from within. Unlike a technical or mathematical solution, you cannot remove uncertainties created by that intelligent opposition or expect that if you find a successful solution to a problem your opposition will not change the conditions and create new problems for you to address. Strategic decision making is prone to error because of what you do not know, cannot know, or will not accept. A good strategy must therefore be born out of a pragmatic and logical review of the situation and must afford those who execute it the flexibility to handle changing conditions, some of that change being created by the very act of executing the strategy itself.

Rolls of the Dice

Another common reason that people experience unexpected results in apparently favorable circumstances is the consequence of stringing together too many dependent objectives along the way to a goal. For example, if for five key objectives necessary to reach a goal you have a 90% probability that you will succeed with any given one, then when taking into account that you have a 10% chance of failure five times instead of once, you have only a 59% chance of reaching that goal. Fifty-nine percent brings much more uncertainty into play than 90%. This means two things:

1. Pay attention to the number of contingent objectives needed to reach a goal, and pay attention to the innate human tendency not to calculate the combined risk that all those contingencies create.

2. Factor out as many contingencies as you can by either making uncertainties certain, or obviating the need for a contingency at all. For example, if you invalidate a competitor's patent, you eliminate a contingency over your possible infringement of that patent.

Patent Strategy Defined

Patent strategy aligns the power of patents to the objectives of your business. It is crafted from your ability and willingness to *gain, exploit,* and *defend* important creations under the system of patent laws. Patent strategy is a solution to get from "A" to "B" that can be composed of all manner of resources and actions.

Although patents represent an important part of most patent strategies, a given patent strategist may not actually employ his or her own patents within his or her patent strategy. Generic pharmaceutical manufacturers, for example, have geared themselves to compete without their own patents, and yet they certainly have patent strategies associated with traditional pharmaceutical companies that do own patents. So an organization does not have to own patents to use patented technology or to be subjected to actions from other patent owners under the system of patent and broader intellectual property laws. Having few or no patents is a legitimate patent strategy for some organizations. Nor is it an all-or-nothing decision. Dell Computer does file for patents, but owns relatively few patents compared to many of its competitors. Dell Computer instead gains access to much of its technology needs by licensing-in the patented technology of others on a worldwide basis.

How to maneuver in a market with patents depends on what works best for the participating organization. As with anything in strategy, there are trade-offs. For example, while Dell perhaps saves money on research and development costs by relying on the research and development of others, it does so at the risk of trading money, a commodity, for inventions, which are one of a kind. The uniqueness of the latter over the former tends to offer more leverage for the invention owner in negotiations.

Value Capture

A patent is an asset, and as with any other asset, you can exploit its intrinsic value and bear the burden of its cost. Your overriding goal in managing the asset, either as an individual asset or as a part of an asset portfolio, is to make the value of ownership or implementation appreciably higher than the cost of ownership or implementation.

If you are the owner of a patent, then you may exploit the patent through the proprietary manufacture, use, or sale of the claimed invention. This is possible because a patent gives you the right to exclude others from making, using, or selling the invention who have not properly attained the right to make, use, or sell that invention. You gain this right to exclude in the countries in which you have patent protection. It requires both that you have some capacity to enforce your rights and that the patenting authority has the legal infrastructure from which you can make your case. You can also effectively lease the patent through a license, or sell the patent outright to another person or organization.

As an asset, patents offer an opportunity to capture commercialization value in two key ways:

- Value 1: Property rights—value obtained from being the owner of the invention
- Value 2: Implementation—value obtained from being the producer, user, or seller of the invention

These two values are in addition to the value obtained by being a consumer of a product or service that is made by incorporating the patented invention in some way; here the focus is on your being an entity intent on commercializing the invention itself.

Depending on whether your focus is as an invention owner or an invention implementer, you should always consider how your company can better capture value from Value 1, Value 2, or both. After making that assessment, put your conclusions into action.

For thousands of years the commercial value of inventions resided primarily with the implementers of the inventions—our Value 2. This was the case because creators of new inventions had practically no means to enforce exclusivity if someone else could recreate their invention. Patents changed this dynamic because they offered the means to enforce exclusivity. However, even before the advent of patents, instances appear of value being obtained by owning inventions. The fundamental method used to capture this ownership value developed through the ages still exists in trade secret practices. Consider the craftsman sword makers in 1600 A.D. as an example. Once a craftsman learned a trade, such as sword making, that craftsman could practice the art and reap the implementation value of that art. To protect intellectual property rights, early craftsmen established rules for the teaching of their trade.[13] Apprentice craftsmen would agree to work for a period of time for a master craftsman in exchange for learning the craft. This was an early way to capture invention value—Value 1—even if for a short period of time. Today, an organization with a trade secret can go even further than the old guild masters, since in many countries it can indefinitely seek to put legal restraints on the dissemination of trade secrets by employees and associates given access to them.

With the advent of the patent system, the inventor no longer needed to produce the invention to capture value from it. The inventor may well have to share a given, and often substantial, percentage of value with the implementer; still, the inventor maintains ownership of the idea and continues to reap value by being the owner of the invention. Taken further, the owner of a patent may sell his or her invention to another person or organization, and this third party can receive considerable value from owning that patent without being either the inventor, maker, user, or seller of the patented invention. With that in mind, you can obtain considerable leverage in your use of patents by choosing to focus your patent strategy on which of either Value 1 or Value 2 requires the least amount or most available of your resources. The ratio of potential value to obtain at Value 1 or Value 2 differs by industry and company. Whereas producing a tractor costs a lot of money even after you have settled on a design, it costs practically nothing to produce software products once you have invested in their creation. On the other hand, if you have a tractor factory already, licensing a patent from an outside owner can prove a highly efficient way to get the most value out of that factory without unduly raising the cost of your research.

Setting a Precedent

On Nov. 21, 2006, a federal jury in Los Angeles awarded damages of $53.5 million to L.G. Philips in a lawsuit over its liquid crystal display (LCD) technology patents. The jury found that Chunghwa Picture Tubes (CPT) and Tatung Co. were infringing on L.G. Philips's patents without properly licensing the technology from the idea owner. The victory over CPT and Tatung provided an opportunity for L.G. Philips to aggressively pursue and implement its licensing program, since it set a precedent for the legitimacy of the L.G. Philips position and the validity of the LCD patent.[14] In other words, L.G. Philips's capacity to capture

(Continued)

the value of ownership at Value 1 increased significantly with the verdict.

Part of any patent strategy is to improve the capacity of the organization to capture value as the owner of the invention, the implementer of the invention, or both, by the scientific, business, and legal means available. The success of any action in patent strategy can be measured not only by immediate patent infringement damages gained, deterred, or avoided, but also by its capacity to enhance one or both value capture positions.

The Nature of a Strategic Solution

Strategy is a solution, but it is not the same as a solution you might use for a technical problem. With a solution to a technical problem, you can all but eliminate uncertainties in your results through experimentation and calculation. It is possible, for example, to design and test an entire jetliner on a computer before building a single airplane so that you already know with almost complete certainty that it will work as intended. This allows you to have confidence in the solution and experience less failure when you implement the solution. Throughout the design process of its 777 and 787 models, Boeing made extensive use of computer modeling to simulate the real thing well before it produced parts and then the whole airplanes. Planners often use computers in strategic simulations as well, but they cannot reproduce the precise predictions that a company such as Boeing can produce for technical problems.[15]

Unlike a technical solution, a strategic solution must address problems created by both external and internal opposition from entities that may not want that solution to succeed. So with a strategic solution, you will always have uncertainty because you cannot know what the opposition will do. In fact, the people who are the opposition may not know what they will do until they face a circumstance you create. A key component of a strategy, therefore, is to manage uncertainty, defined here as:

1. The unknown
2. The unknowable

Due diligence in strategy involves learning what you do not know that is knowable and that you should know—for example, that a competitor has recently published a patent application describing an invention critical for your path forward. You should know what art exists, assess the enforceability of the art, and know who the respective owners are most of the time. Similarly, you want to know that an acquisition you plan to make, in which patents play an important part in justifying that acquisition, will include the people, such as the inventors, who will allow you to make use of those patents. Finally, you should manage and direct the uncertainties of competitors regarding your efforts so that you do not become an open book to competitors, and instead force them to make hard choices about your confidential plans from which you might leverage exploitable mistakes. For example, if you file patents broadly around the world only if you believe an invention has more potential value than other inventions in your portfolio, you create a signal that competitors can use in their analysis of you. Competitors can easily create a subset of patents from your patent portfolio that has larger than average patent family sizes. Your competitor can then examine that subset of patents in more detail. That subset of patents, after all, would be the patents in your portfolio that you consider to be the most important.

The Hard Way

In November of 1994, the author took a scuba diving trip to the San Diego kelp beds. The owner of the boat used to shuttle the divers to the kelp beds recounted how he had dropped a diver into San Diego Bay who had the mission to photograph, from underwater, the secret winged keel of the Australian America's Cup contender before the 1983 competition. Unknown to him and the diver, the Australian patent office had published complete documentation of the secret winged keel before that time, which included all the drawings and specifications of the invention. The time, expense, and risk of putting a diver into the water to take pictures was not nearly as efficient as simply obtaining a copy of the Australian patent application. While the availability of patent

(*Continued*)

documentation may seem obvious to people who have familiarity with patents, the availability of this material was virtually
unknowable to people without that exposure. Part of a patent
strategist's role, therefore, is to educate people within his or
her organization about the patent field and what they can learn
from it.

Regarding the unknowable, you need to set up contingencies. Contingency planning and action, such as pursuing one course of research
while hedging with an investment in the alternative course of research,
is an important strategic way to address the unknowable. Scenario play,
which is covered in more detail in Chapter 4 and the Appendix, can help
you to plan contingencies by allowing you to test how best to handle
circumstances in advance of their actual occurrence. Since you cannot
fully predict what customers and competitors will do with a product or
service until it actually reaches the market, contingencies allow you keep
some options open. In this way, if customers choose the alternative, then
you will still have a stake in the market.

Bottom line: The patent strategist should make a prudent effort to
know what is knowable that decision makers should know and devise
contingencies to address that which is not knowable. The patent strategist
should also manage uncertainty, not only to make any given situation
clearer to the home organization, but also to manage what his or her
own organization makes clear or less clear to people from the outside.
Doing so puts the patent strategy on a solid foundation.

Contingencies

ACell, Inc., the owner of extracellular matrix (ECM) patents,
won a legal victory on August 18, 2006 in an infringement
case against Cook Biotech, Inc. and Purdue Research Foundation. The victory provided a boost to ACell by validating
a patent position the firm had established in 2002. That val-
idation provided ACell, Inc. with a precedent to aggressively
engage potential partners from the life sciences industry that had
been waiting for resolution on the infringement question.[16] The

verdict removed a major unknown, the validity of the patent, which was unknowable until the verdict was reached.

In such circumstances as these, a patent strategist concerned with the situation could speculate on the outcome of the case with his or her own validity opinion, but the master patent strategist would have also prepared contingency plans for both outcomes. This is particularly so when a patent case moves to a jury trial where decisions on validity ultimately rest with people who may have no real background in the technical art. Contingency planning to establish options relates to the fact that one of the surest signs that a strategy is otherwise in jeopardy is when its implementers run out of good options.

On Who Decides? The *Markman v. Westview Instruments, Inc.* Case

The 1996 Supreme Court ruling in the *Markman v. Westview Instruments, Inc.* case showed that the meaning and scope of terms in claims would be determined by the courts as a matter of law and not by a jury. Since the *Markman* case, most parties to an infringement lawsuit have desired to have a *Markman* ruling made as soon as possible. It can be a determining factor as to the merit of pursuing, settling, or withdrawing a lawsuit because it eliminates uncertainties associated with how the scope of patent claims will be viewed by the court in the case. Essentially, the parties involved argue in advance on the meanings of key terms and phrases found in patent claims rather than waiting to see how they are ultimately interpreted as the case progresses or concludes. It is a practical example of an action that eliminates an unknown variable and clarifies important decisions that opposing parties need to make.

Opposites

Strategy is often discussed in terms of opposites. The Chinese gave yin and yang to world culture to describe complementary feminine and masculine forces. Western literature offers its tradition of opposing good and evil. Sports has its winners and losers. These concepts are considered opposites, yet one cannot exist without the other. The patent world also has its corresponding opposites. The profession tends to define inventions as patented or nonpatented, solutions as open or proprietary, and licenses as open or exclusive. As is discussed further on in this book, thinking about patent strategy with these opposites in mind is useful when seeking leverage over competitors or with prospective partners.

Strategy itself is an interplay of two opposites—interaction and isolation; the general goal is to increase your level of interaction and decrease your level of isolation and to see the opposite result for your competition. For example, winning a key account increases your level of interaction with the market in that you have another customer on the books. At the same time, winning a key account also increases the level of isolation for your competitors since they now have one less customer available to them. Strategy also involves direct and indirect action—again, two opposites. For example, you might engage a competitor with a direct action, such as a patent infringement lawsuit, and then win with an indirect action, such as the invalidation of a patent used by that competitor in a countersuit. In patent strategy, patents have both direct and indirect uses, and they play a key role in the interplay between interaction and isolation because they can both isolate competitors if you enforce exclusivity and provide the basis for interaction, such as through licenses or business ventures.

There are additional pairings of opposites. Another important pairing for the strategist is action and inaction. They represent two opposites that have an equal capacity to produce success when skillfully employed together. A strategist should always keep in mind that the attainment of a desired result does not necessarily require purposive action all of the time. In fact, many of the most effective strategies involve *intentionally* doing nothing.

Strategic Inaction

Strategy can be more about what not to do than what to do. The strategic inaction that this implies is a powerful and often overlooked tool of the master strategist. Put another way, an example of a mediocre strategist is the individual who takes action when no action is needed.

Mediocre strategists can have difficulty overriding the compulsion to do something. This can create mistakes for a competitor to exploit, since action often produces more risk than inaction if for no other reason than that it tends to consume limited resources that might not be readily replenished. An example of appropriate inaction was Boeing's response to the Airbus 380. In 2005, Boeing relinquished the title of "seller of the world's largest commercial jetliner," long held by its 747, and a point of pride, to the Airbus 380. While this happened, Boeing focused instead on the smaller 787 Dreamliner. While developing the 787, Boeing produced a number of patents associated with composite-based aircraft, which are likely to have more applicability over the long term than knowledge gained to produce very large aircraft with more conventional materials and methods.[17] If Boeing had reacted to Airbus with action designed to keep or regain the lost title, it would have taken resources away that it could otherwise have used on its 787 venture.

Strategic inaction is a powerful tool because it conserves resources that you can put to use elsewhere. If your goal is to increase your level of interaction with a base of prospective customers, and your competitor takes action that has the effect of isolating itself from that pool of customers, then your competitor in effect does competitive work for you. In both the aforementioned examples of the Taurus and the Airbus 380, the owning organizations took it on themselves to jeopardize their competitiveness in very important market segments—sedans and mid-sized aircraft, respectively. As Napoleon Bonaparte is noted to have said, "Never interrupt your enemy when he is making a mistake."[18] Now, just as Napoleon would prepare his troops for the eventuality that his enemy would realize its mistake, part of what a patent strategist can do while a competitor is making a mistake is to build a patent portfolio that will make it more difficult for that competitor to rebuild its position on its own terms once its decision makers have realized their mistake.

Strategy and Change

Action and inaction are key elements of choice, since in the act of pursuing some options over others you are both doing and not doing what could be done. Through a succession of choices, some perhaps better than others, you are where you are because of what you did or did not do in the past. You operate in the present, making new choices that will produce new results. Change, resulting from your choices and the choices of others, creates an uncertain future. Your strategy must address your present and your uncertain future in context with your past. The patent system magnifies these truths because of the lag time between the conception of an idea and the award of a patent to protect the idea, the latter outcome itself being uncertain. Today you are making your patent portfolio for five and ten years out, and your patent strategy is currently operating on the base of decisions made five or ten years ago. So, unless you have been involved with the patent strategy of a company for 10 years, or plan to be involved with the patent strategy 10 years from now, you are living with the decisions and actions of your predecessors, while at the same time creating the future that your successors will have to live with.

In this uncertain environment, one unifying element allows you to succeed: innovation. Innovation creates your emergent treasures. Through innovation, along with the intellectual property it generates, you can both create the future and, to some degree, mitigate errors of the past. Through innovation, you make the best of what past actions give you today. Even if you or your predecessors did not make the best choices, innovation provides some measure of control over current events. This applies to both the creation and the improvement of inventions and business models. It also applies to creative licensing and acquisitions, which can make up for inevitable errors or shortcomings in research and development choices and successes.

Always have your desired result "B" in mind when you plan your strategy, but put it into context with your current situation "A" and your past. Innovate to make the best of your current situation and your past. Capitalize on the know-how that you have, and remain open-minded to new opportunities. It may, after all, be possible to purchase the innovation track of another entity if you have otherwise missed out on that innovation. Consider the viability of reaching your desired result "B" in light of what you have done and the resources that you have at your disposal. Then take action and pursue goals that make sense with two considerations that will follow:

1. The perfect strategy
2. The good-enough strategy

Knowledge Links

One of the quintessential American inventions is the airplane, patented by the Wright brothers in 1906. Before the Wright Flyer, powered flight of heavier-than-air aircraft did not exist. The Wright brothers themselves were not even in the existing flying businesses of gliders and lighter-than-air balloons. They did, however, have a track record of making both light and strong but fundamentally underpowered machines, namely, efficient human-powered bicycles.[19] Linking this prior experience to research about the dynamics of flight put them in a good position to take the step toward creating the first successful airplane design. The Wright brothers realized that their technology strengths would become key to the success of powered flight, and they had a versatile enough mindset to venture into a new product area. New ideas and businesses do not generally come out of the blue sky; rather, they build on previous experience, even if they take that experience into a completely different direction.

The Perfect Strategy

We all like the idea of perfection. If we are technologists, in fact, we can often achieve perfection. Sometimes perfection is necessary. Consider laser optics, for example: If there is one minor flaw in the lens, the invention does not function. Even in our processes, we seek perfection. Six Sigma, a process variation control methodology, remains a major initiative for a number of organizations in the attempt to reduce errors in processes to almost nonexistent levels.[20] Can we achieve perfection in strategy? Yes, in theory.

To develop this theoretical ideal strategy, we start with the more common actual practice of strategy, which is a system of managing options. As strategy plays out, it involves the decision to take any number of options, and as the number of options increases, it becomes inherently more difficult to predict exactly how things will turn out. For this the famous Prussian strategist Helmuth von Moltke the Elder coined the phrase "No battle plan survives contact with the enemy."[21] After even one new decision, your action might already be significantly different from the original plan. So if you want to develop a perfect strategy, or something that emulates that ideal, you have to eliminate your opponent's options as well as the decisions you need to make in response to those options.

Following that logic, the perfect strategy has succeeded before it has been executed and therefore presents no uncertainties for you and no options for your opponent. This is in keeping with the ideal stated by the famous Chinese strategist, Sun Tzu: "Making no mistakes brings certain victory, for it means conquering an enemy that is already defeated."[22]

In practice, the perfect strategy is a target whereby you eliminate as many of your uncertainties and your opponent's options as expediently possible. This means doing the groundwork and preparation so that the achievement of victory at the time of action is little more than a formality. As a case in point, when defending in a patent infringement suit you could do your patent invalidity work up front. You could build your case to the point where it is all but inarguable what the outcome will be before you seek judgment in a court of law. You have clear prior art and effectively win before the trial begins, which if your opposition believes the same, could lead to a settlement before you even step into the courtroom. To further emphasize the idea of the perfect strategy, every attorney knows the trial maxim "never ask a question unless you already know the answer." This is a form of the same ideal.

Realistically though, the perfect strategy is almost impossible to achieve. You will always be uncertain about what the opposition will do. For example, even when you know the answer to a question, as in the foregoing maxim, and even if the witness knows you know the answer, the witness might lie. You simply cannot control what the opposition will do in the way you can control the tolerance of, say, your manufacturing lathe. You will also have missing information that you cannot know, such as unpublished competitive patent applications sitting at the patent office. So although we like the idea of the perfect strategy, you will spend most of your time in the domain of the "good-enough" strategy.

Sun Tzu

Sun Tzu, the famous Chinese strategist from 2,500 years ago, wrote *The Art of War*.[23] His book is still revered by strategists to this day and was even quoted in the 1987 Oliver Stone movie, *Wall Street*, considered by many movie buffs to be a modern classic. Gordon Gekko, the master strategist investor who mentors the movie's protagonist, Bud Fox, said, "I don't throw darts at a board. I bet on sure things. Read Sun Tzu, *The Art of War*. Every battle is won before it is ever fought."[24] Interpretations of this quote are wide and varied. Hollywood's Gordon Gekko interpreted it as having inside information, legal issues aside, so as to know which way a security will go before he invested. Our real life patent strategists could emulate this ideal through thorough legal research. For example, the author has heard on many occasions, and has seen more than enough evidence to believe in its truth, that 90% of patents can be invalidated, in whole or in part, if someone is willing to invest in finding the prior art. Armed with convincing invalidating prior art, a patent strategist could effectively win a patent litigation case before it is actually tried in court if his or her opponent has anchored that case on the now invalidated art.

The "Good-Enough" Strategy

The "good-enough" strategy takes us from our current situation "A" to our desired situation "B" with enough resources still intact to leverage the success or react to an unknowable once we get there or along the way. As the pragmatic World War II General George S. Patton, Jr. stated, "A good plan, violently executed now, is better than a perfect plan next week."[25] This is in keeping with the idea that after a period of time, added preparation produces minimal returns and could even produce negative returns as the situation and opportunity change. It also comes with the realization that in conflict, uncertainties will always exist, and with those uncertainties come chance and probabilities. Therefore, there comes a time in every strategy to execute a plan, particularly when you have an acceptable probability for success and some measure of control over how the future will look.

Winning is often more about doing a little better than the competition than about being perfect. Doing a little better is itself often achieved simply by focusing on the fundamentals. By doing the fundamentals well, you will have better flexibility to handle changing situations. Vince Lombardi, the late master football coach, said, "Excellence is achieved by the mastery of the fundamentals."[26] It makes sense in his world. If blockers can block, receivers can catch, and the quarterback can throw, all with reliability, then they can adjust to almost anything the opposition throws at them. Likewise, a well-written patent that follows all the fundamentals of the patent prosecution profession will do much better, all things being equal, than a poorly written patent on the same invention. Think about the "good enough" in both business and technical terms. Who would care if you patent and sell the best camera lens on the market if your camera body does not take pictures well? The whole unit must first be good enough to hold its own in the market, and from there you can make it a little more extraordinary, perhaps by adding that special lens.

Of course, alternative methods for success do exist that may be expedient at the time, but are generally neither perfect nor good enough even though they can emulate those results over the long term. These include, among others, insider trading, paying off decision makers, and industrial espionage—appreciating that some cultures view these acts differently than others. Methods such as these are illegal in most industrial countries and would have to be considered cheating, therefore, by the strategist, if not at least highly risky in more accepting cultures. Temptations to cheat occur any time a person or organization is not good enough to succeed or not good enough to succeed as well as envisioned, within the rules of law. The strategist does need to account for such activities when planning. If cheating did not exist, companies as diverse as Dow and Microsoft would not feel pressure from counterfeiters and spies.

Although it's been said that "all is fair in love and war," and "if you ain't cheating, you ain't trying," cheating is an isolating action likely to make it more difficult to interact with people you will need in business over the long term. For example, just having Enron, Worldcom, or Arthur Andersen on your resume can raise the eyebrows of prospective employers, even if you had nothing to do with the shenanigans that ran afoul of the law. By executing strategy well, you can succeed within the rules or decide on more suitable prospects elsewhere.

Strategic Risk

It almost always makes sense to reduce your risk in any endeavor, unless you have specifically chosen to make increased risk a part of your strategy. Raising the stakes, which means to increase the risk beyond your adversary's capacity to accept that risk, is, after all, a universally understood way to keep out the risk averse. In either case, you need to understand what the real risk is and plan accordingly.

Risk calculation is the ratio of the potential usefulness of an action to the potential harm from the consequences of the action or its alternatives. Up until the threshold where delay or the effort to reduce risk itself causes undue risk, you wish to drive the usefulness of the result up toward 100% and harm down toward 0%. From this ratio of percentages, you can calculate risk, which is an integral part of the strategic decision. You talk about this ratio of percentages in terms of probabilities—for example, you have a 90% probability that your action will succeed at an acceptable cost and a 10% probability that it will fail or cost too much. You measure this against the probability and degree of usefulness in the results and the question of whether a given harm is something from which you can recover or if that harm would be catastrophic.

To illustrate risk in patent strategy, we can look at pharmaceutical companies. In the blockbuster world of large pharmaceutical companies, the vast majority of patents ultimately have no commercial value, but the ones that do have commercial value more than make up the difference. Knowing that a useless patent is of little harm to the viability of the company, but that a failure to file for a necessary patent in a highly competitive environment could be harmful or even catastrophic, pharmaceutical companies typically file for patents early and often. Pharmaceutical companies further manage their investments in research and development and hedge the risk inherent in making significant research and development commitments with licenses and acquisitions so that any given failure, while unpleasant, will not be catastrophic.

Even at the level of the individual patent, you need to concern your-self with strategic risk. Every time you file a new patent application, you take a risk that someone has already filed for a patent that covers your invention and will cause difficulties for you in the future. There is little you can do about this. As stated, in any given patent authority, a filed patent application will not appear in the public domain for at least 18 months after the filing date unless specifically opted out as allowable in USPTO procedures. In patent strategy, moving ahead anyway is a cal-culated risk that you have to take at least some of the time. Otherwise, you would not get anything done.

Fear of Catastrophic Loss

The fear of catastrophic loss is one of the important tools avail-able to the strategist who seeks to keep potentially dicey situations under control. On the one hand, if an adversary can be made to fear a catastrophic loss out of proportion to its actual probability, then the strategist can influence the behavior and therefore the performance of that adversary with comparatively little invest-ment of resources to that investment of resources that would be necessary to make the probability of a catastrophic loss a real-ity. One well-executed and publicized lawsuit, for example, can prevent the need to launch many more lawsuits in the future.

The fear of catastrophic loss is another strategic element that needs to be managed and employed well, because as much as it can work for you, it can also work against you if your com-petitor does not have a suitable orientation. A capable adversary that does not fear catastrophic loss—either from ignorance, over-confidence, or a mental framework that allows him or her to accept catastrophic consequences that may happen—becomes a danger that must be addressed in as efficient a manner as possible. This is especially so when the collateral costs of your adversary's catastrophic result, or the means from which it is created, put your own position in jeopardy. Many lawsuits, for example, cre-ate two losers. This adversary needs to be combated, avoided, or in some other way educated to appreciate and respect the gravity of the situation.

Competitive Risk

Risk, both recoverable and catastrophic, comes in two key forms:

1. Risk for surviving
2. Risk for thriving

We can illustrate these forms of risk by starting with the analogy of the relationship between a seal and a great white shark. Let's start from the perspective of the great white shark.

Powerful as it is, muscular and commonly over 16 feet or 5 meters in length, the great white shark uses ambush as a primary hunting technique.[27] It cruises hidden in the depths while it seeks an opportunity presented by a seal swimming above it. When it identifies a suitable target for attack, it rockets vertically to the surface in order to surprise the seal and give the seal no chance to fight back. Certainly the seal is no match for the great white shark once the shark makes physical contact, so why the need for the surprise attack? The first reason is that a fast and agile seal might flee if it becomes aware of the shark and cause the shark to waste energy in a pursuit where the seal will often get away. Second, if the seal had ample opportunity to fight back, as an attack that was not a surprise could allow, the odds of an injury to the shark from the seal's own jaws, however slight, could catch up to the shark over time. Perhaps the seal could cause injury to an eye with one of its long canine teeth, which would prove catastrophic for a shark that relies on vision to hunt. This is a natural version of the "Rolls of the Dice" we discussed earlier that successful sharks have evolved to address. Each time the shark attacks, it is rolling the dice, and it needs to drive its risk to near zero. The shark cannot avoid all risk when it hunts, or it would starve, but it has evolved to take no more risk than necessary to both survive and thrive, both increasing its hit ratio and lowering the possibility of injury by using ambush as its primary hunting technique.

Similarly, for you as someone involved with patent strategy, your company cannot avoid all risk. You cannot know for certain everything that your competitor is doing or will do. But you can take steps to minimize the risk as much as possible through thorough research and by interacting with competitors to lay the groundwork for future trades instead of litigation. After all, even staunch business competitors can be friends on the golf course, particularly when some measure of cooperation reduces the risk of failures for all.

To produce the best outcome in an interaction with your competitors and to fully understand a situation, it pays to look at the situation from the other point of view. Let us now look at the relationship between the seal and the great white shark from the seal's perspective. An overriding goal of a seal is to eat without being eaten. To do the former, it generally exposes itself to the latter, depending on the presence and the disposition of the sharks. With this in mind, if you could ask a seal to make a choice between swimming and feeding where there are sharks, or swimming and feeding where there are no sharks, and the seal could really think through the consequences of its decision, then the seal would have to choose to swim where there are sharks. Why? Because that is where the fish are. An overemphasis on just surviving can lead to self-isolation, and isolation generally leads to entropy and eventual death. A focus on thriving emphasizes interaction, which tends to lead to growth, provided the risk associated with that interaction is survived. So the seal needs to learn how to survive and thrive in the presence of sharks instead of spending time trying to find some mythical place with lots of fish and no sharks.

Such is the challenge for patent strategists: to allow their companies to thrive in a contested environment. Contested environments become contested by the very fact that they have value, and people who execute patent strategy in contested environments tend to become more capable practitioners of the art, since they must operate with a lower margin for error. Companies that cannot thrive in contested environments ultimately see themselves removed from those environments, either by their own mistakes or when they become valuable to someone more capable. A stark example of this is Netscape. For a brief period of time, Netscape dominated the Web browser market. Netscape managers, however, failed to protect Netscape's intellectual property when a few well-prepared patents could have left them in a much less vulnerable position. This left the door open for Microsoft, a highly adept competitor in matters concerning intellectual property, to enter and then dominate the market with Microsoft Explorer.[28] So the master patent strategist must in effect become a shark-savvy seal in order to thrive and survive. A place to develop that savvy is in the decision cycle.

The Strategy Paradox

A balance between surviving and thriving is a key element for determining where the real risk in business lies. To illustrate, Michael Raynor's book *The Strategy Paradox*, shows that while companies with a high degree of focus appear to outperform their more generalist rivals, these same single-minded companies also have the highest number of business failures. Since the failures are no longer independent business entities, they drop from the performance statistics, giving the appearance that a high degree of focus is a better strategy for success. So when business consultants take measure of the most successful companies and compare what they do differently from average performers, the consultants may not take into account the full picture.[29]

A recommendation to overly focus efforts in business could be akin to recommending that a person quit his or her job, fly to Hollywood, and start a career in acting. Successful movie stars certainly make much more than the average person, but considering the high failure rate among movie star hopefuls, is this truly a wise recommendation? Raynor's idea carries over into patents, considering that while focused companies may score big-time with a hit product in their chosen field, they will also have diminished flexibility to address changing environments. The focused companies have less diversity in their patent portfolio to draw from should the environment change. In a world of opposites, between being completely focused or totally diverse, a healthy in-between position needs to exist in most organizations.

Chapter 2

Decision Cycle

his chapter introduces the decision cycle, which forms the backbone of this book. The decision cycle is an ongoing cycle of assessment, decision, and action that pertains to all strategy. It models how we see an opportunity or threat, how we decide what to do about that opportunity or threat, how we execute that decision, and how we assess the results for the next decision cycle. The decision cycle loop is continuous. The strategist seeks to have proficiency in a race of decision cycles that is in some way superior to the proficiency of the competition. That proficiency is achieved by developing the pertinent capabilities of the organization for the strategy being employed and by fostering a suitable orientation for success on the part of decision makers and those other individuals executing the strategy.

To fully develop the decision cycle in patent strategy, we have a few important considerations to make first. These are the costs to participate in patent strategy, the questions to ask when reviewing inventions that you may incorporate into your patent strategy, and the four rules of patent strategy. We will cover these considerations, along with some important related notes, and then expand on the decision cycle itself.

The Question of Cost

Have you ever been to a Las Vegas casino? If not, then perhaps you have seen one on TV or played some rendition of the gambling games themselves elsewhere. When you pull up a chair to gamble, what thought should cross your mind? The possibility of winning aside, if you are like most people, you should ask yourself how much the respective game could cost you.

For many people involved in patent strategy, their orientation on patent strategy is almost entirely cost based and defensive in nature. This is a limiting orientation that has started to change in business circles as patent portfolios become profit centers and integral parts of the corporate strategy infrastructure. But suffice it to say, the further your patent strategy is from being a perfect or ideal strategy, the more it does involve some level of gambling from which you incur costs with no guarantee of a return.

Gambling can generate considerable costs that may or may not be recovered at the conclusion of a given event. This is true even in poker where all outcomes are not necessarily left to chance. While luck is always a factor in poker, it is possible to win with a weak hand and lose with a strong hand, depending on the comparative savvy of the competing players, and this comparative savvy will impact views of cost. For the importance of comparative savvy, among other reasons, the dynamics of poker and patent-based negotiations are often similar; while having strong patents is a plus, you will not necessarily achieve the best possible outcome in any related interaction with competitors, nor does having weak patents necessarily mean you cannot achieve a result you desire from them.

In the patent world, the cost even to be in the game is high. The cost to file for a patent in the United States on anything but the simplest of inventions will run over $10,000 and quite possibly over $25,000 per patent, considering filing and prosecution fees.[1] In some industries, the range can fall into the $25,000 to $50,000 range, depending on the technology. If you decide to seek an additional patent for a given invention in the European patent authority, then you can expect to add another $15,000 to $20,000 dollars and more to the cost.[2] If you choose to file in Japan also, then you can expect to pay a cost similar to that paid for your U.S. or European patent.[3] Each additional patent authority you choose adds to the cost of your overall patent protection. Then there is the issue of maintenance fees if you plan to keep the patent in force for all or part of the usually 20-year period granted for patent protection. Add all of this up, and the total cost of a globally filed patent can easily exceed $100,000. Now marry the cost to protect a single invention to a portfolio of tens, hundreds, or thousands of patents, and you start to see why every decision in patent strategy needs to consider the cost involved. Bottom line: Paying to play in patent strategy can cost a lot of money, all the more so since it rarely suffices to bring just one patent to the table, and you have no certainty associated with the value of the effort.

So considering that you have a limited budget to work with regarding a given invention or collection of inventions, you need to ask within your decision cycle whether to patent at all. This is further complicated by the fact that taken as an independent entity, getting a patent on any one given invention is more likely than not a losing bet, yet your best bet on aggregate when competitors have patents is generally to also have patents of your own. So before you begin to plan your patent strategy, you need to have some appreciation of how much you are willing to spend on your patent portfolio, and then place the best bets you can with the opportunities that you have to create, acquire, advance, and defend patentable inventions. While you make your decisions on whether to patent new inventions, which are essentially for your tomorrow, you fund and play your present situation with the patents you have on hand, even if they are not exactly the patents you would like to have. In so doing, you seek to achieve an ample return on your investment that allows your costs to make sense for the returns to the business.

International Filing Strategies

Part of patent strategy is to determine in which countries to file for patents. This is often a cost driven decision, because of the

(Continued)

high price of obtaining patent protection in multiple countries. It weighs the available budget against the chosen method to prioritize which inventions need international patent protection and in which countries they need that protection. Your considerations on what to protect internationally and where should include both your perspective and the perspective of competitors that may challenge your patent positions legally or commercially. From both perspectives they include the predicted value of a given invention, targeted markets, predicted revenues, production locations, headquarters locations, plus licensing targets and the enforceability of patents in the proposed patent authorities.

Foreign filing strategies very much reside in the domain of seeking a "good-enough" strategy, noting that even the most well-endowed patenting concerns do not protect all of their inventions globally. Patent counsel, when apprised of business needs, can help to assess the level of international protection necessary considering, for example, that obtaining patents in major markets such as the United States, Europe, and Japan plus perhaps a competitor's manufacturing country, such as China, might effectively protect a given invention as much as if you had in theory obtained a patent in every country in the world that grants patents. Your objective in international patent filing, therefore, is to build enough of a deterrent for the technology or product line protected, even if it is not a perfect deterrent, to reasonably expect to inhibit competitive encroachment, all within the confines of your patent budget and other priorities.

Invention Review List

With your cost limitations and risk tolerance in mind, we have in the decision cycle a set of 10 questions on whether or not to patent a given invention. These 10 questions can supplement existing questions that you use for your current invention review process, and your current invention review process probably includes many of them already. All

Exhibit 2.1   Invention Review List: Questions a Patent Strategist Needs to Answer

---

1. Is there existing prior art?
2. Does the invention have commercial potential?
3. Is the invention patentable?
4. Can the invention serve our competitive strategic purpose?
5. Will a patent on this invention deliver a business advantage?
6. Do we have other competitive advantages that reduce or enhance the need to patent this invention?
7. Does a patent on this invention support our position in the technical space?
8. Are we willing and able to litigate over a patent on this invention if challenged?
9. Can we detect a patent infringement on this invention if it occurs?
10. Are the business, legal, or technical risks associated with this invention acceptable?

---

the material we have and will cover in this book addresses one or more of these 10 questions. Since they are important at the beginning of a given decision cycle involving new inventions, they appear here. We will also revisit them toward the end of the book as a part of connecting the loop in the decision cycle. The invention review list is shown in Exhibit 2.1.

The invention review list helps you to screen less promising inventions for your purposes from those with more promise. Your answers to the questions should detail the reasons behind your positive or negative responses. If, on reviewing an invention, you cannot satisfactorily answer any one of the questions on the invention review list in a way that allows patenting to make sense, you should consider correcting the deficiency, protecting the invention another way, or not protecting it at all and using your resources elsewhere. Even if you can answer the invention review questions satisfactorily, you may have to prioritize a given invention based on its expected importance in relation to other opportunities you need to protect. Assuming that you do decide to patent at least some of the time, and that you have or will have patents in your portfolio, we can develop the next consideration for your decision cycle.

Four Rules of Patent Strategy

Given that we have focused our attention on patent strategy and that patent strategy typically involves patents, we can construct four rules of patent strategy for their use. Even if you do not have patents of your own, these rules will impact you if somebody else in your technical domain does have patents. A given patent itself is like one piece in the larger patent strategy game. It is a defined unit of transferable knowledge that you can use for many purposes.

In that light, we can draw some ideas for patent strategy from one of the most popular strategy games in Asia. This is a 3,000-year-old Chinese game called "Go." Go has only four simple rules that govern how players play their pieces; yet playing in accord with these four rules generates so many complex patterns and possibilities that, unlike the more commonly known strategy game of chess, no computer program has yet outperformed a human master.[4]

Go is a great game for the patent strategist to learn, because the way to win is to capture the most territory with the fewest number of pieces (resources). Go strategy includes the tactics of blocking, surrounding, linking, and negating also found in patent strategy. Like Go, patent strategy has four simple rules. Playing in accord with these rules allows you to eliminate, isolate, interact with, or negate (four competitive effects that are detailed further on in this book) competitive patent positions, and to do so within the constraints imposed by your limited patent budget. The four patent strategy rules are:

1. Use a patent to isolate.
2. Threaten to use a patent to isolate.
3. Use a patent to interact.
4. Leverage the possible use of a patent to interact.

All patent strategies can be derived from these four rules. It is important to keep them in mind for patent strategy, because, though their interplay with competitors and facilitators can be highly complex, the rules themselves are not. One of many examples of an action for each rule follows:

1. *Use a patent to isolate.* Enforce your patent in order to isolate your competitor from the invention through an injunction.

2. *Threaten to use a patent to isolate.* Threaten an infringement lawsuit if certain conditions are not met.
3. *Use a patent to interact.* License your technology in order to establish a solid business relationship with another company.
4. *Leverage the possible use of a patent to interact.* Indicate your willingness to license if certain conditions are met so that multiple parties bid for an exclusive license.

Any given action in patent strategy has underlying it one or more of these patent strategy rules. The rules serve as a part of a decision cycle whereby you assess, decide, and then act, with the action in patent strategy being taken in accord with one or a combination of the four rules. Additionally, although the rules as written use the term "patent" in the singular, depending on your industry, you may actually have an aggregate of patents that work together to achieve your objective in your patent strategy. In the pharmaceutical and chemical industries, there is often a one-to-one (or a one-to-a-few) relationship between patents and products, whereas in high-tech and general mechanical industries, you will typically have many patents for each product. So where we use the term "patent" in the rules, the actual implementation of the rules in a given situation may involve more than one patent.

In addition, the predicted usefulness of a given invention in applying these rules can also serve in your assessment of whether to apply for a patent. After all, you do, with any given invention, have the opportunity to keep it as a trade secret or to disclose it, and that would be a factor in how you respond to the four rules that you or your competitors play with other patents in a portfolio. Part of your assessment regarding each given patent authority is whether a patent would help you to use an appropriate and useful rule or to address the use of a rule by a competitor.

Credibility

Central to making the four rules of patent strategy work is credibility. To use a patent to isolate, it must have the quality, coverage, and support to keep your opponent from breaking through the isolation. In intellectual property terms, you must ensure that your competitor cannot easily design around or invalidate your

(Continued)

patent. If you decide to threaten to use a patent to isolate, your opponent must believe that you are willing and able to carry out that threat. This could mean, for example, showing that you have the resources and mindset to sue the opponent for infringement if necessary. Similarly, to use a patent to interact, it must have the quality, coverage, and support to merit that interaction; to leverage the possible use of a patent to interact, the other party must believe you can and would follow through with that interaction if it meets certain conditions. When considering any strategic action, it is important to consider how it will impact or be impacted by your credibility.

Love and War

The four rules of patent strategy are the same underlying four rules in love and war, and for that matter, any strategic contest. Starting with the example of war, you seek to gain a result through actual fighting or through the threat of fighting, keeping in mind that the threat, since it keeps your options open, is often more effective than the actual fighting. In love, you seek a significant interaction with your object of affection, and just the possibility of such interaction can often generate greater leverage than the actual interaction itself. Throughout this book, you will see universal principles of strategy applied to patent strategy. Patent strategy is a unique professional discipline, but the underlying rules that govern it strategically are not.

Shades of Gray

One of the surest ways to fail in strategy is to lock yourself into black and white categorizations of the world or profession of which you are a part. Expert strategists know that the real world operates in shades of gray. So in patent strategy, whenever we talk about patents in the singular in order to make strategic principles clear, the strategist should recognize that what we really need to think about goes beyond the single patent or even an aggregate of patents. We really need to think about the entire body of intellectual property that could be a single patent but could also comprise multiple patents from multiple sources, trade secrets, and perhaps even brands or copyrights that would all come into play as an aggregate whole to foster interaction and isolation activities.

Related to this idea of shades of gray is to appreciate that when we say that an industry, such as the pharmaceutical industry, typically has a one-patent-to-one-product relationship, that is not always the case and may not apply in the future. Computer-assisted pharmaceutical development simulations, used to more rapidly test for new drugs, can raise the number of related patentable compounds associated with a targeted treatment. In addition, the trend toward developing personalized drugs, which takes a base molecule and modifies it such that each person has a custom-made version optimal for his or her physiology, will also determine the type and quantity of intellectual property needed to protect that given class of drugs.

Furthermore, traditionally distinct industries, such as pharmaceuticals and high-technology, have started to overlap. For example, printing technology associated with creating office documents can, by substituting ink with a pharmaceutical, be used to print a treatment regimen of very specific doses onto digestible paper related to the specific condition and specific individual, all at a level of accuracy, variability, and convenience difficult to achieve when splitting pills or measuring liquid doses by other means. That solution involves multiple patents from multiple sources and multiple industries. The underlying rules of patent strategy, however, stay the same. Bottom line: The rules of patent strategy are simple, the aggregate body of technology is not always so simple, and the more you can think and classify in shades of gray instead of black and white, the better your performance in patent strategy and any other strategy is likely to be.

The Definition of a Decision Cycle

The four rules of patent strategy apply to decision cycles. The decision cycle is a continuous loop of:

1. Assessment
2. Decision
3. Action

This loop provides a framework for all strategic activity.[5] You make an assessment of a situation, come to a decision, take action, make a new assessment from the consequences of that action, make a new decision, and so on. Exhibit 2.2 shows the decision cycle, which is a continuing cycle of assessment, decision, and action that provides a framework for all strategic activity.

All patent strategy is built around a continuing cycle of assessment, decision, and action. These three decision cycle elements are influenced by both the current situation and the orientation of the participants. The decision cycle may pertain to individual actions, such as preparing and filing a patent, up to and beyond the entire cycle a corporation goes through to turn an idea into an intellectual property asset. The individuals and organizations that can proficiently move through their decision cycles at a higher tempo than their rivals frequently have significant competitive advantages over those rivals. To better appreciate this definition, let's revisit our seal and shark analogy as it pertains to the decision cycle, and then we will convert that analogy back into patent strategy.

When seal and shark meet, each animal tries to act and react faster than the other to attain its desired result from the encounter. If the shark

All patent strategy is built around a continuous cycle of assessment, decision, and action.

Our orientation has a major impact on how we assess, decide, and act.

Exhibit 2.2 Decision Cycle

attacks the seal in open water and misses, which it often does, the more agile seal will try to stay very close to the flank of the shark and away from its jaws until it finds an opportunity to escape. This tactic works better or worse for the seal, depending on the experience of the shark, the experience of the seal, and other variables such as water clarity. The capacity of either animal to proficiently move through decision cycles at a higher and higher tempo provides a significant competitive advantage, and so they evolve to do so. This proficient tempo improves for both animals as a result of experience—the faster-thinking sharks eat and the faster-thinking seals escape.

All strategy, including patent strategy, is built around a continuing cycle of assessment, decision, and action. Those entities that can proficiently move through these cycles at a better, usually higher, tempo than their rivals usually win in competition. This does not mean that taking immediate action is always the best decision; sometimes the best decision is to wait for more information or a more appropriate time to act. Purposeful inaction, however, is different from not making an assessment or slow decision making. As someone involved with patent strategy, this means that you need to execute the four rules of patent strategy as they pertain to your situation at a better, usually faster pace than your rivals. You want to isolate before you are isolated and interact before others pursue interaction elsewhere, in the way that either activity helps you to reach your overall goals.

With decision cycles, the advantages offered to you from the material in this book can go beyond just the familiarity and knowledge of the material. After all, your competitor can gain the same familiarity and knowledge by reading this same book. In response, you will want to become more adept at using the material so that the knowledge better translates into proficient action. Since most of the time the advantage lies in proficiently moving through decision cycles at a higher tempo than your rivals, that higher tempo will be our focus for this discussion. You seek to go from idea to patent application to asset and implementation faster than your competitor. You hire the people and design the systems that can make this possible.

Throughout this book, we will focus on the speed aspect of the decision cycle—quick assessment, quick decision, and quick action. However, because all strategies have their opposites, keep in mind that sometimes operating at a slower tempo than competitors can operate can be the decisive advantage. For example, investor commitments may prevent a venture-funded competitor from waiting for a market to develop for as long as you can, or perhaps your present market position allows you to let other pioneers test new ideas first so that you can learn from their mistakes. In these examples, your capacity to operate at a slower pace, if you have better funding, more patient investors, or an already established market base, could be your decisive advantage. Still, for the sake of clarity, most patent strategy situations focus on the faster-paced side of the race of decision cycles, and so will we.

Winning the race of decision cycles is critical to strategic success in patent strategy and all other strategic decisions. Because of its importance, the main body of this book is arranged in accordance with the decision cycle model. We will discuss ways to craft a patent strategy using the decision cycle model as our guideline. No matter how complex a topic becomes, you can ground it on the idea that you seek to proficiently execute decision cycles that involve the four rules of patent strategy at a tempo competitors cannot match, and you seek to do so within the constraints of your financial and other resources. We start with "assess."

Chapter 3

Assess

Assess is the first part of the decision cycle. During your assessment, you take stock of the current situation, your available resources, and the possible futures. After your assessment, you should thoroughly understand where you are, "A," and where you want to be, "B." This section on assessment introduces nine key learning points, as follows:

1. *Defining the problem.* To succeed in any strategy, the strategist needs to understand the problem that the strategy must address. All strategy addresses problems, since even not being where you want to be creates problems. But while the need to understand the problem may seem obvious, most strategists in most disciplines, patent strategy included, do not actually focus on the real problem of a given situation. The real problem in any given situation is the effect of not getting from a present situation "A" to a desired situation "B." It is not the opposition that keeps us from getting from "A" to "B," although within our strategy, we may need to address that

opposition. It is also not the condition that we are away from "B" itself, whatever the cause, since we might find the benefits we seek from a new situation other than "B." The real problem is the effect of not getting to "B."

2. *Problem resolution.* When the strategist views the problem as the effect of not getting from "A" to "B" instead of just the cause or the condition, many more strategic options open up for the strategist to explore. You will learn four major classes of solutions from which to craft comprehensive strategies. These solution classes make sense when you take the point of view that the real problem is not necessarily the cause of the effect or the condition of your situation—it is the effect itself.

3. *Identifying the opposition.* Barring good fortune, a strategist can expect to succeed against opponents only if he or she has identified them as opponents. Opposition, however, comes in many forms; some obvious, some not. The patent strategist must address opposition that develops both inside and outside the traditional domain of patents and the traditional domain of what he or she may consider as a competitor. The patent strategist must know how to identify who the opposition is beyond traditional competitors.

4. *Understanding why opposition must exist.* Opposition exists because your day-to-day activities almost always interfere with the plans of others. If you succeed at any endeavor of value, then you capture an opportunity that someone else may not have the opportunity to capture. If you patent an invention, someone else cannot patent that same invention. If you are doing anything or seeking anything of value, you will have opposition, especially if you are succeeding.

5. *Identifying with whom you should cooperate or compete, and why.* At the root of strategy is the desire to raise one's capacity for independent action. Independent people and organizations have a greater latitude to interact at places and times of their choosing, which is a significant advantage. Therefore, you naturally will cooperate with people and organizations that increase your opportunities for independent action and compete with those that restrict your opportunities for independent action. There is rarely a black-and-white differentiation between those with whom you compete or cooperate; in patent strategy you often compete and cooperate with the same entities at

the same time. Licensing is at the core of many such dual relationships in the patent field.

6. *Evaluating resources that are at the heart of cooperation and competition evaluations.* A patent strengthens and is strengthened by any number of additional resources both inside and outside the organization. The patent itself can be used as a tool for gaining access to resources you do not otherwise have, access to resources being a key reason to compete or cooperate. You either compete or cooperate with a given entity depending on which type of interaction you believe will improve your access to needed resources.

7. *Putting cooperation and competition into context with three Centers of Excellence.* Successful companies focus their time and resources on three specific areas that the author calls Centers of Excellence. Three Centers of Excellence in innovation, advancement, and security determine the who, what, when, where, why, and how you should cooperate or compete with other entities, and they ultimately determine the overall success of the organization. These Centers of Excellence operate internal to the organization, external to the organization, or both; from whatever source, the business needs to achieve excellence in these disciplines if it expects to thrive in the marketplace. Patent strategy cannot occur in isolation from broader business strategy, and this model provides an effective way to link the two. It is also possible to compete with an entity along one Center of Excellence while cooperating with the same entity along another. For example, you might jointly work on a new technology but compete to sell that technology within your own respective and competitive products.

8. *Putting the three Centers of Excellence into context with parallel lines of competition as a key to crafting powerful strategies.* Organizations traditionally align themselves into silos that focus on different but parallel lines of competition. Examples of these silos are engineering, sales, finance, marketing, and the like. Head-to-head competition in a single line of competition, while it may seem natural, may not be the best approach to strategy. If a competitor is a marketing giant, then pouring additional resources into your marketing department may give you little to no advantage. But if that same competitor is not focusing on intellectual property protection, then by protecting more of your

own intellectual property, you may create a competitive advantage over that competitor because your intellectual property allows you to impact how your competitor can access those markets. By creating a structure around a situation that leverages parallel lines of competition, you can craft a strategy to create desired changes in that system outside the traditional competitive domain. Strategy is not always about doing something per se: it is about creating the conditions under which that desired something is done. Often another line of competition is an avenue for changing those conditions. This is an important point about achieving goals indirectly, one that is highly relevant to patent strategy and is developed throughout this book.

9. *Dominant and contested positions—assessing where your sanctuaries are and the dominant or contested nature of competition.* To succeed in any strategy, including patent strategy, with both your resources and your objective intact, you seek advantages. These advantages come in the form of overwhelming advantage, surprise, asymmetry, and sanctuary. The proper application of these advantages is critical for creating a first-rate patent operation.

Defining the Problem

Strategic planning begins when you identify a goal. Through the strategic process, you determine *how* to get from your current situation "A" to your desired situation "B," which in turn defines the objectives that you believe will lead to your goal. You also plan for how you will address any interference from opponents. The strategy you select is your solution for how to get from "A" to "B." It differs from a traditional solution, however, where through experimentation you can eliminate most, if not all, uncertainties. Strategy addresses uncertainties caused by often intelligent opposition. It can also address forces, such as forces of nature, that you cannot fully understand and predict and therefore present uncertainties that can appear to be created by intelligent opposition. This last appearance of intelligence from natural forces is illustrated by the fact that we still give hurricanes—the ultimate weather event and one that we do not fully understand—personal names.

People develop solutions because they have problems. A problem represents a threat, an opportunity, or both. A strategy is a solution for a problem that involves opposition. To craft a successful strategy, you must first understand the core problem. More often than not, the apparent problem is not the core problem. For example, hurricanes are considered a problem by many people, but the hurricane itself is really not the core problem. The core problem is loss from injury, death, and property destruction, the effects of the hurricane. Defining the problem as the hurricane and the solution as stopping the hurricane seems, on its face, to make sense. But the time and resources necessary to figure out how to actually stop a hurricane would be astronomical. Even if we could devise a way to stop the hurricane, which would serve as a means to protect people and materials, this obvious solution would likely prove short-sighted and do more harm than good. Wetlands, on which much of our food supply depends, require the occasional flushing of the system that a hurricane provides to stay vital.[1] So stopping the hurricane would then have an unfavorable effect on the ecosystem and would possibly cause more long-term harm to people and materials than the hurricane itself. Focusing on the problems of danger to personal safety and property allows for a more directed solution, one designed toward stopping or reducing the injury, loss of life, or property destruction. This opens many more, and more realistic, possibilities for resolution.

Similarly with patents, if you focus too narrowly on the cause of a problem (e.g., a competitive patent) instead of the effect (isolation from the claimed technology), your solution can easily make your situation worse. For example, let's suppose you define a problem as being your competitor's granted patent since you cannot move forward as you would like without infringing on that patent's claims. One possible solution is to invalidate that patent. If your competitor's patent is invalidated, you will have complete freedom of operation with the claimed technology, which may be true. With that in mind, you spend a lot of time and resources trying to invalidate the patent. On succeeding, you gain the freedom to operate you sought, thus seemingly solving your problem. But your act of invalidation may also serve to open a market to a host of other competitors that also benefit from the invalidation.

Now revisit the situation and focus on the real problem—the effects associated with your isolation from the claimed technology—and consider solutions that do not necessarily consider the patent as a problem. For example, rather than exposing its patent to an invalidation exercise, your competitor might be open to an exclusive licensing relationship. The licensing agreement will eliminate isolation, albeit perhaps with some royalty payment as a trade-off; yet that patent, even though held by a competitor, can usefully still maintain a restrictive market.

Murphy's Laws of Problems and Solutions

$$S = \frac{U}{H}$$

Murphy's Law states that "anything that can go wrong will go wrong."[2] Since this law, as stated, does not provide a limit on time, it rings true for any potential scenario for misfortune. If you drive a car long enough and nothing else catastrophically breaks first, the wheels will eventually fall off. According to one of Murphy's other laws, "the chief cause of problems is solutions."[3] Every solution will attempt to solve a problem, and while perhaps succeeding at solving that problem, it will also create new problems. This concept can be illustrated mathematically. If we accept that a solution (S) is the ratio of usefulness (U) to harm (H), then $S = U/H$. The better solution is one in which the solution is proportionally more useful than harmful, and the ideal solution has all the intended usefulness with no harm whatsoever. In this equation, however, it is mathematically impossible for H to equal zero. In other words, any action will cause some harmful consequences, and to believe that it will not is short-sighted. Since it is impossible to completely eliminate harm from solutions, and strategy is a type of solution, a strategist must always consider the harm involved in the strategy. This means that whenever you devise a solution, you must also plan for the problems that it will create.

The chief cause of most problems is the solutions from previous problems. Your current situation "A" is, in effect, a sum of your solutions, the solutions of people who are trying to help, the solutions of people who are trying to interfere, and the incidental solutions of people and entities who happen to have impacted your space and time.

The usefulness and harm from any given solution is also a matter of perspective. If you invent a way to automate a process, your solution may prove great for the bottom line of the company, shareholders, and many employees, but it may also cause personal distress and financial harm to people who will lose their jobs as a result.

Since a problem is a matter of perspective, it can be useful to start an assessment from your own perspective so that you understand that problem from your point of view, keeping in mind that you will need to evaluate other perspectives as you proceed. For example, consider a problem involving a gap, such as a canyon with a river that keeps you from reaching the other side. The gap causes a problem, but the gap itself is not the real problem on which you should focus. The gap has the effect of isolating you from interacting with something of value to you on the other side, and that isolation is the real problem.

So when defining a problem, ask and answer:

- What is the problem you wish to resolve?
- How is the problem a threat or opportunity?
- What is the cause of the problem?
- What is the effect of the problem?

You wish to cross the gap. The gap keeps you from reaching what lies beyond the gap, which you deem as having value. The cause of your problem is the gap itself, a physical barrier. The effect of the gap is the isolation. To you, the problem is not necessarily the gap itself, but the effect (situation) that the gap creates. This latter concept is key in effective strategizing, because the best solutions focus on core problems, which tend to be effects, not the causes. This concept translates well into the patent world, because a patent that your competitor owns is never itself the core problem you need to address. That core problem is the effect that patent has—that is, to provide the competitor with a means to isolate you from the use of the technology claimed by the patent that you would otherwise use to advance your business.

A Real Problem

On November 21, 2002, a jury awarded NTP, Inc. $23.1 million in a patent infringement lawsuit against Research In Motion (RIM), the maker of the BlackBerry® wireless email device.[4] This represented a problem for RIM, since it would potentially enable NTP to seek a permanent injunction prohibiting RIM from selling BlackBerry® wireless handheld products, software, and services in the United States. An injunction would effectively isolate RIM from the market and seriously impact its financial prospects. The core problem RIM needed to resolve was the potential for isolation from its customer base, and RIM resolved this through a licensing agreement with NTP.

As stated, problems are a matter of perspective, and the core problem from your perspective is how a cause and effect impacts you. After all, people on the other side of the gap may be delighted by your isolation. Your goal is to change some aspect of the cause, the causes of the cause, the effect, or the impact of the effect so that you no longer have the core problem—that is, the isolation.

Assessing the situation from that standpoint opens up many more possible solutions than just concentrating on what to do about the gap. So if a competitive patent is the gap, you can address the effect the patent creates, which may not necessarily require that you do anything to or about the competitive patent at all.

Assessing the effect of a gap, as opposed to the gap itself, opens up more questions for the strategist to consider when plotting a solution. To start, have you done your prior art work so you can fully appreciate the situation? The first step toward assessing a patent-related situation is to understand the related prior art, because from that base you can appreciate and develop your options. With the prior art considered, you have many other questions that you can ask. For example, what do you know about the patent owner? Is the patent owner a competitor? Does the patent owner have the resources necessary to enforce the patent? Do you own any patents of interest to your competitor that you can use as leverage? Do you own any patents arguably close to the blocking patent of interest that you can use as leverage? Could you use the patent as an opportunity to make your relationship with that competitor more cooperative? Would cooperation with this competitor with regard to this patent be a disadvantage to other competitors? How strong is the patent of interest? Have you conducted your own invalidation study and drafted an opinion on the strength of the patent in question? Are there other competitors that would be advantaged by the invalidation of the patent? Can you design around that patent? Finally, what will be the costs, benefits, and risks associated with the possible options you have developed? This last will help you to determine which option you should choose.

Sometimes knowing the problem, its cause, and its effect provides enough information to resolve the problem. That being the case, you might devise and execute a solution and then move on. Sometimes knowing the problem, cause, and effect is not enough, and the problem requires further analysis. That analysis leads to problem resolution.

Problem Resolution

Resolving a problem involves synthesizing strategic operators, a source of which we will introduce later in this book. Although you may not have heard the term "strategic operators," they are something you use. Any time you have solved an existing problem with the same underlying methods you have used to solve previous problems, you have drawn from a body of strategic operators that you have learned through experience. For example, you have probably at some point in your life used, or had used on you, the strategic operator "raise the stakes," which means to threaten someone with a loss that is higher than he or she is willing or able to pay. This is a strategic operator that we learn very young, such as when a teacher threatens to call your parents if you do not finish your work. When people craft solutions, they mostly assemble a body of known-to-them strategic operators, although the particular solution might be a unique arrangement of those strategic operators.

The ease with which people assemble (synthesize) strategic operators to solve problems varies, particularly since formal education systems tend to focus on breaking things down (analysis) rather than putting things together (synthesis). But for a strategist, it is very important to be able to do synthesis well and to truly appreciate that synthesis is what you are doing. For now, understand that strategic operators are universal principles of strategy, such as "raising the stakes" during negotiations with a competitor, that can be used to enhance problem resolution. A strategist synthesizes strategic operators so that the benefits delivered by the operators outweigh any drawbacks the solutions may introduce. Strategic operators, such as "raise the stakes," are specific and definable principles of action that a strategist combines in much the same way that a musician combines the standard notes on a keyboard to create and play something new. "Raise the stakes," for example, appears in poker when one player seeks to cause other players to fold by making the cost to match that player's raised bet more than they are willing to risk. Encouraging a legal settlement by threatening a lawsuit that will cost more than an opponent can afford is a way to "raise the stakes" in patent strategy.

"Raise the stakes" is a very common strategic operator; it appears in contests as serious as military brinksmanship or as trivial as a child's game of Truth or Dare. You might also see it in use at an auction, a recent venue for selling patents, as opposing bids rise. The bidding person hopes to bid higher than the opponent is willing or able to match without exceeding his or her own price limit. So there are any number of other places where the intent is to force an adversary to quit by compelling that adversary to risk more than it can practically, psychologically, or morally afford to lose.

Strategic operators introduce the idea of synthesis, since all problems are resolved by one or a combination of known operators. These operators are at the center of strategy crafting. Strategy, as we have discussed, addresses the possibility of active opposition. A decision to "raise the stakes" (e.g., to raise the bid on an acquisition of a key portfolio of patents) can allow you to get from your current situation "A" to a desired situation "B," the consummation of the purchase, while also defeating an opposing bidder that stands in the way. But as stated, a strategic solution, unlike a technical solution, resides in a world of uncertainty. You might raise the stakes, but you can never be sure that that action will achieve its intended effect until your competitor actually folds. Even your competitor might not know what he or she will do until actually faced with the dilemma. Before you make a decision to "raise the stakes," you must decide how far you are willing and able to go to make it succeed.

Strike With a Borrowed Hand

In the mid-1990s, a major chemical company, Company X, desired to move forward with a plan that required the use of a patented process owned by another competitor, Company Y. It was quickly determined that Company Y's patent had the effect of blocking Company X's plans. During assessment of the problem, Company X also discovered that a larger chemical company with which they had a better relationship, Company Z, was using and had been using the same process Company X wanted to use, and that it might now be infringing on Company Y's patent. Rather than spend their own resources to seek an invalidation of Company Y's patent, Company X brought the patent of Company Y to the attention of Company Z. Company Z, now threatened with the possibility of infringement, used its own resources to successfully invalidate the patent of Company Y. After the action, Company X was able to gain a reasonable license from Company Z, which allowed it to implement its original plan. Company X had spent very little in the way of its own resources to accomplish this. This was an example of a strategic operator called "strike with a borrowed hand."

Synthesis

Synthesis is the flip side of analysis. It is the act of accumulating possibilities from which you will choose to derive a plan and take action. In its opposite, analysis, you take a system and break it down into its core elements. In strategy, we define those core elements as strategic operators. All strategies, when broken down (analyzed), comprise one or more of a limited number of operators. Synthesis in strategy involves putting these operators together, sometimes sequentially, other times in parallel, or both, with the intent to craft a strategy that gets you from "A" to "B." We will explore operators in more detail throughout the course of this book, and introduce each source as we further lay out the groundwork for using them.

For example, let's look at the operators "create something from nothing" (a form of bluffing), "raise the stakes," and "eliminating your adversary" in the context of a patent infringement lawsuit against you. These three operators can be put into a sequential action plan that might proceed as follows:

1. First threaten to countersue.
2. If the opposing party calls your bluff, launch an actual countersuit.
3. If that countersuit does not create a settlement, purchase the litigating company and thereby eliminate it as a threat.

These three operators tie in with the four basic rules of patent strategy. Remember that all patent strategy is composed of four basic rules: (1) use a patent to isolate, (2) threaten to use a patent to isolate, (3) use a patent to interact, and (4) leverage the possible use of a patent to interact. In this example we used the strategic operator of "create something from nothing" (a bluff) to threaten isolation (rule 2), then moved on to actual isolation (rule 1), and finally to an actual interaction through the purchase (rule 3).

Sowing a Discord

In the early 2000s, a Hewlett-Packard (HP) employee reputedly wrote an internal memo warning senior management that Microsoft was planning to launch patent infringement suits against companies distributing open-source software such as Linux and Apache. The memo was apparently based on statements allegedly made by Microsoft employees during a patent licensing negotiation with HP.[5] This alleged lawsuit threat was most likely a bluff to cause HP to reconsider its use of open-source products, although there would have been no way to know that at the time. If this information was purposely planted by Microsoft employees during HP negotiations as indicated by the foregoing reference, then it would appear to be a combination of two strategic operators:

1. "Create something from nothing," which is an element of bluffing to make appear as fact something that is not. This

strategic operator can give positive results with no reduction of resources.

2. "Sow a discord," which is another element of bluffing involving feeding misinformation to people whom you know will report that misinformation to their leadership. Information coming from an internal memo within an organization carries a lot of credibility and in effect endorses the bluff.

Both of these strategic operators can cause issues for a business, but as a strategist, it is important that you understand how they work.

Identifying the Opposition

In strategy planning, the opposition is generally defined as an intelligent, thinking, and planning entity that takes active actions against your plans. While you are crafting a solution to get from "A" to "B," your opposition may be crafting a strategy to block you from "B" or to take "B" for themselves. The actual and potential effects of the opposition's actions are your core problem. In addition, other incidental problems, such as conflicting actions of non-opposition players, or uncontrollable forces, such as the weather or even a political coup d'état in a supplier country, can appear to be active opposition because you cannot predict the effects of those actions with certainty. All potential effects need to be considered when assessing a situation and deciding on a strategy.

As benevolent as we may try to be, we will always have opposition. Maybe it is human nature, or maybe just a truth in business, but we simply cannot get from "A" to "B" without creating opposition or otherwise putting ourselves at risk.

Why Opposition Exists

During an interview with the reporter Bill Moyers, Joseph Campbell, a philosopher and expert in myth and story-telling, noted in a passing comment that "everything you do is evil to somebody."[6] Think about this statement for a moment. Everything you do has a negative impact on somebody or something. Spending time reading this book will, hopefully, prove beneficial to you and people who depend on you, but things you learn here may also have a negative impact on people at competitive organizations. Even the time you spend reading this book may mean you will have a little less time to spend with someone else who wants your time.

This issue captures the heart of why strategy is necessary. On the one hand you need, to counter the "evil" wrought to you by others, and on the other hand, you need to manage the "evil" you cause to others in the process of reaching your goals. There is certainly something beneficial in navigating promising waters without swamping too many people in your wake.

What Do We Do That Is "Evil"?

Without taking the word "evil" too literally, what do we do that is "evil" from the perspective of other people? Let's look at this from someone else's perspective in patent strategy. If you are the first to invent or file for a patent application, then someone else cannot be the first to invent or file. If you claim more technical space or secure better relationships, someone else may not be able to have that technical space or create those beneficial relationships. You may also offer an exclusive license to one organization at the expense of other organizations that would like to license those inventions as well. There is no way that you can implement patent strategy actions without harming someone else in the process. This is why you absolutely need some measure of competency in strategy, particularly as your efforts become more and more valuable to others.

Do No Evil

Google, the company with the motto "Don't be evil," is absolutely considered "evil" in the eyes of some competitive organizations. Google's Internet search page displays the first lines of certain content and gives direction to cached copies of entire articles. These user-friendly search features were considered "evil" by the content-making company called Copiepresse, as

Copiepresse is in the business of selling the cached articles. Copiepresse sued Google for copyright infringement because it displayed partial and cached copies of Copiepresse articles, to the extent that it obviated the need for many people to buy that content. A Belgian court agreed with Copiepresse and ruled that it was Google's responsibility to get permission from Copiepresse before displaying such content.[7] What would seem good to the users of Google was "evil" to Copiepresse. And in actuality, the continued ability for Google users to view Copiepresse's content for free could have been "evil" to Google users as well, for in the long term a decline in revenue to Copiepresse could mean that Copiepresse would no longer be able to produce the sought-after content in the first place.

An Illustration of "Evilness"

Let us say that you are a car salesperson who just sold a brand new Toyota Camry to a customer who is going to use it to commute to and from work. To whom are you an "evildoer"?

The first and most obvious answer is your direct competitors. You are a recognized "evildoer" to anyone who makes a living selling Honda Accords. The Honda Accord that your customer did not buy stays on the lot a little longer than it might otherwise have, and the Honda Accord salesperson does not make as much money. You are also an "evildoer" to alternative use competitors. The seller of a Ford F-150 pickup might have been able to convince your customer that a truck normally used as a work vehicle or for recreation could also be used to commute to work. Direct and alternative-use competitors will always consider you an "evildoer" when you take away potential customers. Being successful in business has this effect. After all, how do you feel about your competitors when they steal a good potential customer away from you?

Substitute and economic competitors may find you to be an "evildoer" as well. The commuter train, bus system, and taxi companies that could take your customer to work by means other than a personal car or truck will not receive a fare when your customer drives the new Camry to work. Also, since there is only so much money in a person's bank account, the purchase of the Camry might postpone other uses for that money. Disney World might now have one less family visit its park this year because the new Camry used up all of your customer's spare dollars.

Even complementary companies might consider you to be an "evildoer," at least in part. Toyota Camrys require a number of products from other companies, such as tires. While your Camry customers may ultimately buy tires from any number of companies, such as Michelin, Goodyear, or Firestone, if your tires come from one supplier and the Honda's from another, your success at selling Camrys may ultimately reduce the tire sales of the supplier to Honda even though your Camry customer might buy tires from that same supplier to Honda in the future.

Those who sell upstream technology from the perspective of the commuter car, such as telecommunication companies, might consider you an "evildoer." Their telecommuting solutions could have potentially eliminated the need for your customer to commute at all. Now your customer might defer telecommuting options that these software companies would like to sell. Stakeholders downstream from your commuter car, such as repair shops, may also consider you to be an "evildoer" since they will lose business they might have received if your customer retained an older car for them to repair.

The list does not stop there. Even noncompetitive entities may consider you an "evildoer." For people in the United States, the purchase of the Camry will mean that profits from the vehicle sale will go to Japan instead of the United States. People in the government of Michigan will have a political base with less money than if your customer had purchased a GM or Ford product, given their Michigan-based headquarters. If too many profits go overseas and the quality of jobs diminish in the United States, that could even have the end result of making your sale "evil" to yourself by eliminating potential future customers from your market. Still further, environmentalists will consider you "evil" for selling what they consider to be a fossil fuel–burning and therefore polluting machine. And finally, your sale of the Camry could even make you an "evildoer" to your customer, since a new car could encourage your customer to drive more instead of walking, precipitating a decline in personal fitness and increased exposure to accidents on the road.

Your sale of a Toyota Camry will benefit a lot of people, including your own family by bringing in income, your customer by having reliable transportation, your state and federal governments by your income taxes and sales taxes on the vehicle, and the global body of Toyota employees, shareholders, and suppliers. However, it will also harm a lot of people or help them less so than other options. If you are "evil" enough, these people will have no choice but to respond, and that response will, more than likely, work against your plans to sell more Camrys. Your direct and alternative use competitors might lower prices on their models, or come out with an actual or perceived better product. Pickup truck makers, for example, started to add cup holders to their models that many coffee drinking commuters find essential. Your substitute and economic competitors might promote their products as being more eco-friendly and lure your customers away. Your complementary companies might promote competitor products more in line with their end goals. Upstream and downstream technology companies might convince your customer that they offer great service, and reliance on their services will unfortunately have a negative impact on you as a Camry salesperson. Your local governments might place tariffs on your product, making it less competitive in the domestic market. No matter what response occurs, you will need to counteract that response with a strategy that impacts both immediate and long-term consequences, prioritized so that you focus most on the most significant threats.

A Deeper Vision

Where there is competition, there are also many facets of "evilness," even beyond what has already been shown. For example, take Microsoft, McKinsey Consulting, and Goldman Sachs, all top companies within their fields, with respect to one "evil" they do to each other. Bill Gates of Microsoft noted that these three companies, even though they are not direct competitors with regard to their products, often find themselves competing for the same top talent to become employees. These employees are also the ones who will ultimately create or implement each respective company's intellectual property. Considering that the

(Continued)

most successful organizations put their priorities on people first, ideas second, and tools third, your ability to recruit top talent from someone else's employment could be your most critical "evilness" factor of all.

"Evilness" Exercise

Following the pattern of the foregoing section, consider one of your major product lines. For each category, list someone to whom you are "evil." Consider the categories as illustrated by the Toyota Camry example:

1. Direct competitor—Honda Accord
2. Alternative use competitor—Ford F-150
3. Substitute competitor—commuter train
4. Economic competitor—Disney World
5. Complementary company—Exxon
6. Technical upstream—telecommuting
7. Technical downstream—repair shops
8. Government—Michigan political base
9. Customer—capacity to walk

Now flip this around and ask who is "evil" to you. Do they know they are "evil" to you? Often "evilness" occurs incidentally, meaning the encroaching parties may not realize they have a conflict with you until you let them know by actively opposing their plans. A gorilla may sit on a mouse without realizing it. Your strategy should address both the "evil" of others and the "evil" that you cause to others if you want to proficiently deal with opposition.

Gorilla and Mouse
The patent information industry is fairly small, with the annual revenues generated by the largest entities being in the millions of dollars as opposed to the billions of dollars. In the mid-1990s, IBM, a company outside the patent information industry,

launched a patent server that allowed people to search for patents through the Internet for free. This had a significant impact on commercial companies that depended on having people pay for patent information. IBM is a multibillion dollar, multinational company that had made single sales of computer equipment comparable to the entire revenue generated by the patent information industry. So why was it even there?

Answer: IBM used its patent server to demonstrate its capacity to build and host very large databases. At the time of its launch, the patent server was the largest database in the world. IBM could give away patent data for a period of time because the primary value of the patent server to IBM was to demonstrate IBM's database creation capabilities, rather than to generate revenue for IBM. Eventually, however, IBM did spin off the patent server into a company called Delphion, which was ultimately acquired by Thomson Information, a leading commercial source of patent information.

When you prepare your full list of who potentially views you as being "evil," you will likely see many of the same entities that you view as being "evil." Such is often the case in competition. However, there are some organizations that do not line up in these categories, and it is these entities that people often miss during strategy planning. Your patent strategy, while it certainly impacts direct competition, needs to address all the possible opposition you may encounter. For example, on their face, automotive dealerships and telecommuting companies do not appear to be in competition; however, if the telecommuting company is able to advance its products and allow more people to work from home, the need for commuter cars declines. If telecommuting appears to be a significant threat to your market for commuting cars, you may need to direct more effort into researching, developing, and promoting the advantages of your product over theirs. After all, telecommuting software cannot be used to transport the kids or carry groceries, and not even the most sophisticated teleconferencing solution beats the quality of communication received from true personal interaction.

The task for you as someone involved with patent strategy is to mirror these concepts shown here into your own industry. The underlying principles used for identifying opponents is the same regardless of industry.

Paying 100 Times More for Less Accuracy

How you compete often changes; and as technology changes, so too must your strategy. For example, it is general knowledge that Swiss watchmakers make very precise mechanical wristwatches. At one time in history, people would pay more for Swiss mechanical wristwatches than watches from other locals because of that reputation for accuracy. Today, no matter how precisely the Swiss watchmakers build an all-mechanical watch, it will not be as accurate a timekeeper as a cheap, all-digital watch. Therefore, Swiss watchmakers no longer compete using accuracy as a primary or sole customer incentive, and have instead moved to elements of style. Why do people buy a Rolex? Your answer to this question, as an element of style, illustrates how Rolex was able to change its strategy to combat the digital wristwatch technology. Even lower-priced Swiss watches, Swatch being an example, focus on elements of style. Swatch combines style with a low price, such that people could buy one watch for every outfit in their closet if they wanted to.

Piracy

Another angle of competition exists in the form of piracy. This is a significant "evil" that is inflicted on many companies; it can live up to the word "evil" in its true form. Microsoft loses billions of dollars in revenue each year from piracy, and that has a trickle-down effect on other companies in the Microsoft software ecosystem of five times the value that Microsoft itself loses.[8] This impacts legitimate jobs. The author has spoken and listened to many people from Microsoft who consider piracy to be their most important competitive threat. Pharmaceutical companies and their customers are also victims of this crime when counterfeit drugs, which may or may not be copies of the actual compounds and which may actually be dangerous, appear in pharmaceutical distribution systems.

A 2004 reference by the U.S. Department of Justice on a study by the World Trade Organization showed that counterfeit products account for up to 10% of pharmaceuticals worldwide.[9] Airlines, likewise, pay special attention to ensure that the parts they put into their planes are from approved vendors, since the approved vendors follow very necessary quality control requirements that counterfeit parts manufacturers often ignore. In one cited case from the International Anti-Counterfeiting Coalition, a bearing seal removed from a United Airlines plane in 1996 had a 600-hour operational life whereas the genuine parts were rated for 21,000 hours.[10] Such piracy is a deliberate and often sophisticated infringement of patents and brands, and defending against that piracy is another important task of a patent strategist and intellectual property strategists in general, both on behalf of his or her organization and customers.

Defending against piracy requires you to protect and police your products. This means taking steps to make your product more difficult to copy, conducting private investigations to root out counterfeiters, and if necessary, working with authorities and the legal system to enforce your rights.

Why We Act

"Act" is the word used for the third element of the patent strategy decision cycle that is covered in detail in a later chapter. When you assess, however, you should understand why you act and understand the core of why other people who will impact and be impacted by your strategy act. The assessment of why we all act leads us to the elements of motivation that are driven by our collective needs to survive and thrive, with the latter encapsulated by the inherent drive to succeed on our own terms.

Succeeding on our own terms is what thriving is all about. It is iconically represented by the independently wealthy person who works if and where he or she wants to work instead of when and where he or she must. It is the company that creates the future by inventing it versus the company that, though it perhaps succeeds, is ever chasing the whims of the market. Many patent strategists with whom the author has worked question how their new intellectual property addresses the market, but the question should be how can their new intellectual property shape the market to the advantage of their organization?

For the past several years, Apple and Google have been shaping markets with their new inventions. Consider the iPod, which is Apple's MP3 player. It, unlike the other MP3 players on the market, often has its own category and section in stores. That category ownership represents a shaped market produced with the benefit of superior technology, solid intellectual property protection, combined with first rate marketing. Google, likewise, continually leads initiatives that change how people view Internet searching. Google has been successful in Internet searching to the extent that people frequently use its company name as a verb—to "google" something on the Web. (Note, this actually creates a dilemma for Google in the sense of being too successful, a condition in strategy we will discuss in more detail later. Google runs the risk of its trademark "Google" becoming deemed "generic" as has happened to other trademarks in the past, such as the mark "Aspirin.")

What We Want

Our overriding aim in strategy is to improve our capacity for independent action. This is what we want. Even making money is really about making options, since money can buy options. Opposition creates the largest obstacle to independent action. That opposition is not just your competition; rather, it is anyone or anything that could negatively affect your capacity for independent action. Facilitators, on the other hand, increase your capacity for independent action. Customers, complementary companies, and even competitors can all serve as facilitators.

A patent affords its owner the right to enforce exclusivity through the patent legal system. Any competitive patent can threaten your capacity for independent action, since you cannot freely use the invention described in that patent or your own patent unless you first address such "blocking" patents. Competitors, by enforcing their patents, restrict you from capturing value you might otherwise capture if you had the freedom to operate with the described invention. When a competitor restricts you from producing a profitable product, it leaves you with less revenue with which to fund other actions you would like to take. Lower revenue means you have fewer options, and fewer options means you have fewer strategic maneuvers available to you and your organization.

Facilitators positively affect you by increasing your capacity for independent action. They are generally entities with which you have built or could build mutually beneficial business relationships, but they could be direct competitors—for example, if they open new markets that you can also exploit. Working with a facilitator can involve trade-offs, such as could occur if you pay a license royalty in order to gain access to a needed technology that you would prefer to have for free. A joint venture, as another example, may give you access to needed technology, but the agreement you sign may restrict the markets in which you can use that technology. As such, it can be easy for an entity to be both a facilitator and a competitor at the same time.

There are very few instances in which any single entity is either solely in opposition or totally a facilitator. As you interact with people and companies, you should evaluate how the planned interactions you have with them open opportunities and create restrictions, with the idea of increasing the former and decreasing the latter. Consider the Toyota Camry salesperson again. He or she might find that other auto dealerships moving in as next-door neighbors actually facilitate the sale of more Camrys. Why? Because more buyers as a whole will come to stores where they can easily comparison shop than would come to an isolated dealership.[11] This highlights that your measure of success as a competitor, in patent strategy and otherwise, is more often about your ability to succeed in contested environments rather than your ability to identify uncontested environments that have value. Even if you do create value in a previously uncontested environment, your success will also create competitors and will not stay uncontested very long. If you have a successful auto dealership that currently stands alone, you can bet that your competitors will notice and set up shop near you. If you patent a successful invention, then you can bet just as well that you will soon have competitors in your midst.

Playing a New Game
Through the early 1990s, Sega profited as a producer of both video games and the video game consoles on which they were played. For the most part, competition included only Nintendo and Atari. As the 1990s ended and the 2000s began, Sony and then Microsoft decided to enter the game console market. Sony and Microsoft used their considerable technical resources to stake growing positions in video game intellectual property ownership. Considering the technical and marketing power these organizations brought to bear, Sega, already suffering from market missteps in previous product releases, found it difficult to keep pace. With the change in the environment under way, Sega took its best option to retain its capacity for independent action; it withdrew from the game box market and focused its effort on producing games for Sony, Microsoft, and Nintendo consoles.

Independent Action

The capacity to operate independently is powerful. Think again about the independently wealthy people who can do almost anything they want whenever they want. Becoming such a wealthy person is an aspiration for many businesspeople who would rather work by choice than by necessity. It also produces one of the most leverageable assets in the negotiation world—the ability to say "no."

In almost all circumstances, you gain independence by working with others. Interaction, not isolation, leads to success. This important fact was noted by Sir Winston S. Churchill during World War II, when he was Prime Minister of a staunchly independent England: "There is at least one thing worse than fighting with allies, and that is to fight without them."[12]

That is not to say that you cannot gain a form of independence by isolating yourself from others; you most certainly can. However, fruitful independence generally develops by interacting with others. Even the most isolated author, writing alone in a cabin on a distant mountain, interacts with people through his or her written words. Otherwise, he or she would not thrive as an author.

Gaining value from patents likewise means sometimes having to interact with the competition. IBM opened up its patent portfolio for licensing to almost anyone who wants such a license. This was an action originally imposed upon the company and its culture by the 1956 consent decree for antitrust that required IBM to offer royalty-free or in other cases reasonable royalty licenses to its patent portfolio.[13] IBM currently uses patents as a powerful interactive tool with which to work with others. The IBM patent portfolio becomes a center for advantage from which others seek the benefits of IBM, as opposed to IBM's needing to seek the benefits of others. Contrary to the old cliché, "it's not what you know, but who you know," for IBM, it is what they know and who knows them from an intellectual property stance that facilitates its success with this model.

Cooperate or Compete

Considering that an overriding motivational goal in strategy is to maximize your capacity for independent action, and considering that you want to succeed on your own terms, you can now assess whether it is to your advantage to compete or cooperate. Always keep in mind, however, that both competition and cooperation can help and hinder your company's goals.

To illustrate the tight link between competition and cooperation, consider Michael Jordan of basketball fame, thought by many to be one of the greatest athletes of all time.[14] His capacity for independent action on the court depended on the mutual cooperation of at least four other competent basketball players on his team. It also depended on having five other competent basketball players as competitors on the court. Opponents on the basketball court cooperated in the sense that they played and abided by the same set of rules, and through their efforts, Jordan could then showcase his superior prowess.

Jordan could not have been as successful if not for the interaction of both his teammates and his competition, and the patent strategist is just as unlikely to succeed without both. In business, the assessment of whether to cooperate or compete is rather straightforward; managing both to your advantage is more of a challenge. In short,

1. Cooperate when the benefits of cooperation exceed the constraints imposed by cooperation, and seek to do so on your terms.
2. Compete when the benefits of independence exceed the constraints imposed by independence, and seek to use the competitor to improve your performance.
3. Do not look at cooperation and competition as a black-and-white issue; you will often cooperate and compete with the same entity at the same time.

Marshall Phelps, who heads Microsoft's IP effort, states that, "Companies are partners, customers, and competitors at the same time." This statement encapsulates the shades of gray we discussed earlier, because while some companies may lean more toward cooperation or competition than others, any attempt to make a black-and-white distinction between the two can lead to problems. For example, viewing a relationship as purely cooperative could cause you to relax your protocols for sharing ideas that you have not yet properly protected through a nondisclosure agreement. This could lead to a loss of a trade secret or lost patentability for disclosed inventions. Viewing relationships as purely competitive could cause you to shun a potential customer for your own products. So these three axioms bring forward questions about constraints that make any given relationship cooperative or competitive, and they are situation-specific more than they are organization-specific.

Shades of Gray on Whites

To return to our sharks and seals for a moment, recent studies have shown that great white sharks often hunt loosely together when they hunt for seals.[15] Traditionally, scientists had considered them solitary hunters. So what is going on here? Great white sharks have not organized for pack hunting in the way the Orca (killer whale) seal hunters have, but they do tend to travel about together. What is happening?

What we have with the great white shark is an almost perfect blend of cooperative and competitive activity that has evolved within the animal. It is revealed by looking at the situation from the perspective of the seal. It is one thing for a seal to track one white shark, but an entirely different and more difficult thing for the seal to deal with two or more sharks. If a seal darts away from one shark and finds itself in the path of another, it will take a moment to recalculate its next move. That moment, that tiniest fraction of hesitation, is often all a shark needs to succeed in its strike. Classical strategists might call this "show part but not all of your plan," meaning that the first observed shark is not a ruse—it will be more than happy to catch the seal if the seal fails to react properly—but if the seal does react, then the part of the plan not observed, the other sharks, can take advantage of its actions.

Of course in this loose gathering, each shark still competes with the others to make the actual kill. Also, a fed shark does not apparently go out of its way to feed another, and a hungry enough shark could conceivably eat its own young. Yet they all tend to eat better when they are somewhat more together than apart, and so that is how they have evolved to travel.

This idea represents a subtle challenge for the patent strategist. Just about every action an opponent undertakes can be turned to advantage. Even IBM's 1956 consent decree to force it to license patents may have precipitated a model for high interactivity. That perhaps was a precursor to the overall trend in patent strategy to leverage the capacity to interact afforded by patents even more so, in many cases, than the capacity to isolate.

What are the constraints associated with cooperation? What are the constraints associated with independence? Starting with cooperation, we usually see constraints as restrictions imposed by the contract to work together, compromises on how to do important activities, or restrictions imposed by agreed-on transfers of wealth between the two parties. Thus when the benefit of producing a patented product exceeds the licensing fees required to produce the product, or when both parties receive balanced enough value in cross-licensing arrangements, it encourages cooperation. If the licensing fees are too high, restrictions on use too binding, or contributions to the effort are unsuitably balanced, then it discourages cooperation.

Restrictions on independence that foster competition usually involve the scarcity of needed resources. It takes money to invent and protect inventions in the patent legal system. Money alone is a key driver of many relationships, and the glue that keeps them together even when parties may prefer to go their own way. So abundant or alternative resources that offer less restrictions to independence can foster competition since entities do not need the other entities to access those resources. If you have superior research and development resources, then you may also decide you can do best by competing in order to get a greater share of the wealth that develops. While setting up a joint venture, along with the possible sharing of intellectual property that goes into and comes out of the joint venture, often proves to be the best option, retaining your freedom of action can be worth more than the resources a partner could deliver. It all depends. Business is ultimately about gaining and retaining good customers. Competitive decisions, even in patent strategy, ultimately need to take measure of the customers for which either or all would like to do business.

How have you cooperated regarding patents with other organizations, including competitors, to improve your capacity for independent action? When and why have you chosen to compete rather than cooperate? What precipitated a change from competition to cooperation or from cooperation to competition?

Evaluating Resources for Cooperate-or-Compete Decisions

Our capacity for independent action revolves around resources. We need resources to use and to trade in order to compete and cooperate. The resources that serve as key reasons for cooperation and competition appear in five major categories:

1. Manpower—people and access to people
2. Money—capital and access to capital

3. Machines—tools and access to tools
4. Methods—ideas and access to ideas
5. Materials—substances and access to substances

Abundant resources typically demand less for a strategist to retain, but when those resources become scarce, strategies should be developed to account for that scarcity. Scarcity has much to do with whether you cooperate or compete as you consider which of the two options gives you better access to needed resources.

Valuation and Return on Investment

Patent strategy is a part of business, and as such, it is conducted for the purpose of gaining a return on investment (ROI). Valuation and ROI are therefore a key part of our discussion related to resources. To begin this evaluation, there is the issue of cost of the investment, where as noted earlier, after filing fees and attorney fees you can expect a patent in one country to cost perhaps $25,000, and international protection to be perhaps $100,000 or even more. This is aside from the costs of creating or acquiring the invention, which often exceeds $1 million and can exceed $1 billion, depending on the industry and the technology. Add to that the cost of associated trade secrets and copyrights, licenses to previous technologies, and marketing costs, and the price tag for even a single invention can become significant before any customer takes delivery on a product or service. Now consider the foregoing as it multiplies within a whole portfolio of inventions, and you can see how important your assessment of resources becomes. Most strategic campaigns, in patent strategy and otherwise, are ultimately won or lost as a result of the proper or improper allocation of resources, or simply when one or another of the competitors runs out of resources.

In the conduct of a patent strategy campaign, you therefore need to consider what financial and other resources you will need to succeed and how to manage two important factors:

1. You need to estimate a cost that makes sense in relationship to the probability of achieving the desired ROI either as an independent project or as an aggregate of projects supported by the stakeholders.

2. No matter what cost you estimate, you should expect that if your estimate meets the criteria of factor number one, it is probably an underestimate of the entire resources you will need to see the opportunity through, and you will need to consider how and when you will justify and access additional resources that you will need to reach your ultimate goal. Generally, the more contingent factors involved in the project (rolls of the dice), the more you should expect this underestimation to be so due to the higher potential for unforeseen problems to develop at any or all of the multiple contingencies. But provided your project is on a trajectory toward success, the potential for unforeseen problems should generally become proportionally less as you resolve contingencies and should make the outcome and therefore the value of the project more certain. With that increased certainty, provided you have been reasonably accurate at assessing the potential value of the project or campaign as a whole, you should have a better draw for more resources. For example, at the outset of your project, you may be able to show a 30% probability of success based on 10 major contingencies, but by the time you need to seek additional resources, you may be able to show a 70% probability of success perhaps based on three remaining contingencies—you ideally will have overcome some of the key obstacles the project or campaign faced—and that could allow you to justify additional resources or partnerships that may have been improbable at the outset of the endeavor.

Assessing the potential end value of a project that would justify the use of any resources at any point in an endeavor is another matter to consider. Many standard methods exist for doing so, and you should consider using more than one method to get the best average result. Net Present Value (NPV) is a way to calculate value that involves probabilities of success and decision trees. A node on a decision tree may, for example, be whether a drug in a clinical trial proved effective enough to proceed to the next phase of experimentation, whereby you may give one percentage probability for success, another for failure, with possibly some gradients in between. Based on the value of the possible outcomes, you predict a value for the project as a whole. So as in our earlier example in "rolls of the dice," if your NPV tree showed five major contingencies where each offered a 90% chance of success, then the entire project would have a 59% chance to succeed, which you would apply to the estimated value of the project if it did succeed in order to obtain your NPV calculation for the project prior to its launch.

A key to making the NPV model useful in the real world is to first remember our "rolls of the dice" discussion and the tendency of even diligent people, when making their trees, to miss a couple of nodes that will ultimately show up during the conduct of the actual project or campaign. This is related to the fact that the NPV decision tree can reliably address only predicted results, and the ultimate success of any strategic endeavor often depends on unpredicted results, which frequently arise from unpredicted nodes. If Pfizer's evaluation of *sildenafil* (Viagra®) contained an NPV decision tree in its original project evaluation, it is a safe bet that it did not include a node regarding the compound's possible success as a sexual dysfunction drug. Bottom line on NPV: It becomes more useful and accurate as the number of unknowns decreases, but it needs to be handled with caution in highly uncertain environments.

Precedents provide another way to assess the potential value of a project. The success of known products in a market provides a base from which to assess the potential value of new but related products. For example, if you wish to develop a consumer electronics product and can show that the existing market for that type of product is $15 billion, then you can estimate the portion of that overall market that you believe you can obtain or grow. The key to making precedents work is to appreciate that people typically overestimate what they can actually achieve. Some basic marketing laws can help to ensure more accuracy. For example, if you are the fifth entrant into this consumer electronics arena, then with a reasonably successful product, you can expect to have the fifth largest share of that market.

A general law of marketing, shown by the research of Al Ries and Jack Trout, is that market share is usually determined by the order of entrance into the market, not necessarily by being somehow better than the competition.[16] According to Reis and Trout, as a new entrant to this consumer electronics arena, you should expect the predicted market share result to be different only if your consumer electronics product is significantly better in some way from those products already out on the market to the degree that you could create a new category in which to be the first entrant. The Apple iPhone is an example of such a new category product that allowed Apple to obtain substantially more market share in the cell phone market than if Apple had just launched yet another more conventional phone.

All methods for calculating value aside, intuition is often key when determining potential value and the allocation of resources, married to some probability strategies that serve as a hedge or reality check on that intuition. If standing in the shoes of Steve Jobs, for example, you look at your iPhone concept, appreciate that the business goals for the product as conceived are achievable, perhaps do some market surveys to assess levels of interest, but ultimately intuitively know that if successful, the ROI on the iPhone will more than cover the cost. You recognize that the product could in fact be a blockbuster if you can deliver on its full potential. With that appreciation, you take the risk and proceed with the project, making the best estimates that you can. If there were truly better ways to assess the value of an invention tomorrow as it exists in its present form today, then venture capitalists, who often fund new intellectual property–based endeavors, would have better business models available to them than that of expecting 90% of their new ventures to fail.[17]

So using the means available to make the estimates that you can, you combine those estimates with the intuitive feel of your own evaluations and those of appropriate experts. You have your views challenged by contrarians skilled at pointing out details that you might have missed. You appreciate that the unpredicted results in your efforts may actually produce the biggest returns if you keep your eyes open. And finally, you appreciate that to advance you need to create and attain inventions somewhere that you believe—with ample evidence for the truth of that belief and with a plan for success—will provide you with the value you seek.

Application of the Patent Resource

Patents, by creating an asset from knowledge, facilitate your capacity to cooperate and compete. In the former, *cooperate*, they provide a quantifiable vehicle for trade—that is, you can license the right to make, use, or sell an invention as described by the patent to someone in exchange for another resource. In the latter, *compete*, they provide a quantifiable vehicle from which to enforce exclusivity, which essentially denies a desired resource to your competitor. Your capacity to enforce exclusivity often provides the key point of leverage from which to set up cooperative relationships. One alternative, owning value in the form of a trade secret, tends to foster competition, not cooperation, which is fine if competing is what you want to do. Another alternative, putting inventions into the public domain without patenting them, can foster cooperation if thoughtfully approached; this is most suitable when you seek only to gain or maintain your freedom to operate as opposed to your right to enforce exclusivity.

Patents themselves are a resource that their owners can use to secure other resources. Some of these methods are more direct than others. For example, patent holders can sell patents outright or license them as a way to bring in money that itself can be used to secure other resources. Patent holders can also use patents as a basis to cross-license technology and therefore gain access to other needed technology and know-how. Indirectly, patents can attract important resources such as talented people. Companies that have a well-developed patent process within the organization tend to apply for and have patents awarded on a regular basis. As a result, the outside world typically views such companies as showing patent leadership and therefore as innovative. Successful innovative companies naturally draw innovative people, not just because successful companies may pay more for good talent, but because innovative people want to work in an environment with other innovative people who will value, promote, and develop their ideas. This creates a virtuous cycle of superior talent creating more and better inventions that attract yet more superior talent that brings even better ideas from which to access other needed resources.

All individuals and groups compete for resources, whereby the improved capacity for independent action by one party invariably reduces the capacity for independent action of another and therefore sows the seeds of competition. This is one of the things that happens when you hire an engineer who will produce some of your future patents. By hiring that engineer, you keep that talent away from your competitor. With your competitor's objectives in mind, you therefore need to take some precautions for your business. Although we want to trust the intentions of others, you need to appreciate that some organizations may use the guise of cooperation as a competitive move. As an example, consider a small start-up company that patented a marketable invention without having the financial wherewithal to bring that product to market. The start-up company signs an exclusive license with a larger company, expecting that the larger company will dedicate resources to market the product. Instead, the larger company puts the licensed technology on the shelf and markets an alternative technology, having through its agreement effectively eliminated the rival start-up's technology. In this scenario, the start-up will want to defect from that relationship, but the ability to do so without proper exit clauses may prove challenging. This scenario is a very real possibility for a small start-up. It is common enough that a prominent New York-based investment bank asked the author how to detect it before consummating deals involving their start-up ventures.

Now since the people with whom you interact also make cooperate-or-compete decisions, consider the other side of the foregoing story. In a conflict between two parties, there is always another perspective. From the perspective of the larger player, acquiring and putting that start-up's technology on the shelf could mean quashing a pending "evil" from an uninvited entity in a market that the larger company had, through no small effort, created on its own. From the perspective of the larger company, this small start-up would have destabilized that market with an alternative technology, perhaps just at a time when its customers were trying to settle on a universal standard. This would mean that the larger company would have a new competitor in the form of either the start-up company itself or another competitor that licensed the new technology in its place, and that the market would stay confused a little longer in the absence of a final standard. Furthermore, since every misfortune has the chance to be somebody else's good news, the large company's other major competitors may also have benefited from this quashing of the start-up, given that they may benefit from the adoption of a universal standard as well. Of course whether the standard is best for the consumer is yet another question and yet another link in the chain to consider. Bottom line: Truly comprehensive assessments are no small tasks.

So, this status of cooperation and competition represents both opportunity and threat to all interested parties, from the raw materials producer to the customer, and needs to be managed on all counts, considering all points of view. It lives in the spirit of the late President Ronald Reagan, whose approach, even to friends, was, "Trust but verify." The need to manage relationships is a reason why people often formalize the distinction that they are cooperating with each other by signing contracts between the parties and then announcing this cooperation to other would-be suitors. They want a way to enforce that cooperation when necessary, and they also want those who will find that cooperation "evil" to know that it is their tough luck.

In patent strategy and otherwise, when you contemplate cooperation and competition, you should always assess who will find your actions "evil" and take measures to address the potential consequences. Your patents are a vehicle to further isolate or interact with that opposition as best suits your objectives. You must keep in mind that you also compete with those with whom you cooperate and vice versa. You can see the anomalies that develop in day-to-day life in which competition can actually foster a benefit greater than cooperation. Consider a tailgating party interview where a Washington Redskins fan sincerely describes how much he or she hates the opposing Dallas Cowboys. But who would the Redskins be without the Cowboys? Similarly, part of the allure for BMW drivers that boosts BMW sales is the very fact that not everyone can afford to own a BMW. Part of what makes Apple users more loyal to Apple is the presence of Microsoft. Think about the popular Mac versus PC commercials that seek to showcase the "evils" of the Microsoft-based PC. Competitors can give your efforts meaning.

Hindsight and Foresight

Strategies of cooperation and competition can appear to work or not work depending on when you look at the results. Just as strategies can change, so can the apparent results of those strategies over time. With the split-up into the "Baby Bells," AT&T found itself in the difficult position of competing for long-distance telephone services with key customers of its telephone equipment business. In 1996, AT&T spun off Lucent Technologies to eliminate this anomaly, since it is generally best not to compete in critical areas with key customers. Lucent Technologies took with it the venerable Bell Labs and most of the patents. Lucent Technologies's market value soared, for a while.

(Continued)

Things changed. During the downturn in telecommunications in the early 2000s, the stock price of Lucent Technologies dropped from $84 to 55 cents. Significant issues had developed concerning the market viability of products in the Lucent Technologies portfolio as well as its business practices, irrespective of whether the spin-off from AT&T made strategic sense.[18]

As an apparent part of a patent assertion campaign, perhaps related to the downturn in its business and the need to find new revenues, Lucent Technologies filed suit against Gateway, Dell, and Microsoft to assert patent U.S. 5,341,457 relating to MP3 players. Microsoft showed that it had received a license for MP3 technology from Bell Lab's parent research organization, Fraunhofer Institute, for a flat $17 million, but the court agreed with now Alcatel-Lucent that MP3 had been invented at Bell Labs before joining with Fraunhofer. (Alcatel merged with Lucent Technologies in 2006 to create Alcatel-Lucent.) In February 2007, the court awarded Alcatel-Lucent $1.5 billion from Microsoft for non-willful patent infringement. This ruling was overturned in August of 2007 for lack of sufficient evidence.[19] Those who may judge the efficacy of the assertion strategy for Lucent Technologies, at least for this case, would likely have different opinions had they made their judgment in February of 2007 or August of 2007.

Centers of Excellence

With the prevalence of contracting, outsourcing, consulting, and joint venturing, the boundaries of where one company ends and another company begins are less distinct than they were a decade or more ago. One piece that will always be inherent to a given company, however, is the central idea that defines that company or significant and definable parts thereof. This central idea is most often represented by the brand, its associated trademarks, and often its key patents. Nike, for example, has its registered trademark "swoosh" logo, the trademarked "Just Do It®" slogan associated with sports and competition, and many patents associated with its products. Around this central idea, Nike is also well known for cooperating in joint ventures, and outside of its trademarks and patents, it can be very difficult to determine where exactly the Nike company begins or ends.[20]

To whatever extent companies keep work in-house or out of house, all successful companies share a common structure. Whether internal to the organization, external to the organization, or both, they have three distinct operational areas around the central idea that is the company that we can call Centers of Excellence. In larger conglomerates, there may functionally be several of these Centers of Excellence that support several central ideas, but the core structure regarding a distinct division, subsidiary, or even a single product line, remains the same. The three Centers of Excellence, illustrated in Exhibit 3.1, are as follows:

1. Innovation
2. Advancement
3. Security

The three Centers of Excellence support the central idea that is the core reason for the business's existence from the market's perspective. That core, if described well, provides the business's identity and defines the benefit of the business to customers. Nike's "Just Do It®," for example, when combined with sports images and images of its products, gets to the heart of what Nike means and therefore its central idea. It is the

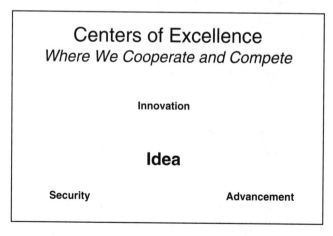

Exhibit 3.1 Centers of Excellence

company that makes products for the people who challenge themselves in sports. The three Centers of Excellence that support this core can be internal, external, or both. As such, the Centers of Excellence model accounts for the graying of corporate boundaries where, for example, the innovation arm may include both an internal research and development team and a licensing group that brings in innovation from the outside. It also accounts for the possibility that a business may cooperate with another business at one Center of Excellence, such as innovation, while competing at another, such as advancement.

At the Center of Excellence in innovation, we have derived the products and services that companies sell. Having a Center of Excellence in innovation does not always mean that the company itself is creating innovative ideas; rather, some companies keep a sharp eye out for new technologies as they emerge and quickly move into exclusive contracts to license and sell the technology of others. So what it means is that the company has a source for innovation through one, the other, or a combination of internal and external sources. Traditionally organized companies often create their own products and services and spend a considerable amount of resources on predicting future trends and directing research and development to actively respond to those trends. Sometimes that innovation will actually create the future trends, as in the previous examples of the iPod and the iPhone. So having a Center of Excellence for innovation means that the company has a way to create or acquire products and services to sell that buyers want to buy by whatever means that company uses.

Regarding a Center of Excellence in advancement, successful companies need to proficiently market their products. Once an organization has a product, a product line, or services, it needs to sell those products and services to make its efforts worthwhile. It may do so through an internal marketing and sales force, an external marketing and sales force, through both, or by some other means. However this is accomplished, all companies need to advance (promote) their products into the marketplace. All things being otherwise equal, the company with superior advancement capabilities will most likely sell more products and services.

Once an organization has products and services in its portfolio, along with a way to advance them into the marketplace, it will need security to protect the value of that success. Securing your intellectual property through patents and other means is one critical component of that defense for protecting company value, although this component will integrate into many other aspects of corporate security. In the absence of intellectual property rights, your competition may quickly follow you into the market by simply backward engineering your products and imitating your services. If your innovation is easy to copy, then a patent on the associated inventions can afford some security. If your innovation is nearly impossible to copy, then perhaps maintaining it as a trade secret in whole or part will provide more security than patenting the associated inventions. The ease with which you can design around associated inventions also merits some consideration regarding how you patent or whether you may better serve your security efforts by allowing easy licensing or opening up the technology all together.

Regardless of the preceding, you need a security plan and should be active in your role of security. If your organization is not policing your intellectual property rights, then any protective value is passive in that all an associated patent may do is prevent someone else from getting a patent if the patent examiner reviews it. In all cases, some of your security may be internal—for example, in-house legal counsel working together with the engineers to file and police patents. Some of that security may be external—for example, the hiring of an outside law firm or private investigating firm to perform specified enforcement tasks. Much of that security, as is discussed later, will come from other aspects of an organization's power than intellectual property. However arrayed, all successful organizations need a way to protect value.

Successful organizations seek proficiency in all three Centers of Excellence in accord with how they fit into the chosen business model. Viewing companies through the lens of the three Centers of Excellence opens up several possibilities for the strategist when assessing situations and potential actions. To start, the graying of company boundaries expands the scope through which a company can interact with customers, suppliers, facilitators, and competitors. A master strategist could, in essence, put even competitors on the same team for a marketing effort. This means that the entire world becomes a potential source for innovation, advancement, and security. Every mind in the world could potentially be tapped for new innovation. Every person on the planet, through word of mouth promotion or more, could potentially serve to advance your products into the marketplace. Finally, since more people have the opportunity to participate in your success, and therefore less interest in seeing you fail, your security can improve as well. To illustrate Centers of Excellence, take a look at Federal Express.

Federal Express as a Centers-of-Excellence Model

Federal Express anchored itself on one of the best descriptions of a central idea ever written, "When it absolutely, positively has to be there overnight®." This is a trademarked tag line that described exactly what the customer could expect from the company while it was in use. This tag line also psychologically positioned customers to decide, should they choose a competitor, that they must not really care whether their package made it there overnight. It both advanced and secured the business at the same time.

Federal Express patents are oriented around fulfilling the promise of this idea. A review of Federal Express patents will show that they describe packaging, labeling, and logistic methods oriented toward getting packages from point A to point B proficiently and at high (i.e., overnight) speed. Its entire intellectual property suite—the brand name, the trademarked tag line, the patents, plus trade secrets—both categorized and inherent but undocumented in the know-how of people—are all oriented toward delivering that promise.

The Center of Excellence for Federal Express in innovation focuses on improving logistics, and this is still the case since its merger with Kinko's that it positions as an office for people on the road. The focus on improving logistics is so advanced that Federal Express consults on logistics for noncompeting organizations as well.[21] Furthermore, key components of its logistical operation also provide the prime ingredient of its Center of Excellence in advancement. Each box, truck, and store prominently displays the Federal Express trademarked logo to keep it top-of-mind for prospective customers. But Federal Express does not stop there; it also focuses on advancement by having an effective program for creating and supporting corporate accounts.[22] The Center of Excellence in security focuses on protecting the brand, the patents, its trade secrets, and, most importantly, delivering on the promise of reliable overnight delivery so that the brand and the promise become intimately linked.

With Federal Express, or any other organization, should any Center of Excellence underperform, or should the core idea become unclear, the organization will run into trouble. For the patent strategist, there are two key guidelines to follow:

1. An ample number of patents within a patent portfolio should align with the central idea of the supported products and services. If not, either the patents or the central idea probably should be shifted. By *ample*, we need to recognize that while the example company, Federal Express, has a reasonably clear focus as an outsource logistical service, an organization with many dimensions could have several ideas to support from several different bodies of patents. Johnson & Johnson is a prime example of a large corporation that is in many ways a confederation of smaller companies, each with its own Centers of Excellence.

2. Just as patents support the central idea and the Centers of Excellence, the central idea and the Centers of Excellence need to support the patents. New innovation, effective advancement, and effective security make a patent valuable, and good patents provide a base from which to innovate, a base to create marketable products and services, and a tool from which to build security. The chicken and the egg, so to speak, emerge at the same time.

When all the Centers of Excellence operate in accord with "excellence," a great opportunity arises to create and capture value. Should even one element underperform, however, it can shake apart the whole system. Atari, which had been a major video game developer and manufacturer since its launch of Pong® in 1975, was effectively out-innovated by Nintendo and Sega in the video game market by the time Atari exited the market in 1996. After Nintendo had the lead with its Nintendo Entertainment System®, introduced in 1985, Nintendo was out-innovated for a time by Sega when Sega introduced its Sega Genesis® system in 1989. Both found their capacity to advance challenged by the innovation and marketing powerhouses of Sony starting in 1995 with its Sony Playstation® and then Microsoft starting in 2001 with its Microsoft XBox®.[23] Nintendo stood up to this challenge with the Nintendo Wii® and prepared a solid battery of patents to protect it. Sega took another course when it chose to focus on making games instead of whole gaming systems.[24] Fortunes changed respectively, and what is "excellence" also depends on the comparative performance of competitors at critical points in time.

Parallel Lines of Competition

Underlying the Centers of Excellence are several parallel lines of competition in which all companies participate in some way. Twelve parallel lines of competition appear in the following list, but how you configure them, as well as inclusions and deletions of competitive lines, is open to modification for your industry and company. The principles that follow stay the same. For the focus of this book, one of these parallel lines of competition is called the patent line of competition. With others included, we could have the following:

1. Leadership—the competition for initiative and access to initiative
2. Human resources—the competition for talent and access to talent
3. Branding—the competition for identity and access to identity
4. Patents—the competition for inventions and access to inventions
5. Sales—the competition for customers and access to customers
6. Marketing—the competition for markets and access to markets
7. Finance—the competition for capital and access to capital
8. Research—the competition for ideas and access to ideas
9. Development—the competition for innovation and access to innovation
10. Supply—the competition for materials and access to materials
11. Logistics—the competition for distribution and access to distribution
12. Manufacturing—the competition for production and access to production

Part of your challenge when crafting a patent strategy is to ensure that these parallel lines of competition work well together. By doing so, you can ensure that your patented or patentable inventions also receive protection in terms of market penetration, complementary relationships, know-how support, branding, and any number of other means to protect inventions besides or in addition to patents. The risk is that these lines of competition can become silos that tend to be isolating in nature instead of interactive. If you have started to subscribe to the idea that interaction, not isolation, leads to growth, you should recognize the issues that silos within an organization can create. If the people leading the charge in their respective silos do not communicate and are unwilling to share resources with the other silos, then it will be difficult to implement any line of competition well. Your patent strategy needs to involve all of the parallel lines of competition in your field and your company, which means you will need to interact with all of the people so associated.

By linking your patent line of competition to other sources of power in your organization, you can craft some very powerful asymmetric strategies. Asymmetric strategies are a way of using strength against weakness. If a competitor is strong in one line of competition, you could focus your competitive efforts on another line of competition where your competitor is comparatively weak. So if your competitor has a powerful marketing force, you could focus on the patent line of competition, for example, to which that competitor may not pay adequate attention. By winning in the patent line of competition, you could leverage the exclusivity your patents afford to undercut your competitor's market position. Done well, you could advance your own marketing agenda much more efficiently than you could have by launching a competing marketing campaign. In the comparative game of "rock, paper, scissors," where rock trumps scissors, scissors trumps paper, and paper trumps rock, if your competitor plays "rock," then you play "paper" to win.

Rock, Paper, Scissors

When Microsoft decided to enter the video game console business, it faced formidable marketing powerhouses Sony, Nintendo, and Sega. A traditional approach to enter the market that Microsoft did put into play was to use its own considerable market presence and financial resources to push its way into the space. A quick study of the patent files shows that Microsoft may have intentionally put an asymmetrical strategy into play in parallel. Microsoft invented and patented a large number of game console patents that built on earlier Sega inventions for which it had some earlier collaboration.[25] In fact, during the past

(Continued)

10 years, Microsoft applied for over 150 U.S. patents of its own having to do with video gaming and consoles. While not exclusively a competitive issue for Sega alone, these Microsoft patents served to reduce Sega's maneuvering room in innovation at a time when Sega's own releases of otherwise excellent console products were not as well received by the market.[26] Microsoft created a situation in which Sega had less space to innovate without infringing on one of Microsoft's newly issued patents. Microsoft's patent landscape could only give further impetus for Sega to withdraw from the game console marketplace and focus on making games for all game box makers, which is what Sega did. While from Microsoft's perspective, Sony and Nintendo were its most formidable competitors, with relatively low cost—Microsoft desired to innovate and create a base of patents in video game consoles anyway—a third potential competitor vanished as a competitor and effectively became an important facilitator instead.

Parallel lines of competition take place simultaneously, with patents being one of those lines. Unless you truly have no better choice, the only reason you would want to initiate a patent-versus-patent battle with a competitor is that you have an overwhelming advantage in that line of competition. Such an overwhelming advantage in the patent line of competition is generally anchored by the strength of a given patent or the sheer volume of good-enough patents owned by an entity. In the absence of an overwhelming advantage, or to supplement that overwhelming advantage, you want to leverage other advantages you may have elsewhere.

When competing, it makes sense to use a different line of competition against your opponent whenever possible. Do this in the spirit of "rock, paper, scissors" to minimize direct contests in the same lines of competitions that can prove expensive. As stated, the only exception to this rule is when you have an overwhelming advantage in that line of competition, the equivalent to playing rock against rock but having a much bigger "rock." Hewlett-Packard, for example, has a massive patent portfolio and may countersue with 20 patents a suit brought on by a smaller company that has only one patent. In a scenario such as that, you can often compete in a direct line of competition and win relatively cheaply. Given here perhaps that patents are paper, even though you have pitted "paper" against "paper," you have much more "paper."

Any number of approaches can work to find asymmetrical advantages. A powerful brand can impact a competitor's patent strategy. Having a deeper pool of talented engineers can impact a competitor's patent strategy. Your superior access to capital can impact a competitor's patent strategy. Any source of advantage can work in your favor if you create the conditions to make that so. Still, although asymmetric strategies are powerful, to protect the integrity of a resource, that resource should have the capacity to stand up to like resources from the same line of competition. Since they operate in the same universe, they will run into each other. So for patents, while you may want to move the focus of your competition with another organization from the patent line of competition to, say, the innovation or human resources line of competition, that competitor may at some point call you to the table in the patent area. A well-written patent, integrated with other sources of organizational power, will still prove essential.

All Aspects of Power

The success of your patent strategy will depend on how well you can link the power of patents to other aspects of your company's power and the appropriate organizational power of others. When you interact with others, you tend to foster growth, if for no other reason than that interaction exposes you to more opportunities. When you isolate yourself, you tend to foster decline, if for no other reason than that you miss opportunities you may have had. This does not mean you always want to interact and never want to isolate yourself, but the overall trend should lean heavily toward the former and away from the latter.

Your success in patent strategy in relation to other sources of power is enhanced the more those other sources of power discourage or prevent the imitation of your patented ideas versus requiring you to enforce your patents after the fact. The cliché that "an ounce of prevention is worth a pound of cure" holds well here since, for example, competitors may be less inclined than otherwise to challenge a strong first-mover success from your organization where they would have to fight both your patent and your early recognition as the market leader rather than either one alone. Your success in patent strategy is also enhanced by the appreciation that all the intellectual property in the world really is potentially a resource to advance your own interests. Accessing the world's intellectual property requires interaction with its owners and creators.

Creating and Using
Qualcomm's patent strategy emphasizes creating its own patents for licensing and having few of its own actual products.[27] Dell Computer's patent strategy revolves around creating new products and is supported by relatively few of its own patents as compared with its competitors.[28] Both patent strategies work because the companies have linked patents to other sources of business power: Qualcomm's patents are linked to the businesses of others, and Dell's business is linked to the patents of others.

A viable patent strategy can be not to have any patents. Under Armour®, started in 1995, established a strong product and brand position in compression sportswear in the face of brand-based sports competitors such as Nike without filing for any patents, although Under Armour® has recently started to patent as Nike and others recognize the value of Under Armour®'s compression sportswear space.[29] While this perhaps left Under Armour® vulnerable had Nike and others responded to the new market sooner, it is arguable whether Under Armour®, even if it had filed for patents during the initial phase of its growth, would have had the resources to defend them. Although now a multimillion dollar operation, Under Armour®'s first market was literally just the members of the University of Maryland football team.[30] So a viable patent strategy can be not to have patents.

Standing on a Whale, Fishing for Minnows

In addition to linking your patents to other sources of power within an organization, success with a patent strategy also requires fully appreciating the full potential power of inventions that you have within your patents. You do not want to figuratively starve in the wild because you do not recognize what is food. Xerox®, as a case in point, invented the foundation of the DOS operating system and the document software ultimately marketed by Adobe®, yet in the course of business decisions made with the people who would develop those technologies, Xerox® received little of the value.[31]

"Standing on a whale, fishing for minnows" is a Polynesian idea about focusing on small opportunities without considering the greater opportunity on which you are standing.[32] Missing out on large opportunities that are right in front of an organization can create real financial loss and heartache. So your assessment for how best to secure value means appreciating and pursuing value in your intellectual property wherever and however it exists. Consider the following five cases in which people got it right and saw the figurative whale beneath their feet:

Post-it® Notes—originally a music place holder[33]

Coca-Cola®—originally a patent medicine brain tonic[34]

Viagra®—originally an inconsequential heart medication[35]

Microwave oven—originally conceived from magnetron sets for radar[36]

NutraSweet®—originally an anti-ulcer drug candidate[37]

When crafting a patent strategy, take some time to appreciate the greater potential of what you have with any given invention. What other gaps could the "bridge" that is your invention cross? How might your invention obviate the need for someone else to cross a gap? Are you spending resources fishing for minnows when there is a larger whale right underneath you?

Dominant and Contested Positions

As an additional part of your assessment, and before deciding on a plan, take into account whether your current position at "A" is a dominant position or a contested position. That will affect the wisdom of choosing your desired position "B." Whether a position is a dominant position is open to interpretation, but we do have some indicators, which will follow. For example, having 200 patents in your patent portfolio will have an entirely different meaning depending on whether they are for golf club heads, which are represented by relatively few patents worldwide, or for stents, which are represented by relatively many. Furthermore, your evaluation would need to account both for the quality of the technology covered and the quality of the patents themselves. In considering a decision to pursue a market, some questions to ask include:

- Is the field contested?
- Who are the competitors?
- If contested, what conditions will create a dominant competitor?
- Is there a dominant competitor?
- Who is the dominant competitor?
- If it is a dominant situation, which conditions will create a contested situation?

One way to determine whether you are in a contested position or a position with a dominant player is to examine common patent benchmarks, such as the patent count or market share. But you need to look a little deeper than just the count. Let's suppose that you see a distribution of patents in a technical field such that the leading patent holder has 20 patents, the second leading patent holder has 10, the third has 7, and the fourth has 5. At first glance, and quality of patents aside for the moment, it might seem that the patent holder with 20 patents has the dominant position. Odds are this is not true. In most cases, you have a normally contested situation. Zipf's Law, a ranking methodology similar to Pareto's Law or Power Law Distribution, predicts that in a system that has many random variables (which is the case with patents), the largest representative of that system will have twice as many elements as the next, three times as many as the next, and so on.[38]

The observed pattern conforms to the predicted pattern and would indicate a market situation that is neither overly competitive nor dominated by any one or more competitors. If the highest patent holder has 40 patents instead of 20, four times as many patents as the next ranked patent-holding competitor, then the holder of 40 patents is likely in the dominant position, pending further qualitative analysis. However, the real determinant is the quality of the claims of a given patent. A single "pioneering" patent can dominate a field much more than the sheer numbers of patents of a competitor. So you need to go beyond simple patent counting.

On qualitative analysis, there is probably no better way to assess a patent than to have qualified people actually read the document. It can, however, take a day to do this really well, which is likely to hinder any effort to assess hundreds or thousands of patents. Even a more cursory read-through of one patent document per hour limits any one person to reading 40 to 60 patent documents per week if the intent is to make a real qualitative analysis. Here we have some indicators to work with to narrow down the field so that a patent analyst can focus on the patent documents most likely to be important for them to read. Indicators of importance include the number of claims associated with a patent. A seminal patent often has a substantially greater number of claims as compared with a less important patent in its industry. It will have more claims because, if the invention is truly groundbreaking, it will generally have comparatively more for the inventor to describe than the related art and less competitive art to narrow the scope of the invention. The word "generally" is used because there are exceptions. Indicators of importance also include claim size, given that a broad patent, which patent holders typically like to have, often has comparatively shorter claims than a narrow patent in the related art. The broader patent generally has shorter claims because fewer technical specifics are needed in order to fit the described invention within the existing prior art.[39]

Patent citations, both from examiners and inventors, also serve as an indicator of importance. A patent citation is a record found on a patent document that shows that the patent examiner or the inventor has reviewed a prior patent document as prior art when making an assessment of the patentability of the newer invention. Considering that litigated patents have characteristics shared by other patents, as evidenced by the fact that people are willing to pay the cost of litigation, important patents often cite more earlier patents, are often cited by more later patents, and cite more internal patents belonging to the home organization than comparable patents in their art.[40] As people develop important technology further and file new patent applications around that technology, patent examiners and other inventors will likely cite the prior important patents and cite them more frequently than less important patents. Since people tend not to further develop patents of lesser importance, the patent examiners generally see fewer similar patent applications related to that technology, nor will inventors find as frequent a need to cite the less important

patent documents; therefore all will cite the less important patents infrequently, if at all.

Yet another indicator of patent importance is patent family information. A patent family is the collection of individual patent documents
from different authorities that describe the same invention. For a given
invention that you feel is important, you might seek a U.S. patent, a
Japanese patent, a European patent, and, perhaps because you have a
market in Brazil, a Brazilian patent. In this case, you would have four
patent family members for that one invention. Typically, a company that
considers a given invention more important to its business than other
inventions will file for patents on that invention in more patent authorities than otherwise and thereby create larger patent families. When a
company starts to patent in countries outside its standard practice, such
as Brazil if it does not patent in Brazil as a matter of course, that creates
an even stronger signal of an invention's importance. If that patent is also
highly cited, it has the right claims profiles, and experts who read it also
see importance in the invention, then you have a "lighthouse" patent
that shines above the rest within a patent portfolio, clearly visible for
those who seek to peer through the fog for important patents.

When using any of the indicators such as these, however, keep in
mind that they are all just indicators. They are like having all the statistics of a sports game to assess who won a game except for the score.
Usually the side with the better statistics wins, but not always. Quantitative analyses, such as patent count, claims analysis, citations analysis,
and patent family analysis do not give you qualitative values such as
the actual strength or coverage of each given patent, which itself may
not be fully tested until challenged in court. All these require further
qualitative analysis of the market to confirm or refute the quantitative
evaluations. It also requires studying the patents and constructing the
claims of the patents, the legal property "metes and bounds" of a given
patent. This would focus first on those patents that have risen to the top in
your analysis and perhaps further investigating the work of the inventors
associated with the art. However, when you find a patent that claims analysis, citations analysis, and patent family analysis all indicate is important,
and that a study of the patent by an expert also shows is both important
and well written, the odds are pretty good that you have a patent of value
in hand.

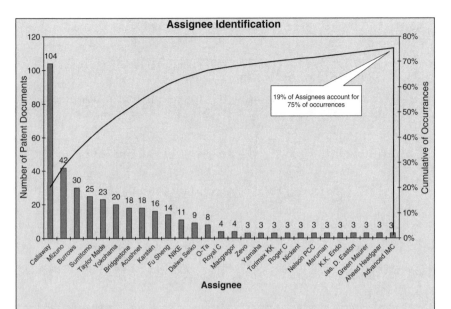

Assignee Identification

19% of Assignees account for 75% of occurrences

Golf Contenders

The above chart of golf club head patents over a five-year period shows that Callaway Golf had 104 U.S. patents, followed by Mizuno with 42, Burrows with 30, Sumitomo with 25, Taylor Made with 23, and so on. At first glance it could appear that Callaway Golf dominates the field—it does, after all, have more than twice as many patents as its nearest competitor—the distribution pattern is close enough to Zipf's (power) Law of expected distribution to indicate a contested market. Any visit to a golf superstore would confirm the contested nature of the marketplace. So as someone involved with patent strategy in the golf club space, if you do not like the contested situation indicated by the patent analysis, you ask what you can do to change the contested space into a dominant space as a whole or within a niche that you care about. For example, a strategic acquisition could change the distribution and actual balance of power significantly by combining patent portfolios, provided there is not too much duplication of the types of inventions and corresponding solutions.

(Continued)

Now take any other technology and count the patents that belong to the lead patenting companies. More times than not, you will see a similar distribution pattern as that predicted by Zipf's Law, indicating a contested market with no true dominant-positioned player. However, if you come across a patent count result outside of Zipf's Law, you need to understand what variables allow for or prevent the existence of a dominant position. When you understand these variables, you can influence them. Make sure, however, to always consider the quality and actual subject matter of the patents when comparing quantitative numbers. The total is only an indicator of performance. A single quality patent's claims will always carry a lot of weight if they cover an important invention, and thus you should also take the quality of the patent claims into consideration.

Between the Lines
Around 1995, the author conducted an experiment to show that you could break down the majority of a pharmaceutical company's patents into distinct areas of research simply by clustering which inventors patented together. He did by hand what a number of computer programs can do automatically now. To explore what to do with these clusters, the author focused on an apparent Merck research team involved in Angiotensin II Receptor Antagonists. He read all of their patents and papers and had a pretty good understanding of what the research team wanted to do and the problems they needed to overcome. By pure coincidence, during a high-technology conference given by IBM, members of this Merck research team gave a presentation that discussed how they were using an IBM computer-assisted research system to accelerate their research efforts. Inasmuch as the team practiced their art in a highly competitive therapeutic area, they sought not to tell too much about their actual research results. Having read all their patents, however, the author found it very easy to fill in the blank space between the lines of their

discussion, such that using this approach for competitor investigation became a major recommendation given to people at his pharmaceutical competitive intelligence courses. It is always easier to listen and learn at the bleeding edge when you have already thoroughly investigated the track record and apparent direction of the researchers' work.

Sanctuary and the Dominant Position

Competition is actually a form of interaction that can keep a market vital. Competition can help you to become stronger, since without that competition you can become isolated either in a place others have abandoned or in a monopolistic position that could eventually displease customers and result in your breakup or the creation of new competitors. That stated, you do want a meaningful position of dominance somewhere, in at least one significant niche, to reasonably expect to survive and thrive in the market.

For example, when you think of the automobile manufacturer Volvo, what do you think is the main reason people buy and drive Volvos? A large base of Volvo customers buy Volvos specifically for safety, and safety issues are important enough to a large enough segment of automobile purchasers to make safety a significant niche for Volvo. Volvo should and does, therefore, keep a demonstrably significant portion of its research and corresponding patents oriented around securing that sanctuary. From that base, engineers can explore additional possibilities to make Volvos more appealing to buyers outside the safety niche. So if, for example, Volvo were to make an exotic sports car, it would still want to start from a base of superior safety so as not to dilute that sanctuary in the minds of the buyers. Volvo would want to keep safety in mind as well, even in marketing an exotic sports car. Such an exotic sports car could have many features that also make it safe, and in turn, the high safety demands of such a sports car could lead to the development of new safety features that Volvo could use on its standard car models.

Any position of value without a sanctuary likely rests in jeopardy. This is true of patent strategy, as well as many other strategic environments.

Think about the seal that has at least one safe place to go, the shoreline, where it is out of reach of sharks. You simply cannot expect to survive long without a sanctuary, nor can you expect to defeat an adversary until that adversary has nowhere safe to go.

Take a moment to consider some of your own technologies and markets. What are your sanctuaries, and how do you secure them? What areas would you like to have as your sanctuaries? Are you or another competitor the dominant player, or is it a contested field? If contested, how can you take the dominant position? If someone else is dominant, how can you make their position contested?

Licensing to a Competitor

Microsoft licensed Word and Excel for use on the Apple operating system.[41] Although it could appear to be against Microsoft's interests to facilitate the use of a competing operating system by allowing Apple Macintosh® users to have the opportunity to use these popular programs, Microsoft effectively prevented anyone else from establishing a presence in the word processing market by developing a word processing product for the Macintosh®. Such a hypothetical competitor, if successful, might have chosen to launch a PC version of its word processing software from the sanctuary of its position with Apple. This decision therefore served to maintain Microsoft's near monopoly in its own sanctuary in the PC word processing and data spreadsheet market.[42] It also serves as another example where seeking strategic cooperation with a competitor, positive interaction, was more successful than seeking to isolate that competitor from both corporations' point of view. Both companies benefited, and so both made the agreement.

In Summary

In Chapter 3, Assess, we discussed how to define a problem, showing that the real problem is not the gap itself, but rather the effect of that gap in keeping you from something of value. From this we discussed that if you focus problem resolution on the effects of a gap, not just on the gap itself, you can develop many more strategic options. We identified nine types of opposition and discussed why opposition exists. We identified how to determine whether you should cooperate or compete and why. To better assess cooperation and competition, we evaluated resources, the scarcity of which fosters both cooperation and competition. We put all these strategic ideas, which are universal in nature, into context with patent strategy.

In this chapter, we also discussed a model of business as being a core idea supported by three Centers of Excellence in innovation, advancement, and defense, in order to link patent strategy to other aspects of business power. In doing so, we learned how patents should both support, be supported by, and in fact help define the core idea that is the company and everything that happens within the Centers of Excellence. We also discussed the key idea that all the intellectual property in the world, including that belonging to your competitors, can potentially be used within one or more of the Centers of Excellence belonging to your organization, especially considering that it is possible to be cooperative at one Center of Excellence while being competitive at another. We further put the three Centers of Excellence into context with 12 parallel lines of competition that are key to crafting powerful strategies. By considering parallel lines of competition in the spirit of the game "rock, paper, scissors," we learned that you can devise powerful asymmetric strategies for focusing competition in areas where you are strong and avoiding areas where competitors are strong. Finally, we discussed the nature and importance of dominant and contested positions, and showed that you should develop and defend a sanctuary somewhere from which you can venture to compete in other areas.

We now take what we determined in Assess and move to Decide.

Never Tell Me the Odds

When have we assessed too much or too little? In the movie *Star Wars Episode V: The Empire Strikes Back*, the robot character C-3PO calculates the odds of success for seemingly every risky action that the character Han Solo—a pilot seeking to
(Continued)

smuggle C-3PO and other key characters through a hostile empire—undertakes; the robot does this to the point of distraction, whereupon Han Solo says, "Never tell me the odds!"[43] The interaction between these two characters illustrates a contradiction between the benefits of a fully informed decision and the impulse to take some action at some point to make things happen. C-3PO adeptly calculates all the risks and invariably advises that any action is too risky. Han Solo prefers not to know the odds so that they do not keep him from acting. Neither extreme represents good decision making. That stated, however, business, like the natural world, which is often willing to trade thousands to millions of a species' young to create one surviving adult, does seem to favor the big risk. When looked at individually, a Han Solo decision is almost always a bad idea. When looked at collectively, if there are enough Han Solos, then enough will beat the odds to deliver the benefits of success that collective inaction would never deliver. Business will make heroes out of these fortunate few, and they may even write books to tell how they succeeded, perhaps without due consideration of the role that luck may have played. The question will always remain, therefore, whether you are crazy to follow their example or crazy not to.

Many patent attorneys, focused on keeping people under their watch out of trouble, take the position of C-3PO to calculate and avoid undue risk, and many business executives can picture themselves as a Han Solo able to defy the odds, whatever they may be. Attorney-to-executive dialog about proposed actions can follow the same underlying pattern as that expressed in the dialog from the movie. All parties need to be cognizant of the shortcomings of being either overly risk averse or overly dismissive of risk and concentrate on finding that balance of assessment that is good enough for making appropriate decisions.

Chapter 4

Decide

From Assess, we move to Decide. This is where we make our plans. Key learning points for Decide include:

1. *Defining the goal.* If strategy is a solution to get from "A" to "B," you need to know what "B" is and why you want to arrive there. You also determine the objectives you will need to reach along the way. In the Decide part of the decision cycle, you determine which "B" to select.

2. *Fundamental competitive strategy—an interplay between interaction and isolation.* With the selection of "B," you can now decide who you need to interact with and who you need to isolate in order to reach your objectives and the desired result "B."

3. *Four key effects for proficient strategy.* Isolation leads to entropy, which can lead to elimination from the environment. Interaction leads to growth, which can negate the adversarial plans of competitors. Elimination, isolation, interaction, and negation represent the four

key effects of any strategic action. In the Decide part of the decision cycle, you choose the effects you want to see happen and make your plans accordingly.

4. *Competitive equilibrium and disequilibrium—how to decide when to push for change.* Does the current trend help you or hurt you? When planning, you can decide whether to support equilibrium, the current trend, or disequilibrium, something to change the trend, based on whether the current environment is beneficial to you or not.

5. *Leveraging the three Centers of Excellence to craft a strategy.* Patent strategy encompasses the entire business. Here, we discuss how specifically to use other aspects of business power to support the patent strategy and how to use the patent strategy to support other aspects of business power.

Philosophy of the Cheshire Cat

When planning strategy, you want to decide how to get from "A" to "B." This necessarily means that you need to know what "B" is before you set out and that you have a purpose for reaching "B." Consider Lewis Carroll's Cheshire Cat in *Alice's Adventures in Wonderland*, which highlights that we all head somewhere even if we have no apparent direction. The question is whether we can make that somewhere important.

> "Would you tell me, please, which way I ought to go from here?" said Alice.
> "That depends a good deal on where you want to get to," said the Cat.
> "I don't much care where," said Alice.
> "Then it doesn't matter which way you go," said the Cat.[1]

Bottom line: To make a good decision, you should know where you want to go.

Defining the Goal

You should leave your Assess phase of the decision cycle with a clear understanding of your desired result "B." If you know where you want to go, then you can determine your objectives and decide what actions will allow you to reach your goal.

Definition of "B"

To get from your current situation "A" to your desired situation "B," you need to define "B." Only then can you devise a solution (strategy) to reach "B," one that has acceptable risks. When approving a strategy, there are three areas of risk that you should find acceptable:

1. *Probability of success.* You reach "B" or something close enough.
2. *Probability of failure.* You fail to reach "B" but continue to operate.
3. *Probability of catastrophic failure.* You fail to reach "B" and cannot continue to operate.

We can use a patent infringement scenario to illustrate these three risks. Suppose a competitor sued you for patent infringement. One example of a successful outcome from that lawsuit would be to have a court rule that you did not infringe your competitor's patent claims, and further that you attain this positive ruling before you have critically exhausted your resources in the fight. This latter condition is important so that you have the necessary resources left to continue to conduct business after the infringement case ends. An example of a failure would be to have the court rule that you did infringe on your competitor's patent claims and that you should pay damages. It is a failure, but perhaps not a catastrophic failure if you have other viable lines of business. Further to this, perhaps you license or design around the patents of issue, and through that stay in the line of business where the patent infringement occurred. An example of a catastrophic failure would be to have the court rule that you did infringe on your competitor's patent claims and that you should suffer an injunction on your products that effectively puts you out of business. Yet another example of a catastrophic failure, to illustrate a subtlety, is to win the case but to have so depleted your resources in doing so that you fundamentally go out of business anyway, a concept classical strategists call the "pyrrhic victory."

It is important as you make your strategic decisions that you plan your strategy to influence the three risks in a positive way. For example, settling with a competitor instead of taking a fight to court, while it may eliminate all probability of proving that you did not infringe, may also eliminate the probability of a catastrophic failure that could put you out of business. Taking this example a little further, whereas your desired result "B" may be to get a court ruling that you did not infringe, you may decide an acceptable result "B2" should be your target—for example, the result that you pay a nominal royalty. Your objective, therefore, becomes not the acquittal for infringement but the license that keeps you in business and avoids the possibility of a catastrophic injunction that might occur in the absence of that license. That objective, the license, creates the desired result "B"—the nominal royalty that affords you the opportunity to stay in business.

Winning the Race to the Waterfall

Actually, there is even more to defining "B" than knowing what "B" is. It also means appreciating the consequences of reaching "B." It is easy to get so focused on where you want to go that the reason behind getting there falls by the wayside. This is commonly seen in patent strategy when the goal to file a defined number of patents takes on a life of its own at the expense of the purpose for filing patents. "Winning the race to the waterfall" means to use the good execution of a bad or obsolete plan to hasten disaster. It is often a component of a strategic operator, used by many astute competitors, called "Burden Your Adversary with Victory," whereby you can picture the metaphorical competitors of this race to the waterfall realizing the impending danger, pulling their own boats to the safety of shore, and then tipping their hats to their leading adversary as their adversary's boat plunges over the waterfall's edge.

In the patent field, this can happen when companies continue lines of research that no longer make sense. Such was apparently the case concerning Motorola's mid-1990s decision to focus on improving analog cell phones when the rest of the cell phone industry had shifted toward digital networks. This apparent misstep from Motorola's management, which led to a major decline in the company's fortunes, did not come without warning, given that Motorola was licensing some of its own digital cell phone network patents at the time.[2] Bottom line: Know the why behind the "B" so that reaching it makes sense and continues to make sense.

Strategic vs. Technical Solutions

Strategic planning, on the surface, is not that different from other types of planning, such as planning to address a technical problem. You have a problem and decide on a solution. The difference in strategic planning involves the presence of active opposition to your plans as well as uncertainties that you may not be able to eliminate. For example, a technical problem that requires a technical solution could be the undesirable loosening of an attachment bolt due to excessive vibration. One solution to that technical problem would be to apply a damper to the system. If the damper is designed properly to eliminate all uncertainty regarding the efficacy of the solution, the system will stop vibrating and the bolt will no longer loosen, thus solving the technical problem.

In strategic planning, however, you could have an opponent who wants to loosen the bolt. After you apply the damper to the system, that opponent may change the vibration cycle, add more mass to the system, try to remove the damper, or use a welder's torch to cut through the bolt altogether. Not only is this opponent reacting to your solutions, it may also anticipate your solutions so that when implemented they fail. So whereas in a technical solution you may be able to test all uncertainty out of the situation and fix that bolt, the strategic solution must address some level of continued uncertainty about how your opponent will oppose you and perhaps even the efficacy of your solution as a whole. Fruitfully interacting with your opposition so it becomes a facilitator instead of a competitor may be a way of getting to your desired result "B," as could isolating your opposition, keeping your opposition away from the bolt, so to speak, if your opponent otherwise threatens to keep you from reaching "B."

Actions associated with technical solutions can come into play with strategic solutions. The idea to "remove unnecessary parts" commonly applies to technical solutions—say, to make an engine more reliable by lessening the number of parts that can break.[3] It could also apply to a strategic solution by removing unnecessary people from a confidential project to reduce the probability that someone will leak information. So although strategic solutions address uncertainty and opposition, they can draw ideas from the practices of technical disciplines.

Fundamental Competitive Strategy

Earlier in this book we discussed that all strategy is an interplay between interaction and isolation. We have seen examples in which interaction led more to growth, and isolation led more to entropy (decline). These correlate directly with our capacity for independent action and, therefore, our capacity to succeed on our own terms.

Expand succeeding on your own terms further and think about two equally well-off people—one who has achieved success doing what he or she loves, and another who is compelled to work at something he or she does not love in order to maintain that well-off status. The person doing what he or she loves is succeeding on his or her own terms, whereas the other person, while successful on paper, sacrifices his or her quality of life by doing something that is not enjoyable. How much compromise is the second person willing to give to actually succeed on his or her own terms?

So, your decisions should gravitate toward increasing useful interaction and decreasing harmful isolation with a directional bent toward succeeding on your own terms and not someone else's terms. This applies both to individuals and organizations. Interaction tends to lead to more opportunity, and opportunity raises the probability that you will indeed find success on your own terms. Interaction brings in fresh new possibilities and allows you to discard burdens that might otherwise weigh you down. In patent strategy, interaction is essential if the entire body of the world's intellectual property is to be potentially useful to you.

Isolation, in contrast, leads to entropy. Competitors will try to isolate you with varying degrees of success, and you will have to deal with that. A solid first step to deal with isolation is to avoid self-isolation. Not Invented Here (NIH) syndrome is one condition that leads to self-isolation. To illustrate, we can start with a leading source of innovation for industry through the years—government and defense institutions and companies.

The U.S. government's Key West decision in 1948, which defined the role of the new Air Force (formerly the U.S. Army Air Corps part of the U.S. Army), stated that the U.S. Army should not have fleets of fixed-winged aircraft, since that would be the exclusive domain of the Air Force.[4] This has caused the Army to rely on helicopters to the present day, such as the Apache Attack Helicopter, to perform tasks that fixed-wing aircraft might perform better. For example, the Army cannot fly the armored A-10 attack planes that it wants for very close air support where helicopters are vulnerable, and the Air Force does not necessarily want to fly the A-10s that fill this Army role.[5] This has created a 60-year old institutionalized form of NIH that gets in the way of innovation for present-day Army requirements. It contrasts with a current decision to build the Joint Strike Fighter for the Air Force, Navy, and Marine service branches as a highly innovative modular aircraft that shares its major components but can also be customized to even include a vertical take-off variant for the U.S. Marine Corps.

Self-isolating activities are not necessarily restricted to large bureaucracies such as the military staff. As an often-referenced case of NIH, an otherwise nimble and adaptive company in most regards, Apple Computer, stayed with its one-button mouse until 2005, long after the two-button mouse was available and desired by the public. Apple Computer stood by its single-button mouse despite calls by its customers for the two-button variant.[6,7]

To illustrate why isolation causes so much trouble, picture what happens when a population of people becomes isolated from another population, as has happened throughout human history. Over time, their languages and cultures diverge until they can no longer understand each other. In the same vein, think about the progress of your engineers, executives, and other professionals over time if you isolate them from customers. Their appreciation of customer needs will diminish the longer they are isolated.

So, bottom line: Favor decisions that lead to increased interaction and discourage decisions that lead to isolation. In addition, take advantage of good ideas from other sources; such interaction leads to growth. As an example, most of the flagship products for Microsoft actually had their origins outside the company. MS-DOS®, Windows®, Internet Explorer®, FrontPage®, SQL Server®, and PowerPoint® all began with licenses or purchases of technology from outside sources.[8]

To Sue or Not to Sue

An estimate by experts in the field showed that open-source software likely infringed up to 235 Microsoft patents and that Microsoft has considered litigation since the early 2000s.[9] The problem with doing so is that such litigation would get in the way of Microsoft's connections with other companies, systems interoperability, and the desires of customers. Suing people who are also customers tends to drive them away, not to mention the possibility that a judge and jury could produce a negative result in a verdict that would set a damaging precedent for other cases. All things taken into consideration, Microsoft's management has chosen nonaction with regard to these infringements. Nonaction makes sense, since the risk is too high that the consequences of litigation, even with a win, could diminish interaction and increase isolation in the market space. Also, the continuing threat that Microsoft has the power to litigate if an open-source provider were to push its boundaries too far has leverageable value that the precedent of a loss would destroy.

Fundamental Competitive Strategy, the Objective, and the Desired Result "B"

Interaction and isolation are the fundamental elements of competitive strategy. In most circumstances, your competition wants to see you isolated from your desired result "B," isolated from the means to achieve your desired result "B," or isolated from the opportunity to leverage your desired result "B" if you reach it. You, on the other hand, want to reach your desired result "B," a form of interaction, and then use your desired result "B" to leverage additional desired results, which will most likely include additional forms of interaction.

So your plan should raise the level of your interaction, which, since everything we do is "evil" to somebody, will have the deliberate or incidental effect of raising the level of isolation in the opposition. As in the previous example, winning a good customer raises your level of interaction (you have the customer) and raises the competitor's level of isolation (it does not have that customer).

Your synthesis of strategic operators that we explored in Chapter 3, Assess, will be oriented around this interplay of interaction and isolation. A useful product that describes strategic operators is the *Art of War: Sun Tzu Strategy Card Deck*.[10] This is a literal and useable playing card deck produced by the author of this book. It was designed around the concept that if you analyze strategic actions, you find they are derived from one or a combination of ideas (strategic operators) in much the same way that all musical melodies are derived from a combination of notes in a musical scale. Learning these strategic operators, most of which have been known in classical strategy for thousands of years, raises your proficiency in strategy because you can better appreciate both what you and your opponents are doing when competing and why. You can find reference to all of these strategies in Sun Tzu's *The Art of War*, for which the author wrote a companion book, *Understanding Sun Tzu on the Art of War*.[11] That book is part of the curriculum reading at the National Defense University, where much effort goes into classical strategy instruction and research.

The isolate and interact cards in the *Art of War: Sun Tzu Strategy Card Deck*, are respectively, the Ace of Diamonds, "Isolate Your Adversary," and the Ace of Clubs, "Create a Center for Advantage." This last card, the Ace of Clubs, "Create a Center for Advantage," focuses on the idea that the best way for you to interact with others is for them to want to interact with you. For your patent strategy, you look to create a center for advantage such that people want to interact with you and thereby help you to succeed. IBM, as noted earlier, has taken this idea to a high level by presenting a huge patent portfolio that is open to pretty much anyone for licensing. On isolating in business, you preferably want your isolating of those who are "evil" to you to be less a targeted activity and more a by-product of your positive efforts to interact with desirable customers and facilitators. Doing so is equivalent to winning a game by outscoring the opponent instead of injuring the opponent and then scoring, which, aside from the ethics involved, also means risking injury to yourself.

Art of War: Sun Tzu Strategy Card Deck

The *Art of War: Sun Tzu Strategy Card Deck* is a card set of winning strategies designed to improve your ability to succeed when faced with adversaries. It is also a playing card deck made from casino grade card stock.

The *Art of War: Sun Tzu Strategy Card Deck* has been rigorously peer reviewed and acclaimed by professional strategists, including instructors from the National Defense University at Ft. McNair, Washington, D.C. It has also found a home at several top intellectual property strategy and management departments worldwide.

Many anthropologists believe that human intelligence evolved to make people successively better able to deceive and defeat their neighbors. The *Art of War: Sun Tzu Strategy Card Deck* contains the strategies men and women have used to deceive and defeat their neighbors since the dawn of time.

So why do we use the *Art of War: Sun Tzu Strategy Card Deck* here? Bottom line: The better you are at applying classic adversarial strategies, the less likely you are to need them, and the more positively interactive you can safely be. Winning in patent strategy ultimately is about high interactivity with selective customers, facilitators, and competitors. Knowing the strategies is also a matter of survival; other people will use the described strategies against you to keep you from where you want to be, and if you understand what they are doing, you can better counteract or preempt them.

How to Be Proficient at Decision Making

When making your decisions, you will wish to derive a proficient solution. To do so, as noted at the end of Chapter 3, you will need to strike a balance between being informed enough to act and not being so fully entangled in the details as to be unable to see a clear picture of the whole situation. Some people call this being able to "see the forest for the trees." The best way to strike this balance is to have some base conditions for success on which you can actually make decisions when there is either too much or too little information.

In patent strategy, you will want your decisions to create one of four basic conditions from which you can derive proficient solutions. If you have any or all of these conditions, you raise the probability that you will succeed with both your objective and your resources intact. If you do not have any one of these conditions, you can still win the contest, but more than likely at a higher cost than you would have wanted. The four conditions are:

1. Overwhelming Advantage
2. Surprise
3. Asymmetry
4. Sanctuary

Overwhelming Advantage   The competitor with an Overwhelming Advantage has the opportunity to dominate a situation. In the *Art of War: Sun Tzu Strategy Card Deck* Overwhelming Advantage is best represented by the Queen of Spades, "Use Overwhelming Force." The principle behind overwhelming force is to employ more physical, psychological, or moral power than the opponent can resist. For example, the patent portfolios owned by Hewlett-Packard, Canon, Intel, or Samsung can often overwhelm that of smaller competitors in a patent assertion contest.

In a litigious environment, it makes sense to have a portfolio of sufficient size to counteract competitive patent assertion attempts. However, Overwhelming Advantage comes in more forms than just numbers. A single, well-written patent, particularly in the pharmaceutical or chemical industries, may prove to be beyond a competitor's ability or willingness to challenge. A specific legal team could outclass an opposing legal team. One entity could have considerably more time to deal with a problem than another that needs a decision right now. The side with the Overwhelming Advantage has the opportunity to dictate terms.

Surprise   Surprise often pairs with Overwhelming Advantage to enhance it, but just as often may serve as a tool to overcome weakness caused by an absence of Overwhelming Advantage. Surprise creates a temporary advantage because your opposition is not expecting your action, or at least not expecting it at the time, at the place, or in the way you execute it.

In the *Art of War: Sun Tzu Strategy Card Deck*, Surprise is best represented by the Jack of Spades, "Catch Your Adversary Sleeping." The principle behind Surprise is to act with deliberation at a place and time of your choosing to force your opponent, for the period of time it takes to defeat that opponent, to engage you on your terms. Much of the success in Surprise depends on the timing of the event. Consider the case where you choose to threaten patent infringement litigation against a competitor that has a larger patent portfolio than your own. This could be a surprise to your competitor if you have not otherwise tipped your hand or the competitor has not otherwise detected the danger, but the impact of that surprise could vary. In the absence of a pending event, such as that competitor's consummation of a merger with another company, the surprised competitor may take all the time needed to examine its own portfolio for patents to support a countersuit, or it may undertake a project to invalidate your patent. If you wait and surprise that competitor by initiating an infringement lawsuit just before a pending event, such as when that competitor desires to complete the merger, that competitor may not have the time to do anything but settle on your terms.

Surprise requires secrecy as well as timing to work. You need to have stealth so that your competitor cannot learn your intent before you take action. Surprise also has a short shelf life. Once your opponent becomes aware of a situation, then if your opponent survives the surprise, the opponent will adjust and possibly counteract your approach. In light of that, you should be thorough in your planning and proficient in your execution when you determine to use Surprise so that it succeeds before your opponent can effectively respond.

The Hidden Army Behind the Hill

In the late 1990s, an intellectual asset management company called Aurigin, originally named SmartPatents, threatened to sue Thomson Information for patent infringement on a patent search product, Patent Explorer®. Aurigin asserted that

Patent Explorer® used software code patented by Aurigin. Patent Explorer® started out as a Microsoft product that Microsoft sold to Thomson Information. Through a previously negotiated agreement between Thomson Information and Microsoft, Microsoft promised to stand behind any intellectual property disputes that arose from Patent Explorer®. Any suit by Aurigin against Thomson Information over Patent Explorer®, therefore, became a suit against Microsoft. Suing Microsoft was not in Aurigin's interest for a number of reasons. According to members from the Thomson side, this arrangement between Thomson and Microsoft became the defining reason for Aurigin not to pursue the case. It also illustrates how the wise strategist is pragmatic when making decisions; in this case, the decision of Aurigin's management to withdraw from a situation that could have been expensive because of the cost of litigation and the potential damage to its market relationships.

Asymmetry Asymmetry is a strategic tool derived from the condition that you or your competition are stronger in one area and weaker in another. The proficient decision maker will use this condition to take action that lines up strengths against weaknesses to his or her advantage. Asymmetry comes in many different forms and is not represented by any one card in the *Art of War: Sun Tzu Strategy Card Deck*. A central theme of the idea, however, appears on the Eight of Diamonds card, "Lure the Tiger Out of the Mountain." The core idea behind this card is to take a formidable adversary and entice it to engage you on your terms, meaning to fight you when, where, or how you have the advantage. For example, if your competitor sells a technology product that it keeps proprietary, you could launch a competing and noninfringing product as an open and nonproprietary product.

Being open rather than proprietary was one of two key factors in the success of Matsushita's VHS video recording technology format over Sony's Betamax in the late 1980s. Sony kept the Betamax format proprietary, whereas Matsushita offered VHS licenses to a large number of companies. Matsushita used Sony's self-imposed isolation against them by offering a license to every other company wanting to enter the videocassette market, ultimately including Sony. Although Sony had the upper hand in the Betamax market from a technical quality and first-mover point of view, that was not a sufficient advantage over Matsushita's offering of a more open alternative with its more than good enough quality VHS technology. Critically, VHS videotapes could also record longer, the second factor. This longer recording capability was also an asymmetrical advantage that was important for recording television shows, a major sought-after utility from consumers who wanted to do more with their videotape systems than just watch movies.[12]

The condition of Asymmetry can also mean using patents to address the marketing line of competition, which Polaroid did to knock Kodak out of the instant camera market. Kodak's instant camera was succeeding in the marketplace, but a 1976 patent infringement verdict in Polaroid's favor forced Kodak to exit that market.[13] The infringement verdict put Kodak, a strong company in the area of traditional film photography that sought a position in the instant camera market, into a nonexistent position in the instant camera market. This unbalanced condition allowed Polaroid to dominate the instant camera marketplace on its own terms.

Asymmetry is how, in business, you put the often quoted Sun Tzu maxim, "Attack where you are strong and your enemy is weak," into actual practice. The side that knows its competitors' strengths and weaknesses, as well as its own, will have the opportunity to be more proficient in its strategic decision making.

Asymmetric Vulnerabilities

In the fall of 2006, RFID World used U.S. Patent No. 6,967,563, Inventory Control System, to bring suit against Wal-Mart, Gillette, Michelin, Home Depot, Target, and Pfizer in the Eastern District of Texas for use of inventory control tags. A traditional approach to such lawsuits for the defendant is to review the home patent portfolio and launch a countersuit against the litigator's products. RFID World, however, had no products and, therefore, no vulnerability associated with products. This provided an asymmetrical advantage to RFID World in terms of unbalanced vulnerabilities. Those with nothing to lose can be

much braver in the attack than those who may have to put
something or someone else in jeopardy.

Sanctuary   The last key condition is Sanctuary. Sanctuary is a safe place
to rest and recover. Any entity without a sanctuary has no place to rest
and recover, meaning it will eventually wear down or get caught. In the
Art of War: Sun Tzu Strategy Card Deck, the offensive side of the concept
of Sanctuary appears on the Nine of Spades card, "Allow Your Adversary
No Sanctuary."

In business, Sanctuary has a somewhat nuanced meaning that is just
as likely to be in the mind of buyers as in actual technical advantages.
We discussed Volvo's sanctuary in the field of safety, meaning that whatever Volvo may try to do in the market, it has a loyal set of buyers who
will always buy Volvos because of their reputation for safety. Nikon and
Canon, respectively, also have sanctuaries in the single-lens reflex SLR
and digital single-lens reflex dSLR space favored by their customers,
many of whom have made considerable financial investments in expensive lenses that are incompatible with each other's cameras. As the two
companies advance their camera technology into the marketplace and
compete with other camera makers, this base of existing customers provides a cushion against mistakes and competitive encroachments that
is difficult for others to penetrate. In standard marketing lexicon, the
switching costs are higher than most existing customers will bear.

Of course, the viability of sanctuaries can change. Wang had a sanctuary in word processing equipment that became meaningless with the
advent of personal computers; similarly, Polaroid's sanctuary in the instant
camera marketplace that it solidified with the patent infringement victory over Kodak became all but irrelevant when digital cameras gained
prominence.

Sanctuary Lost
The Wang word processor, introduced in 1976, was a technological breakthrough and an instant success. Wang was able to
dominate this market and retain this sanctuary up until the advent
(Continued)

of the personal computer, which allowed for word processing software to replicate the function of a stand-alone word processor. When the stand-alone word processor became obsolete, so, too, did the Wang sanctuary. In the absence of new products or services from which to build a new sanctuary, everything that Wang sold was vulnerable to better positioned competitors, and so Wang disappeared.

A patent itself can and does provide sanctuary for a period of time if the owners of that patent can use it to enforce product exclusivity. Take AstraZeneca's patent on Lipitor® as an example. The AstraZeneca patent provided a lucrative sanctuary in the sense that AstraZeneca could profit highly from the sale of the drug without competition for the same underlying drug compound. The patent strategist needs to make sure that the company both gains and maintains adequate patent protections on the technologies associated with its sanctuaries, while at the same time developing future sanctuaries in case the current sanctuary becomes obsolete. The patent strategist also needs to sound the alarm if his or her organization allows overdependence on a sanctuary to cause self-isolation from which a competitor could take advantage, such as Polaroid's over-reliance on the instant camera sanctuary. The competitor that understands its own sanctuaries, and the sanctuaries of others, will have the opportunity to be more proficient in the decision-making process than those less informed.

Accepting the Inevitable

Two thousand one was the last year that Nikon produced its venerable Nikonos-V underwater camera, which had been the standard for consumer underwater photography for nearly 20 years.[14] Although this product line represented a fraction of Nikon's business, it had built a base of loyal customers who continue to trade used and refurbished equipment to this day. Nikon, however, apparently read the tea leaves and withdrew from the market just as camera housing makers, such as competitors

Sea & Sea and Ikelite, started to introduce inexpensive camera housings for consumer digital cameras. For both consumers and professionals, the market was headed to digital camera housings versus dedicated waterproof cameras, and within four years the Nikonos-V would not have had a sustainable position. Sanctuaries are important, but only so long as they can remain as such.

Enemy at the Gate

In 2006, the U.S. Supreme Court reviewed an infringement verdict made against eBay in favor of MercExchange on patents associated with the Buy It Now® feature.[15] However, the details of this verdict put into greater vulnerability companies that make their business suing for infringement on patents they own but do not use in their own products. Many people feared that a permanent injunction against eBay would negatively impact the e-commerce industry as a whole, and it is that fear of injunction, in this case and others, that made the MercExchange business model powerful, especially since its targeted companies could not threaten an injunction in return. The Court held that an infringement ruling did not necessarily dictate imposing a permanent injunction, but it also showed that the infringed company did not need to be practicing the art for an injunction to be considered. At issue was the threshold for injunction, which the Court reaffirmed, such that the plaintiff needed to prove (1) that a company has suffered an irreparable injury; (2) that remedies available at law, such as monetary damages, are inadequate to compensate for that injury; (3) that considering the balance of hardships between the plaintiff and defendant, a remedy in equity, such as a permanent injunction, is warranted; and (4) that the public interest would not be disserved by a permanent injunction. The Court upheld the infringement but did not uphold the permanent injunction against eBay. After the Court's decision was handed down, eBay and

(Continued)

> MercExchange were able to come to an agreement on the licensing and eventual ownership of the patented material; however, the sanctuary of value afforded by just owning a strong patent instead of both owning and practicing it had diminished.

Leveraging Conditions

The advantage in patent strategy can come from any line of competition within the organization. The goal is to identify conditions inside and outside of your organization that you can use to improve your capacity for success.

Consider how the example conditions that follow can make an organization's patent strategy stronger.

1. Pfizer is thought by many to have a preeminent sales force. The Overwhelming Advantage the Pfizer sales force provides enables it to gain access to markets for patented products that only a few other companies in its industry can match. As a result, a patent owned by or licensed to Pfizer can become correspondingly more valuable than if it had been owned by or licensed to a company with a lesser sales reach.

2. Apple utilized the conditions of Surprise and Overwhelming Advantage involving both the innovation and marketing lines of competition within the organization. Apple's launch of the innovative iPhone proved to be surprise enough to the industry that competitors apparently had insufficient time to respond to counteract the first mover advantage. To further reinforce its position, Apple filed patents that would make it even more difficult for competitors to respond once the surprise wore off.

3. The capacity of Linux to use open software development and draw on the collective brainpower of the world provides a potential Asymmetrical Advantage over Microsoft and its Windows® product. The Microsoft business model is based on owning and enforcing intellectual property rights and is not geared for open software development.

4. India and China allow non–patent-owning drug manufacturers to produce and sell drugs within their own borders without the

requirement of a license to the patent owner. The patent owners have patent protection in the other major world markets that bars the Indian and Chinese manufacturers from entering those markets, but the manufacturers still have a Sanctuary to set up a base of production from which to launch products into other countries as soon as corresponding patents expire.

As stated, lacking a significant advantage, you can still succeed with your plans, but your success will likely be inefficient. In strategy, part of your goal is to craft plans to gain a lot for little expense. Take a moment to reflect and ask how you might create any or all of the four conditions discussed in this section in your patent strategy.

Developing the Situation

Now that you have gone through your assessment, decided on your objective and your desired result "B," and ideally have one or more advantageous conditions in play from a patent or other line of competition, you can further develop your strategy. We have some standard considerations you should make to develop the situation, and as with other parts of strategy, the core elements that make up the decision, and therefore the plan, are relatively few. The process of going from a current situation "A" to a desired situation "B" in strategy follows a consistent and universal pattern. Developing the situation, in sequence, means to:

1. *Prepare yourself.* You optimize yourself to pursue "B."
2. *Shape the field.* You create the conditions whereby you can proficiently get *to* "B."
3. *Isolate on the objective.* You focus on the most important aspect of getting to "B."
4. *Close on the objective.* You succeed in getting to "B."

To illustrate, we can start with the way this pattern appears in nature. The wolf, through genetics and experience, has matured to become a proficient pack predator of large game. When hunting large game, the wolf pursues its quarry from an optimal position, perhaps downwind so the herd cannot smell it. Furthermore, it interacts with the other members of its pack that share its objective. The wolf and the other members of the pack isolate one member of the target herd from the rest in a place where it is more difficult for any other member of the herd to intervene. Then, with the assistance of its brethren, the wolf brings down and kills that member. The objective of the wolf was to kill a member of the herd. The desired result "B" was to eat.

A patent lawyer, similarly, through education and experience learns to become the best lawyer he or she can. In the case of prosecuting an infringement lawsuit, the lawyer attempts to influence the shape of the field, including selecting, as is possible, the venue of the trial and consistency of the jury. Perhaps the lawyer chooses the Eastern District of Texas to try the case, because it has proven on aggregate to give rulings that an infringement has occurred. Next, the lawyer isolates a specific aspect of the infringed technology that a jury can understand in order to make his or her best case. The lawyer uses that aspect of the infringed technology to win the case. The lawyer's objective is to convince the jury that an infringement has occurred. The lawyer's desired result "B" is to win the case and gain the personal benefits associated with winning.

Move up the scale, and you can picture executives deciding where to focus their research and development efforts. Given the uncertainty associated with predicting the future, they may ask themselves how they would like the future to look and then explore the avenues of research that would help to create that environment. As that environment actually takes shape, and the future becomes less mysterious, they will isolate those initiatives that have, by chance or design, the most promising positions for commercial development. Then they will close on that development with actual products that enter the market.

Notice how the pattern is consistent. As stated earlier, strategy is an interplay between interaction and isolation. Preparing yourself and the field of contest is an interactive exercise that builds your strength. The isolation and elimination activity, while it certainly can have competitive implications, is also how you narrow down your own options so that you ultimately actually accomplish something and choose which relationships to build. If strategy involves a management of options, then you decide on or eliminate options until you reach the end goal and start the process all over again.

Who Is "I"?

For better or worse, the U.S. Army launched an advertisement campaign called "Army of One." The phrase had a double meaning, a subtlety unusual for such a pragmatic organization. One person was both the soldier and the unified army that supported the soldier at the same time. Rudyard Kipling illustrated the same idea when he wrote, "For the strength of the pack is the wolf, and the strength of the wolf is the pack."[16]

This is an important thought to consider when developing a situation, since it likewise makes sense for a company or law firm and the individual people within. The strength of the organization is in the person, and the strength of the person is in the organization. Both emerge from each other at the same time.

Tale of Two Searches

In the preparation phase of a plan, when is a patent search good enough for your patent strategy? That depends on your point of view. If you seek to pursue a patent on an invention, you may consider the good-enough search to be searching the major patent offices, key sources of research papers and conference notes, and perhaps the major databases that a patent examiner would be expected to search. Practitioners of the arts may even say that going beyond that level of search puts you at a disadvantage with a competitor who may come along later with the same invention, be less thorough in his or her investigation, and be granted a dubious patent that is too expensive for you to challenge.

If you are doing an invalidity search, perhaps because you have been sued for infringement with multimillion dollar stakes on the outcome, then no search is comprehensive (good) enough until you have found invalidating prior art or have truly exhausted possible sources of prior art. You will put in much more time than the 8 to 25 hours a patent examiner typically uses to

(Continued)

examine a case, and will very specifically seek out sources of prior art that patent examiners would normally miss, such as less accessible libraries and publications, research papers from less widely read sources, less prominent conference proceedings, brochures, facts pertaining to sale of prior inventions, and third-party documentation. You do this because no matter the cost of the search, being able to invalidate a patent that you allegedly infringed will be the most effective and least expensive way to win most of the time.

Four Key Effects: Eliminate, Isolate, Interact, Negate

There are four key effects we wish to achieve from our strategy. By this we mean that when you take any action, at its barest level, you will have accomplished one of these four things. The first of these that has been a part of our discussion, isolation, leads to entropy, which, if it goes far enough, leads to the second, elimination. The third that has been a part of our discussion, interaction, leads to growth, which if robust enough leads to the fourth, negation, or, in a sense, invulnerability. To understand what we mean by this, think about it from a seller–customer relationship. If you can isolate a competitor from enough customers by winning the business of those customers (a sought-after interaction), then your competitor, now without those customers, will become financially stressed (a form of entropy) and if distressed enough, will go out of business (a form of elimination). Along with this, if you interact with enough customers and prospective customers, then your business success becomes all but certain, given that a certain percentage of those interactions will lead to closed sales (this being a form of invulnerability). So the actions of the opposition become less and less dangerous, because with more interactions you depend less and less on any one customer or prospect for your sales. This all but assures the viability of your endeavor. Furthermore, the two interplays, isolation and interaction, also work hand in hand because your interacting with customers and prospects can serve to isolate your competitor from doing so at the same time your interactions serve to spur your growth.

The four key effects, eliminate, isolate, interact, and negate, are represented by the four aces in the *Art of War: Sun Tzu Strategy Card Deck*:

1. Ace of Spades, "Eliminate Your Adversary"
2. Ace of Diamonds, "Isolate Your Adversary"
3. Ace of Clubs, "Create a Center for Advantage"
4. Ace of Hearts, "Let the Tiger Find No Place to Sink Its Claws"

These four key effects are part of classical strategy and have been understood by expert strategists, if not actually described in this way, for thousands of years. As evidence, you need only look as far as the two quintessential games of strategy passed down through the centuries called chess and Go. In the game of chess, the overriding goal is to effectively eliminate the opposing king by isolating him in a checkmate. The goal of a checkmate is facilitated by the unique movement capabilities of each of the individual pieces and how they interact with and isolate each other and the pieces of your opponent. In Go, the 3,000-year-old Asian game of strategy that has a following in the East similar to that of chess in the West, you isolate competitive positions and gain territory by interacting and linking your pieces together. In Go you can also eliminate enemy pieces by surrounding them, and you can negate attempts to eliminate your pieces by creating an invulnerable position known in the game as "having two eyes."

You can use patents for real-life strategy plays in the same way that you might play chess and Go pieces. You can use a patent to eliminate a competitor by taking such actions as suing for an injunction. This happened with Polaroid's action against Kodak's instant camera, described earlier, which completely removed Kodak from the instant camera market. You can isolate a competitor from a market, as Innogenetics did to Abbott Laboratories, by enjoining a product line (though not Abbott Laboratories' participation in the market). You can interact with patents as Sepracor did with Eli Lilly to extend the patent life of Prozac® by creating a purified (chiral) form of the original drug worthy of a new patent.[17] You can negate the opportunity for a competitor to sue for infringement by designing around the claims of its patents and, therefore, by not infringing.

> **Elimination**
>
> To expand on the aforementioned case, Polaroid eliminated Kodak from the instant camera market with a patent infringement lawsuit filed on April 26, 1976 at the U.S. District Court for the District of Massachusetts in Boston. On October 11, 1985, after five years of pretrial activity and 75 days of trial, seven Polaroid patents were found to be infringed. This knocked Kodak out of the instant picture market, leaving customers with useless cameras and no film. The $873 million damages awarded and upheld in the case is higher than in any other case thus far at the time of writing.[18]

> **Isolation**
>
> In September 2005, Innogenetics sued Abbott Laboratories, alleging that Abbott was infringing the company's U.S. patent No. 5,846,704. This patent covers a method of genotyping the Hepatitis-C virus. Innogenetics wanted to stop Abbott Laboratories from using its patented invention, which is a form of isolation (i.e., Abbott Laboratories would be legally isolated from that invention). The court found that Abbott's product did indeed infringe on the Innogenetics patent, and on January 10, 2007, the judge affirmed Innogenetics's request for a permanent injunction against Abbott from further production. Abbott Laboratories was barred from any further sales, use, or export of products, including components, that infringe on Innogenetics's patented genotyping technology. The isolation from the invention meant prospective Abbott Laboratories customers for this product line needed to go elsewhere, but it did not eliminate Abbott Laboratories from the field, because U.S. patent No. 5,846,704 did not describe the only possible solution to the disease that Abbott Laboratories could pursue.

You have many options for achieving the four key effects of eliminate, isolate, interact, and negate in patents. To begin with, you can achieve the key effects both directly and indirectly. Indirect approaches, in particular, can be highly efficient and are often based on previously described asymmetrical advantages. As we have illustrated, if you want to eliminate a competitor from a market, then you can use a patent that isolates that competitor from a given invention, which has the same effect indirectly as if you had sought to push them out directly through a market-on-market contest. You can also achieve effects through actual action or threatened action as noted by the four rules of patent strategy.

This last, actual and threatened actions, itself brings up another set of possibilities to explore; we have touched on these previously, and we can expand further. Succeeding against opposition through threatened action leverages the psychological fear of that action irrespective of whether you actually follow through or even could follow through with the threat. Threatened action can often be more efficient than actual action, since actual action costs time, money, and other resources, along with the risk that the action might not succeed. To make threats work, as we have noted, your competitor must believe in the credibility of your threat, especially if you choose to bluff.

Considering that in cases where a bluff worked we would not necessarily know the bluff happened, just as in poker, you are not required to reveal your hand if everyone else folds, we can instead illustrate the importance of a credible threat with a bluff that failed. In the case of *Walker Process Equipment, Inc. v. Food Machinery & Chemical Corp.*, where Food Machinery & Chemical Corp. used an invalid patent to challenge Walker Process Equipment, Inc. from entering a market, Walker called the bluff and showed that Food Machinery had been using its patented invention earlier than the one-year window for which it could have applied for a U.S. patent.[19] Food Machinery did not have a credible threat when it chose to bluff and therefore did not succeed with its strategy.

Done properly, winning by threat versus action is in keeping with a strategic ideal of winning battles without fighting. Most often in infringement lawsuits, for example, an organization will prefer to settle with some advantage either gained or not lost than to go to court once the threat of court looms large enough. So if you can achieve the desired effect with a threatened action rather than with an actual action, you generally come out ahead. A threatened action will not generally require the same expenditure of resources, nor will you lose the mystery of just how good your threat was by having it tested in practice.

The following table (Exhibit 4.1) is a sample of causes and effects associated with the eliminate, isolate, interact, negate model. The pairings provide a guideline of possibilities for you to consider as you translate them to your own particular situation. Like so much in strategy, these are guidelines with gray distinctions in many cases. Their purpose, however you get there, is to make sure you comprehensively review all of your possible options before you decide on an action. If a key component of strategy is the management of options, then it pays to know what your options are and to step into the shoes of your adversaries to know the options they have.

Exhibit 4.1   A List of Possible Options Associated with Combining Eliminate, Isolate, Interact, and Negate Effects

Eliminate, Isolate, Interact, Negate

Eliminate by Eliminating	Obtain an injunction
Eliminate by Isolating	Gain market share with a patented technology
Eliminate by Interacting	Acquire a competitor
Eliminate by Negating	Pursue a new and disruptive technology
Isolate by Eliminating	Invalidate a patent
Isolate by Isolating	Obtain a patent that keeps a competitor from the market
Isolate by Interacting	Offer a license that keeps a competitor from developing an alternative
Isolate by Negating	Gain control of a standard
Interact by Eliminating	Out-compete and hire a competitor's former staff
Interact by Isolating	Offer a license to a standard you own
Interact by Interacting	Establish a mutually agreeable license
Interact by Negating	Offer a license to a better competitive approach
Negate by Eliminating	Offer a superior technical solution
Negate by Isolating	Pursue an alternative market
Negate by Interacting	Set up an alliance
Negate by Negating	Withdraw from the market

Competitive Equilibrium and Disequilibrium

This brings us to the important issue of competitive equilibrium. As stated, the existence of competitors can actually make you stronger, provided you have a sanctuary from which to build your advantages. In the absence of competition, businesses often underperform. However, the existence of competition also means the existence of opposition, and the impact of that opposition is something you will need to manage. Since you cannot directly manage your competitor, then you must manage your own performance and expectations and influence the decisions of your competitor through your own actions.

Equilibrium

Although change is inevitable, you may wish to maintain the status quo for a period of time by creating a balanced environment called a competitive equilibrium. This is equivalent to the balanced environment of predator and prey populations found in nature. The predators actually keep the prey healthier by weeding out the sick and slower members of the population, thus allowing the fitter genes to pass on to future offspring of the prey. In nature, predators and prey keep each other in check and at optimal levels of fitness unless something upsets that balance.

The marketplace is similar to nature. Look at the impact of succeeding in the presence of a major competitor where you have attained an acceptable equilibrium. Continuing to succeed and maintaining that equilibrium means finding the continued wherewithal to perform well enough against your competitors in at least one critical aspect of your market. It can also mean finding a way aside from your competitors so that you do not compete directly. Consider a case where there are two major competitors, such as in the case of the long-time rivalry between Pfizer and Merck. Both companies have ample resources in terms of researchers, patents, finance, sales, and marketing to compete directly with each other when and where they so choose, and they often do compete directly with drugs that solve similar health problems for patients. A smaller start-up, on the other hand, might have to consider finding a niche pharmaceutical to develop, one that Pfizer or Merck are not currently producing, so as to step aside from directly competing with them, or alternatively to attract the attention of one or the other as a potential partner in a field in which Pfizer or Merck may be interested. This latter is a key business plan component of many pharmaceutical and biotech start-ups. Once they show promise in their research and establish a quality patent portfolio associated with that research, they will develop a business partnership and interact exclusively with one of the many pharmaceutical giants.

Icos and Lilly

Icos was a small biotech company, cofounded by Dr. George B. Rathmann and based in Bothell, Washington, that started operations in 1990. The company developed the erectile dysfunction treatment drug called Cialis (phosphodiesterase type 5 inhibitor (PDE5)) within a 50–50 joint venture with Eli Lilly. This joint venture positioned Icos, which had the scientists to handle the research, to have access to an established marketing force through Eli Lilly. As the Cialis venture proved itself, other initiatives by Icos failed and Eli Lilly launched a takeover bid for the whole of Icos. While such a takeover is often a sought-after outcome for a small pharmaceutical company, a takeover was not the result originally intended by Rathmann, who had built Amgen and sought similar results with Icos.[20]

The results of this change from the equilibrium of the joint venture to the disequilibrium of the merger became a matter of perspective. Prominent Icos executives, based on SEC filings, presumably did well for their efforts. However, Icos's failure to have other options in its drug development pipeline meant that Eli Lilly had a strong position from which to negotiate a favorable, or from the perspective of Icos's individual and institutional shareholders, a low offer of $34 per share. Eli Lilly also terminated about 550 Icos employees, which threw them into very personal disequilibriums. For Eli Lilly shareholders, it proved a positive transaction. That is often the real nature of a shift from equilibrium to disequilibrium. Some people do well by it; some people do not.

When you are the strongest competitor in an environment that has reached equilibrium, you want to continue performing well, but you might also need to manage your competitiveness. Isolating competitors too much or creating a vacuum by eliminating them altogether will create change and disequilibrium. Change, while inevitable, is not always expedient. A distressed competitor could do something drastic to stay in the market; it could, for example, forge an exclusive relationship with an entity with much deeper pockets and marketing strength than yours. If the market becomes too monopolistic, it could also attract the attention of the Federal Trade Commission or the Department of Justice, as the FTC and DOJ desire that all markets provide viable customer alternatives. Just as may happen to a population of a species once all of its competition disappears, your becoming so good as to create monopolistic conditions in your market space could easily lead to complacency toward new possibilities. You could become less fit over time. Complacency leaves potential value unguarded, which if valuable enough, will lead to new competition and the introduction into your environment of a "devil you don't know," in place of the "devil you do know."

An example of useful competition appears with Microsoft and Apple Computer. To an outsider, a person might believe that Microsoft would be better off if Apple did not exist at all; in truth, however, it is just the opposite. Apple serves a very useful purpose for Microsoft in its desire to retain a high percentage of market share for software in the personal computer market. Apple provides a viable customer alternative to many Microsoft products that the FTC desires to see, and it provides a performance benchmark with which Microsoft development can keep pace. Apple Computer is also the "devil you know" to Microsoft leadership in that Microsoft thoroughly understands Apple both from a technical and personal standpoint.

Agent 86

The TV espionage spoof series *Get Smart* was popular in the 1960s. The show was certainly interesting from an innovation standpoint because of the spy gadgets, such as the shoe phone or the cone of silence used in the show. But the show was also

(Continued)

interesting from a strategy standpoint, since the show focused on the interaction between two main rivals:

1. Control, equivalent to equilibrium
2. KAOS (Chaos), equivalent to disequilibrium

In the show, KAOS was always trying to upset the equilibrium, and Control was always successful, although haphazardly, in thwarting its plans and maintaining equilibrium. As citizens of a country in which things are going well, there is a natural tendency for Americans to identify with Control, because it represents equilibrium. For countries that do not have it as good, citizens may well identify with disequilibrium, because chaos brings change and change brings hope to the discontented that something better may emerge. The same dynamic can play out in markets where the market leaders have a natural tendency to identify with Control and will fight to maintain the status quo. Start-up companies and others trying to become more successful in a specific market may want the disequilibrium that a little chaos can bring.

Disequilibrium

When the status quo does not suffice, you may choose to deliberately create disequilibrium in order to foster change. For example, you may enter a new technical space, picket fence a competitor's patent with patents of your own, acquire a company, or otherwise do something that challenges the balance of power. This becomes most telling when you target a competitor's center of gravity, which in the *Art of War: Sun Tzu Strategy Card Deck*, is best represented by the Jack of Diamonds, "Target a Center of Gravity." This means to pursue or attain an objective your adversary will seek to protect or recover. For example, the recent NTP, Inc. patent infringement lawsuit against Research In Motion (RIM) filed in 2001 that threatened its entire BlackBerry® network created a competitive disequilibrium from which NTP could develop a better negotiating position. The BlackBerry® network was the center of gravity on which

RIM's future depended, and RIM took efforts to protect and recover that position. NTP benefited from RIM's efforts by forcing RIM to secure a license to NTP's technology.

IAM Poster Child

Texas Instruments became the poster child for the fledgling Intellectual Asset Management (IAM) consulting practices that developed in the 1990s when it built a significant stream of royalty revenue from a patent assertion licensing campaign. This avenue for business success caught the attention of many CEOs who sought to launch patent assertion campaigns of their own. These patent assertion campaigns brought a lot of chaos (disequilibrium) to the market. The annual amount of royalty revenue received by Texas Instruments is currently estimated at over U.S. $1 billion, and this became a benchmark that many other CEOs sought to achieve.[21] So what happened that led to this?

Texas Instruments, a pioneer in many technologies, had suffered a period of steep decline in its conventional business fortunes; if it kept to the status quo, it would go out of business. If the status quo (equilibrium) will produce a bad result, then a natural next move, for those with the courage to make it, is to stir things up, create some disequilibrium, and see whether something better can emerge from the new conditions. The patent assertion campaign created a disequilibrium in the market from which Texas Instruments crafted a new environment and new success.

Texas Instruments' success created a wave of companies, including Lucent Technologies, AGFA, and IBM, that also successfully exploited the patent assertion model. IAM consulting practices, such as those housed by Andersen Consulting, PricewaterhouseCoopers, and Intellectual Capital Management Group (ICMG) advised many of their clients to pursue the practice of patent assertion. It also spurred the creation of a body of companies whose entire business model is based on patent assertion and nothing else. These companies are often called "patent trolls," a derogatory term used by people

(Continued)

in the industry who have found themselves on the wrong end of their assertion tactics.

The common definition of a "patent troll" is an organization that purchases the rights to a patent or patents and waits under that figurative technology bridge for an unsuspecting manufacturer to cross and infringe on the patent. Oftentimes, these patents have negligible value to the product in proportion to the damages sought by the owners. Furthermore, those owners may not have materially contributed to the research and development of the patented invention or have any plans to use the patented invention within their own products. Instead, when a manufacturer starts to cross their bridge, the "patent troll" pops up and demands a toll to finish crossing. At this point, the unsuspecting manufacturer has already crossed most of the bridge, has too much invested to turn back, and must either fight or pay the toll in order to license the patent.

Disequilibrium is also created by the introduction of disruptive technologies. These are technologies that start out underperforming the traditional state-of-the-art technology, but by surviving in a suitable niche (sanctuary), grow to outperform and eventually displace that state-of-the-art technology. As noted in Clayton Christensen's book, *Innovator's Dilemma*, steamships developed in rivers where sailing ships found maneuvering to catch the wind difficult.[22] Steamships, however, were inefficient and had to make frequent stops for fuel. While inefficiency was not as much of a problem on rivers where a steamship could make frequent stops for more coal (fuel), it was certainly a problem on the open ocean where steamships could not make those stops. As steamships became more efficient, however, they became commercially able to compete with and then displace sailing ships, even in environments with ample wind. Likewise, while the quality of early digital photography hardly compared to the quality of film photography, it was only a matter of time before its performance caught up with and surpassed that of film. In their times, steamships and digital photography were both disruptive technologies in their respective markets.

A long-standing rivalry between dominant photographic film producers Kodak and Fuji in photographic film products became all but irrelevant with the introduction of consumer digital cameras capable of producing the same or better quality photographs than film cameras.[23] A highly competitive but relatively stable market-share balance between the two companies, reliant on highly profitable consumable film, became a market dominated by camera and memory card producers such as Nikon, Canon, and SanDisk. This forced Kodak and Fuji to change, although the transition did not appear easy. In that light, when change is inevitable, it is better for companies that wish to stay in the market to seek the initiative in some aspect of the drivers of that disruptive change.

Kodak and Fuji now offer digital photo printers and accessories to support the technology that disrupted their original film business, as well as some of the same products that caused the disruption. Outside the film industry, it appears that several of the major oil companies, such as British Petroleum, have chosen to invest in alternative fuels that will eventually become competitive with oil. Here, however, the amount actually invested in alternative fuels is tiny compared to the amount invested in the traditional oil business, and the current investment may further relate to political or public relations benefits. It does, however, give British Petroleum a stake in the technology and therefore the future.

With regard to patent strategy and disruption, it is often useful for the patent portfolio to reflect the trajectory of an important disruption. For Kodak, Fuji, and British Petroleum to succeed in a disruptive environment, they could create or acquire the intellectual property base from which to build a position in the disruptive technology to the extent that it makes sense for their business. Two possible sanctuaries exist from which to build the future:

1. The sanctuary that the existing state of the art creates prior to its eventual disruption (this is often the cash cow that is presently viable enough to provide money to invest in the future).
2. The sanctuary developed from created or acquired inventions and patents in a new (disruptive) field.

For an example of the former, the oil business is highly profitable, and British Petroleum has ample market share to make billions of dollars directly from oil.[24] That revenue stream gives British Petroleum the flexibility to invest in any number of options both in its main line of business and possible alternatives. Any well-conceived investments British Petroleum makes in alternative fuels now will likely leave it in a better position to address the eventual disruption of the oil market than it will likely be after that disruption begins, even though that disruption may take some time to reach full effect. At a minimum, the strategists at British Petroleum would keep themselves apprised of trends in alternative fuels so they could buy into promising outside ventures at the right time.

Bottom line: As someone involved with patent strategy, you consider the current situation of your company as a business and whether equilibrium or disequilibrium is the more desirable state. If your level of interaction is stable or increasing, you will tend to favor equilibrium (i.e., you will want to keep things relatively as they are), appreciating that growth requires some measure of change. If your level of isolation is increasing, or if you are a new entrant, you will, provided you have the courage to do so, tend to favor disequilibrium (i.e., you will want to stir things up to create lots of change and potential opportunity).

So as someone involved with patent strategy, you should ask how you can use patents as a stabilizing tool to protect your core technology. Ask also how you can use patents as a destabilizing tool, such as by patenting a disruptive technology or patenting into the heart of someone else's core technology for which you might seek valuable cross-licenses. Further ask whether you should manage your competitiveness. This last question addresses the point that while planning and executing your strategy, you need to monitor not only those who wish to do "evil" to you, but also the "evil" you intentionally or unintentionally do to others. Remember, "everything you do is evil to somebody," and you want to be able to anticipate the reactions of those who may not have your best interests in mind so as not make a situation worse that you intended to make better.

Keep Your Friends Close, but Your Enemies Closer

Competing is expensive, especially in the patent assertion arena where lawsuits routinely cost millions of dollars to resolve. The impact from the Texas Instruments patent assertion campaign and those that followed from other companies has caused companies to make some adjustments that have been monitored and scrutinized by the government. The semiconductor industry, for example, currently relies on cross-licensing agreements not to sue one another.[25] This creates what many people call "patent pools" from which all participants contribute and withdraw, designed in accord with present antitrust rules. The business relationship of declining to sue rather than asserting patents to generate a royalty stream has arisen because it is in the interest of all parties involved and competition as a whole to do so rather than become involved in endless and unproductive suits and countersuits. The practice is now widespread throughout many industries and serves as a patent-based enactment of the quote from the movie, *The Godfather*: "Keep your friends close, but your enemies closer." Participants in patent pools are often otherwise highly competitive with each other. The agreements further a useful dynamic toward equilibrium for its participants, given that those outside of the sharing agreements often find it hard to break into patent pools created by several well-endowed competitors. Prospective new participants may not have at their disposal the likely millions of dollars needed to license existing patents and are correspondingly unlikely to have a large enough base of patents to make a useful contribution to the pool. Their resources will effectively be pitted against an ongoing collective which can discourage them from making the effort.[26]

These cross-licensing and nonlitigation agreements tend to foster cooperation among participants in the agreements, since it will not be in the interest of any member if one member should suffer a decline in fortunes such that it defects from the arrangement or has its assets dispersed to less cooperative ventures. A variation on the patent pool idea that makes cooperation more universal is the patent commons idea, whereby no one is excluded from the pool of patents put there by other organizations. Such a patent commons was proposed in November of 2005 for open-source software in collaboration with Novell, Philips, Red Hat, and Sony.[27] These patent commons can develop when organizations are not interested in using patents to exclude others but are interested in maintaining their freedom to operate by keeping others from building proprietary competitive positions.

A Sample Cause and Effect Sequence

Change happens constantly, so in a sense there is always a degree of disequilibrium in any competitive system. A key to success is to deliberately use or create disequilibrium to achieve an advantageous effect. A sample (eliminate, isolate, interact, negate) cause and effect sequence might proceed like the following example:

1. A patent isolates a competitor from a critical invention.
2. Without the invention, the isolated competitor cannot serve customers.
3. Customers defect to the patent holder.
4. The patent holder integrates customers into its base and isolates the competitor from them.

The competitor's isolation becomes the catalyst that will force that competitor to do something. This is where a key uncertainty in strategy lies, because at this point you cannot be 100% sure what your competitor, or other entities that can affect the situation, will do. Two of many possibilities follow:

Scenario 1. Isolation causes the competitor to withdraw from the market, thereby eliminating it as a competitor. This could be viewed as a positive consequence.

Scenario 2. The weakened competitor is purchased by a large multinational that is ready to invest funds for a turnaround. This may be viewed as a negative consequence.

Scenario 2 illustrates a scenario in which your very success leads to a greater competitive challenge, so you want to appreciate just how well you are doing. Conversely, scenario 1 could lead to some very favorable things for you, perhaps including the opportunity to acquire intellectual property from the competitor at a bargain price. In the *Art of War: Sun Tzu Strategy Card Deck*, this concept is represented by the Jack of Hearts, "Loot a Burning House." Looting a burning house can be an effective business strategy and strategic operator in the sense that a company in distress or failing often will not have the capacity to say "no" to your offers. They may have to accept your terms as their best possible outcome and typically will not be in a position to dictate terms back.

Looting a Burning House
In December 2004, JGR Acquisitions won the rights to 39 Commerce One Internet business method patents for $15.5 million in bankruptcy court. The opportunity to make this purchase was presented by the distress of Commerce One. JGR Acquisitions's purpose at the time was suspected to be to use the patents in patent assertion. At least one losing bid involved companies that planned to acquire and retire the patents to avoid such a circumstance. Commerce One had not asserted its patents.[28] The outcome here illustrates that even the act of falling into distress can create "evil" for others, if those who gain access to your patents use them differently from the way you did.

(This chapter has so far introduced several strategic operators. The Appendix of this book further describes IP Strategy Boarding and Scenario Play through the use of two card decks written by the author that expands on the strategic operator idea. These are highly effective strategy-creation tools and techniques that focus on the fundamentals of interaction and isolation. They are available for your review and application.)

Leveraging the Three Centers of Excellence When Crafting a Strategy

Where We Cooperate and Compete

Revisiting the Centers of Excellence model, we have a way to better plan where we cooperate and where we compete. As stated earlier, we cooperate with people when our interaction tends to increase our capacity for independent action. We compete with people when our interaction decreases, or threatens to decrease, our capacity for independent action. In the real world, however, exclusively cooperative or competitive relationships are rare. Companies can and do aggressively compete directly with each other to advance their businesses, while at the same time cooperating in joint ventures to produce the next generation of products from which all will benefit. Companies rarely do anything completely by themselves anymore. Contrary to popular perceptions, we live in a world where it is possible for a Japanese-branded car to have more American-made components in it than a Chevrolet pickup truck.

The Centers of Excellence model, in which the areas of innovation, advancement, and security all revolve around a central idea, provides an easy way for us to deal with shades of gray in corporate structure and boundaries. We will start with innovation.

Innovation

The three Centers of Excellence provide a framework for deciding which internal and external resources to leverage to enact your strategy. They will also help you to grasp where you should be competitive and where you should be cooperative, especially with the organizations with which you both compete and cooperate at the same time. Innovation is one of the Centers of Excellence from which we can derive many strategic solutions and their enablers. Innovation is the broad process by which people find better, faster, and cheaper ways to solve problems, provide benefits, or both. It is inclusive of inventing patentable inventions as well as related developments such as creating the right business model for that invention's use. These solutions follow as Solution Quadrants.

Four Innovation Approaches (Solution Quadrants)

As stated earlier in this book, strategy is a type of solution used to address the existence of uncertainties and opposition. Whether they be strategic or technical, solutions appear from one of four places that we will here call solution quadrants. These solution quadrants provide a visual tool for planning. You can organize the solution quadrants on a white board divided into four squares. Whenever you explore solutions of any type, if you have not examined all four solution quadrants, then you cannot really say you have examined all of your options.

Let's start by looking at solution quadrants using the illustration of a river—a gap that prevents you from getting from your current bank to something of value on the other side. For a basic example, let's suppose that something of value on the other side is food. If you wish to cross the gap, then a solution that pops into mind is to bridge that gap with a literal bridge. That literal bridge becomes your base solution from which to develop the four solution quadrants, as follows:

Quadrant 1—base solution. If the base solution is a bridge, then this would include how you make the bridge: beam, cantilever, arch, cable-stayed, suspension, or trestle. With a bridge in place, you can cross the gap to reach the food.

Quadrant 2—alternative solution. This would include other ways to cross the gap that are not a bridge such as a ferry boat or a helicopter. Using these alternative means to cross the gap, you can also reach the food on the other side.

Quadrant 3—inverse solution. This would involve having the reason you need to cross the gap cross over to you instead. For example, instead of you crossing the gap by bridge, boat, or other means to buy food, someone else brings the food across to you so you can buy it on your side of the gap.

Quadrant 4—obviating the need. This would involve making the reason for crossing the gap irrelevant. For example, you grow your own food so you do not need to buy it on either side of the gap.

That is it—four basic solution quadrants to resolve. Yet within these four types of solution quadrants you can derive a variety of possible specific solutions. You can also craft strategic solutions, such as isolating your competition, and then craft technical solutions that might underlie your strategic solutions. For example, you might create a new and patentable invention that will give you an exploitable technical advantage in the marketplace, such as being able to cross the hypothetical gap (you own the bridge) when your competitor cannot (you enforce exclusivity).

Solution quadrants are similarly useful in creating design-around ideas to address blocking competitive patents, since you can effectively design around a competitive solution in one quadrant by finding a useful solution in another. Of these, no better way to design around a patented invention exists than to find a way to obviate any need for the patented invention at all—Quadrant 4. Let's suppose that your competitor owns the patent on a corrosion-resistant ceramic container that allows you to treat the surface of a metal in an acid bath without cross-contaminating the metal, the solution, or the ceramic walls. A way to obviate the need for the special ceramic container is to shape the metal itself into the form of a container and pour the acid onto the metal surface within. Even though building another type of container with a different ceramic material could still bring about contention to the patent, and if the design does not function as well, bring cross-contamination in to destroy the purpose of treating the metal, this design-around of making the metal itself also the container obviates the need for a ceramic container or any ceramic at all, and thus could not be challenged on the basis of the ceramic container patent.

Solution Quadrants Illustration

Booksellers, major players that do have an involvement with patents, illustrate the creation of strategic solutions in all four quadrants to compete against other bookstore types. The quadrants are as follows:

Quadrant 1—base solution. Traditional brick and mortar bookstores with all forms of author-written content on the shelves for customers to browse and purchase

Quadrant 2—alternative solution. Author-written content on shelves at coffee shops, department stores, grocery stores, and other retail establishments

Quadrant 3—inverse solution. Online sites from which purchased content is shipped to the buyer instead of the buyer traveling to the content

Quadrant 4—obviating the need. Content distribution that involves no stores

At Quadrant 1, Barnes & Noble competes with, among others, another large bookstore chain called Borders for the sale of media-based content such as traditional books, audio books, e-books, CDs, and videos. A third company, Amazon.com, exploited an opening in Quadrant 3 to create an inverse business model whereby customers order books online and the books go to the people instead of the people going to the books. Barnes & Noble addressed this threat and opportunity opened by Amazon.com by creating a competing online bookstore called BN.com. Borders addressed this threat and opportunity from Amazon.com and BN.com from 2001 until 2007 by setting up a partnership with Amazon.com, although since that time Borders has launched its own Borders.com e-commerce Web site.[29]

Quadrant 2 may be a universal concern as well as representing a potential opportunity for Barnes & Noble, Borders, and Amazon.com, as more and more people purchase their books, CDs, and movies from department stores (e.g., Wal-Mart), grocery stores (e.g., Safeway), and specialty stores (e.g., Starbucks). Quadrant 4 may be a universal concern for all media-selling companies in that digital copying methods can allow people to more easily distribute content without going to any store at all. Whereas Barnes & Noble's interaction with Borders and Amazon.com is most likely competitive at solution Quadrants 1 and 3, and each will compete or cooperate in its own way with the likes of Wal-Mart, Safeway, or Starbucks at Quadrant 2, it is more likely cooperative at solution Quadrant 4. All parties wish for customers to seek their types of stores for their media needs, and all wish to combat piracy, which obviates the need to purchase content from any legitimate source. All will also want to influence how and when libraries gain access to content that allows people to borrow content instead of buy it.

The Amazon.com One-Click Patent

Even the book world has made news in patents and patent strategy. The disputed One-Click patent created a disagreement between Jeff Bezos, CEO of Amazon.com, and Tim O'Reilly of O'Reilly & Associates. The One-Click patent covers a software invention that allows a person to buy a book or other product from Amazon.com with one click of the mouse, thereby making purchases from Amazon.com exceptionally easy. O'Reilly was an outspoken critic of the One-Click patent, and Bezos was a staunch defender of it. They both turned to a start-up called BountyQuest.com to see just how valid the patent really was. The now defunct BountyQuest.com was built around an idea that people could post a patent they wished to invalidate on the BountyQuest.com Web site and offer a reward for any person anywhere in the world who brought forward invalidating prior art.

(Continued)

The One-Click patent, U.S. 5,960,411, is a patent that describes a method whereby a customer can make a complete online purchase transaction with just one click of a button. With Jeff Bezos's blessing, Tim O'Reilly posted the One-Click patent on BountyQuest.com with a $10,000 reward, yet no one brought forward any invalidating prior art. This seemed to prove Jeff Bezos's point as to the patent's validity.

As a side note, BountyQuest.com folded shortly thereafter, ostensibly because the major companies that could afford to pay meaningful bounties preferred to keep their invalidation efforts confidential. It had also served its more important purpose for Bezos, an important backer of the start-up, who had a much larger enterprise to focus on in Amazon.com itself. It thus became one of many dot com start-up enterprises with an interesting idea that did not quite work out as its management team intended.

As an exercise for yourself, pick a solution sold by your business and identify who and what is at each of the four solution quadrants. How does or should this impact the disposition of your patents? *Hint*: If a quadrant is open and has value, someone will occupy it. It represents an area often termed as "white space" by research and development professionals in search of new areas to explore, since such open areas often require technical enablers.

In the previous example, if Jeff Bezos had not launched Amazon.com in the open Quadrant 3, someone else would have launched such an online bookstore. If Barnes & Noble had considered and launched its online bookstore first, then Barnes & Noble, not Amazon.com, would probably be the number-one online bookstore. This supposition is based on the known business statistic referenced earlier by Al Ries and Jack Trout that market share often follows the order of entrance into a marketplace.[30] Had Borders then responded with an online bookstore of its own, there might not have been room for an Amazon.com at all unless Amazon.com had introduced appreciable differentiated and useful innovations, noting another observation of Ries and Trout that major markets often develop into two-competitor races between the primary and the alternative in the spirit of Coke versus Pepsi, leaving little room for third players such as RC Cola.[31] (Of course, Amazon.com has become more than just a bookstore, but that original bookstore was and is Amazon.com's sanctuary from which it successfully explored new possibilities in other markets.)

The competitive approach of Amazon.com is captured in the King of Clubs card from the *Art of War: Sun Tzu Strategy Card Deck*, "Take the Hill While No One Is There." This strategic operator is based on the observation that it is easier to occupy a hill before a competitor occupies it than after a competitor has established itself there. The most difficult aspect of doing so is to recognize which hill will become important before a competitor makes its importance apparent. In this case, an inverse solution to bookselling at Quadrant 3 represented the unoccupied hill that Amazon.com occupied first. Had Barnes & Noble or Borders occupied it first, Amazon.com would have been less likely to succeed.

Taken one step further, now that Amazon.com sells all manner of products, you could even say that Amazon.com occupied another hill that Sears and JCPenney, with their catalog business, had left some years earlier. The catalog business was a pre-Internet Quadrant 3 solution from the perspective of the brick and mortar store that allowed products to go to people instead of people going to the products. Ideas themselves often are not new, just the enablers that affect their presentation. Further to Amazon.com's position and associated with the enablers as they apply to its business, Amazon.com has established a modest patent portfolio of nearly 100 patents as of the time of writing this book.

Skating Where the Puck Will Be

To innovate strategically, it is useful to innovate ahead of change. We have just illustrated one example—Amazon.com was the first to capitalize on an inverse solution that changed bookselling, a position it further reinforced with patents in an industry not generally associated with patenting. The rise of the Internet enabled a viable inverse business model for people going to bookstores to get books, whereby they could order books over the Internet and have those books delivered to them. Someone was going to occupy that space; the puck was going to go there. The question was who?

Wayne Gretzky, the world-class hockey player, stated the reason for his success: "Skate to where the puck is going to be, not where it has been."[32] This same principle holds just as true for innovation and the patent strategy as it does within the National Hockey League. Being ahead of the curve offers significant advantages in innovation, since it allows you to be the first mover or to, with deliberation, allow others to test the market so that you can be a fast follower, benefiting from their experiences.

To get the most out of Wayne Gretzky's statement, however, it pays to appreciate the full depth of his message. Gretzky was not a passive observer in his effort to skate to where the puck would be, he was a participant in the game and a major influencer in the puck's path. So he was not only skating to where the puck was going to be, he was very much influencing where the puck was going to be. The act of skating to a shooting position where another player will pass the puck for the score is a very deliberate and coordinated effort based on an understanding of and interaction with the other players in the game.

What this means for you as an innovator and patenting entity is that you are also an influencer who both seeks to get to where the innovation puck will be and, in deference to where you would like the puck to be, taking inventive and patenting efforts to make that desired position a reality. You take your best shot at where you would like innovation to be, and your very inventive activities may serve to drive it there. Think about the makers of computer processors. While they may not be able to predict which new applications will arise from faster processors, they can predict that faster processors will give rise to new applications. Taking their best shot to innovate in that space, therefore, will advance their businesses.

To most effectively skate to where the puck is going to be and to influence its path, you identify patterns in technology evolution that you can leverage. These patterns are not absolutes; rather, they are generalities. The patterns tell generally where the puck should be, if not its precise coordinates, and continued adjustment is required along the way. Hindsight tells us that someone was going to create an online bookstore; it was only a matter of time. However, this hindsight could have been foresight since the vacant position of an inverse solution could have been seen many years ahead of time if viewed through the right lens. It was only a matter of finding or creating the technical enablers and the business model to make it work. Still, unless you are an innovator making the next move in the market, you cannot predict exactly who or when someone will occupy the space, just that someone will. Provided Barnes & Noble's management was interested in doing so at the time, Barnes & Noble could have skated to where this puck was going to be by launching an online bookstore first, if for no other reason than that it already had a book warehousing and distribution system in place, noting that the distribution system was associated with sending books to stores instead of individual customers. The base technology of the Internet that enabled an online bookstore to exist was available for either Barnes & Noble or Amazon.com to access at the same time. Instead, Amazon.com moved first and defined the online bookselling category, all the while building a book distribution system of its own from scratch.

So when you become proficient at skating to where the puck will be, you do more than innovate ahead of the curve. You influence the curve itself through your innovation; you create the future. Your own presence and actions influence where the puck is going to be because you participate in the game that moves it. As a strategist, you can know that an online bookstore will come into being because you can see that no one has explored a type of solution represented by the inverse (Quadrant 3). You can likewise know that alternative fuels will be competitive with oil, so it is possible to invest in projects designed to make that happen. The pattern is consistent. Who, if really paying attention, could possibly have thought that digital imaging technology would not eventually displace film for most general photography purposes?

Part of being successful when predicting change in your industry is to more broadly frame who you are. Are you a bookstore or a content seller? Are you an oil company or an energy company? Are you a film company or an imaging company? Once you make the mental leap to the broader topic, things become clearer. If, for example, a film company decides it is an imaging company, it can innovate and patent in a wider variety of technologies associated with taking pictures. If, as another example, an oil company decides to become an energy company, it can innovate and patent outside of petroleum to give the words "energy company" meaning. Otherwise, it can choose to focus on oil and make the best out of that.

Still, there is always a balance, and as with everything in strategy, nothing should be considered an absolute. Focus is also a viable and often recommended strategy even in highly innovative markets, particularly if the current business is lucrative and you also watch the future. In business, given enough capital to do so, you can buy into where the puck is right now and let others take the effort and risk to get it there. It is simply better to do so with intent rather than to do so because you missed something and need to catch up.

Henry Ford

Inventions are a key part of patent strategy, and thus it is important to further develop associated technical solutions, keeping in mind that what pertains to a technical solution almost always pertains to the strategic solution itself. Technical solutions and strategic solutions often intermix; strategy can drive the need for a technology, and technology can enable the implementation of a strategy. Henry Ford provides a case in point.

From 1903 to 1908, automobiles were considered a toy for the rich.[33] Ford saw the proverbial puck sailing across the ice and recognized that where the puck was going to be was cheaper cars that almost anyone could own. Ford adopted the existing concept of interchangeable parts, an idea that had been pioneered by the famous inventor Eli Whitney in such industries as weapons manufacturing before the American Civil War.[34] By using interchangeable parts for automobile manufacturing, Ford was able to create the assembly line, where each worker performed a limited task in the process of building an entire vehicle, and could learn to perform that task with extreme efficiency. Ford was able to assemble automobiles for much less cost per unit than if a craftsman had built each car individually.[35] Ford skated to where the puck was going to be, or in effect brought it there, by creating the mass-production assembly line process; he was thus able to invent the future of automobiles for the masses. Hindsight makes it easy for us to see that the masses would someday all be able to purchase and own automobiles, and if Henry Ford had not skated to where that puck was going to be, then somebody else ultimately would have.

Technically, the adoption of an assembly line can also be seen as a natural line of evolution on which any automobile manufacturer at the time could have capitalized. For Ford and his strategy to make a business from mass automobile production, uncertainty did exist at the time of inception as to whether the public would buy into his technical solution and buy into it soon enough for Ford to prosper. People did, and through this, Ford illustrated a useful strategic operator discussed previously. Enabled by the use of interchangeable parts and Ford's assembly line, Ford played the King of Clubs, "Take the Hill While No One Is There."

Time and Timing

The Henry Ford example also illustrates the importance of time and timing. Henry Ford was in a position to act at the right time, considering that if he had acted sooner, important aspects of the automotive and complementary technology might not have been ready for mass-produced automobiles, and if he had chosen to act later, someone else might have beaten him to the assembly line idea. Of note, however, is that as time progressed and Ford continued to make Model T cars from 1908 through 1927, he did not skate to where the puck would be next—namely, cars of a wider variety that could take advantage of the better road infrastructures that had since developed. That left the door open for Alfred Sloan to launch General Motors and overtake Ford by providing more automobile model variations of the type that the public sought at that time. Ford never regained a market share lead over General Motors during the many decades when they and Chrysler were the big three automotive competitors in the United States, before the puck started to move to yet another place in quality and efficiency, led by Japanese competitors.

Altshuller's Laws of Technical Evolution

The most innovative aspect of a strategic solution in patent strategy is often technical. Technical innovation gives us the very products and services we sell. Genrich Altshuller, who created the theory of inventive problem solving (TRIZ) in the 1940s, illustrated that technology follows predictable tracks of evolution that can greatly facilitate your capacity to predict future trends (skate to where the puck will be) when used in tandem with an appreciation of the market. Altshuller taught that a system of which an invention is a part will always be complete, meaning that within every invention, or an accounted-for outside influence, there is an engine, a transmission, a working body, and an instrument of control.[36] This includes biological systems that form the domain of pharmaceutical and biotechnology innovations as well as mechanical or electrical systems that form the domain for more traditional manufacturing or product inventions. For example, the transmission in a car, which goes by the same component name of "transmission" in an Altshuller system, delivers power from the engine to the wheels. The bloodstream is the transmission element for a pharmaceutical that delivers the active drug element from the injection site to points throughout the body.

Altshuller noted that as technology improves within a system, the transfer of energy from the engine to the working body grows more efficient through means inherent in all of the system components. Altshuller used the first steamships in an illustration of this law.[37] The first steamships relied on inefficient coal and wood-burning steam engines that turned inefficient paddle wheels. Carrying the amount of fuel that would be necessary for ocean travel left little space for cargo or passengers, so the early steamships initially operated on rivers where they could make frequent stops to refuel.[38] However, over time the efficiency of steam-powered engines improved and steamships became even more useful for cross-ocean travel than sailing ships.

The importance of this law of improved energy transfer links over into Clayton Christensen's bestselling book, *The Innovator's Dilemma*.[39] Christensen applied fundamentally the same underlying law of initial evolutionary efficiencies that Altshuller described to business economics. In *The Innovator's Dilemma*, Christensen also uses the steamship example as a disruptive technology and to illustrate why established companies, in this case the clipper ship cargo companies that used sailboats to cross the ocean, could not adjust to the emerging disruptive technologies of steam that, according to Altshuller's observation, would evolve to have the efficiency needed for ocean travel over time. The clipper ship companies focused on improving sail technology until it was economically too late to make the transition to the improved steam engines through which new competitors had already established themselves.

A patent strategist should track this law in relation to the technology he or she protects. Capturing the enablers that allow for more efficient transmission development is a way to patent where the puck is going to be. Investing in disruptive technologies that can emerge from these may provide a way to evolve into markets that will change even if your business stakeholders would rather they not.

Another law of technology evolution that Altshuller noted is that different parts of a system will evolve at different speeds, meaning that at times certain parts of a system will become too good, or not good enough, relative to other parts of the system. Adrian Slywotzky tied this same principle to business in his bestselling book, *Value Migration*. Slywotzky showed how as systems evolve, the places to earn the highest profits appear at the points where technology is not good enough compared to the rest of the system.[40] As a case in point, when the microprocessor was not yet good enough for the potential applications computer users wanted, it generated high profits for Intel and AMD. People would pay a premium for chips that offered the top performance at a given point in time. Now that existing microprocessor speeds are good enough for most people, profit margins have lessened for these companies, because not everyone needs to buy the fastest microprocessor on the market.[41] From this law, the patent strategist can again seek to capture the enablers that will allow a lagging technology to catch up to the rest of the system. After all, the technology will catch up over time. That is where the puck will be.

Yet another law that Altshuller described states that as a system reaches the limits of its own development, it becomes a subsystem of a more general system.[42] Cell phones show this trend now, with the recently launched iPhone being a current state of the art for the trend. As the technology used for actually calling people has developed to the point where that primary function cannot much improve, the cell phone has evolved from a voice-only system into an overall general electronic communications system. This general communications system links the Internet, image creation and dissemination tools, music players, video players, photo displays, and more into a comprehensive communications package that goes far beyond voice communication alone. The cell phone device has, for many people, become an indispensable extension of human communication. The next evolution up as this current system reaches its limits may be a more direct link to the human body itself, as evidenced by introduction of single ear headsets that can be worn by people all day. Think about dialing function alone for a moment in telephony. We have evolved from operator-directed connections, to rotary dial direct connections, to push button dial, to speed dial, to voice command dialing. Could the next step involve dialing by thought?

Another commonly visible trend in technical evolution described by an Altshuller law is the tendency for technology to evolve from macro to micro; in other words, as a technology evolves, the products get smaller.[43] Consider the evolution of the cassette tape player that Sony, with its Walkman®, almost reduced to the size of a cassette itself; a size improvement not matched until MP3 players eliminated the need for portable cassette players and equally bulky portable CD players. Researchers are testing current size limits in many fields. All technologies typically evolve in this direction in whole or in part unless a larger size itself provides some important advantage. What will be the enablers in your industry that can make certain components smaller? Can you capture them within your patents?

Altshuller also noted that technology evolves from mechanical to electromagnetic.[44] The transition from the cassette player to the MP3 player also follows this pattern. The cassette player is a highly mechanical device with many moving parts, whereas the latest MP3 players have eliminated even spinning hard drives through the use of flash technology. Presently, automotive manufacturers are directing the evolution of cars to include full electromagnetic or hybrid electromechanical power supplies. The question, therefore, is not if cars will become all electronic, but when.

As Altshuller continued, he noted that technology also becomes more dynamic.[45] The wristwatch illustrates this law. The first mechanical wristwatches told time, and that was pretty much it. A digital electric watch, such as those made popular by Casio, now serves as a stop watch, alarm clock, pulse monitor, countdown timer, and more, all in one package. Likewise, the previously cited Sony Walkman® allows you to play cassette tapes and listen to the radio. Compare that to the myriad of operations allowed by the Apple iTouch®. Cars, originally only a form of transportation, can now serve as mobile office, command, and entertainment centers.

In the last of Altshuller's laws that will serve as a centerpiece for the rest of this discussion on patent strategy, Altshuller noted that all technology evolves toward a theoretical ideal state, that being an invention that provides all the desired benefits to its users without any drawbacks.[46] This ideal state is theoretical, because to truly have no drawbacks, the invention would have to deliver the desired benefits yet have no underlying mechanism that could create a footprint. Put another way, you receive all the benefits of the invention, but the invention itself does not exist. This condition is difficult to impossible to achieve in practice, but is always a direction to aim for in technology development.

Altshuller and Ideality

Altshuller's ideality concept, as stated by TRIZ expert Semyon Savransky, requires an open mind to understand and accept. It is extremely beneficial, particularly in the sense that it often leads to obviating the need to cross gaps, which is a particularly useful way to design around competitive patents and disrupt competitive businesses for the benefit of your own customers and stakeholders. According to Savransky's interpretation of ideality,

1. The ideal machine has no mass or volume, but accomplishes the required work.
2. The ideal method expends no energy or time, but obtains the necessary effect in a self-regulating manner.
3. The ideal process is actually only the result of the process without the process itself.
4. The ideal substance is actually no substance (a vacuum) but whose function is performed.
5. The ideal technique occupies no space, has no weight, requires no labor or maintenance, delivers benefit without harm, and "does it itself" without any additional energy, mechanisms, cost, or raw materials.[47]

One of the most influential Chinese philosophers, Lao Tzu, stated 2,500 years ago that, "The master does nothing, yet he leaves nothing undone."[48] This is a statement that refers to the ideal and is one of the most powerful strategic statements ever made. It is at the heart of his contemporary Sun Tzu's philosophy, that of winning without fighting which can be rephrased to mean achieving all the benefits of winning without the drawbacks of actually fighting. Suffice it to say here, the master strategy achieves its results seemingly without the strategist doing anything. The strategist is in control but without being in control as generally defined by most people. The ideal strategy delivers 100% of the desired benefit with none of the drawbacks of purposive action, and as such, is completely results-driven.

A Technical Progression Toward the Ideal

The ideal form of travel across the Atlantic is to arrive across the Atlantic at the same instant the thought comes to mind, without any mechanism for having done so. Implausible at this time, yes, but imagine what a captain of a sailing ship would have thought in 1740 if told that people would relatively soon travel across the Atlantic in just a few hours, and that they would do so through the air instead of on the water. As transatlantic travel has evolved from sailing ships to airliners, it has become faster, cheaper, more convenient, more reliable, and, in short, closer to the ideal. Using a telephone with video capability, a voice and image can make the trip across the Atlantic almost as fast as the thought to send it. What is next? For the science fiction-minded, if the telephone evolves as predicted by Altshuller's law to become a system reaching its maximum potential, then we will be able to communicate with anyone in the world instantly as soon as we think to do so with tools integrated into our bodies.

The Optimal

Earlier in the book, we talked about the perfect strategy and the optimal "good-enough" strategy. Considering the ideal as the truly perfect technical solution, we see the same pattern for technical solutions that we see for strategic solutions. While technical systems evolve toward the ideal, the most commercially viable inventions reside at the threshold of "good enough," which we will here call optimal. Although the ideal state is theoretical, the optimal or "good-enough" state is very real. In a given market, the most competitive technologies reside at this threshold of optimal. Optimal means that the technology is neither too good (so that the customer ends up paying for more performance than needed or desired) nor not good enough (so that customer becomes frustrated or left wanting) to solve the existing problem users need the technology to solve.

The existence of an optimal solution is well illustrated in aircraft design. During the first 50 years of flight, air cargo transport aircraft evolved rapidly toward the ideal from little more than powered kites able to lift one man and perhaps a mail bag into the sky to the C-130 Hercules that can carry a light armored tank. Now in 2008, over 50 years after its maiden flight in 1954, the C-130, an optimal air cargo airframe, is still in production as the mainstay aircraft for military cargo transportation in much of the world.[49,50] Lockheed Martin has been building C-130s for more than half the time human flight has even existed. To put it another way, to do as well, the Sopwith Camel biplane that Snoopy purportedly flew against the Red Baron would have had to stay relevant as a British fighter plane past the last 1972 Apollo landing on the moon!

This rapid evolution to "good enough," followed by long periods of stability, is also a way of things in the natural world. Consider the wolf and the dog as natural examples. The wolf is neither more nor less a hunter than necessary to survive as a hunter, and so it has been fundamentally unchanged for some 300,000 years. It is smarter than the dog that evolved from it in the past few thousand years because the expense of maintaining a larger brain has a payoff on the hunt for the wolf that it does not have for a dog that can depend on humans for food.

Having a large brain is expensive for an animal because that brain uses a lot of calories. Intelligence needs to be supported by a solid return on the investment of its development. It is suspected that early dogs evolved from wolves that learned they could make a living by rummaging through the scraps and offerings of people.[51] Rummaging for scraps of food would have eased the pressure on them to hunt and therefore lessened the need for them to be overly intelligent to deal with evading prey. In fact, a too-smart dog, having the higher intelligence of the wolf, would compete at a disadvantage with other dogs in this rummaging lifestyle because the larger brain that supported that added intelligence would tax the dog for extra calories without providing it with a meaningful payoff in getting those calories. The larger brain would make the dog too good for its environment. Through evolutionary forces "dumbing down" the dog and giving it a smaller brain, it essentially reached a more optimal state in the opposite way that we would normally think of as evolution. Put another way, the story of Lassie outsmarting a pack of wolves to save Timmy is just not likely.

Similarly, the return on investment of an inventive effort diminishes or could go negative beyond the optimal threshold of "good enough" for most customers. This means that a decision to develop an invention beyond that threshold should correspond with, or in fact spur the conditions to advance the market as a whole so that the "good-enough" invention of today becomes the "not-good-enough" invention of tomorrow in order to drive demand for the higher performing solution. For example, the rise of computer video gaming made the Pentium® III chip suboptimal shortly after its introduction and paved the way for the next generation of Pentium chips that followed. Correspondingly, as technology evolves, it can make sense to see whether a "dumbed down" version (e.g., a Celeron® processor) makes sense for enough buyers who will find it just right for their needs.

Alternatively, and again tying the patent strategy to marketing strategy, stakeholders could create the conditions whereby the physically optimal technology is no longer the psychologically or morally optimal technology. The continual drive to improve the performance of cars that already offer more than ample performance needed to handle the speed limits of American roads exemplifies this latter example on psychological grounds. Most drivers will never see the speedometer needle of their own cars actually reach 160 mph, but an ample number like to know they could. And although an ample market exists for people who want a car that can reach 160 mph, there is also a moral consideration to factor considering the harm people could do to themselves and others if even a handful of these buyers actually drive that fast on the roads. This situation stands in contrast to fuel efficiency, where the most fuel-efficient cars on the market still are not as physically fuel-efficient as people would like them to be. In this case, since people would be delighted to have a car that required no fuel at all, the optimal position is that level of efficiency that most of the market will bear, given the psychologically accepted state of the art at the time. If people believe that 30 miles per gallon is good mileage, they will accept that, but if they believe 60 miles per gallon is good mileage, then the 30 miles per gallon vehicle would fare poorly.

Overkill?

The C-17, designed and built by Boeing on behalf of its Pentagon customers, was intended to be a replacement for the C-130 for general military air transport. Even though the C-17 is in many ways a more modern aircraft than the C-130, production of the C-17 was scheduled to cease in 2009. Meanwhile orders continued to come in for the C-130s, which Lockheed Martin plans to keep in production well beyond 2009.[52] The C-17 can do things the C-130 cannot—after all, the C-17 can carry over three times more weight than the C-130. But for most air forces and even for the U.S. military that ordered the majority of the C-17s built, the C-17 is more airplane than necessary most of the time. According to people who fly them, the C-130 is also a better plane for pilots; it just responds better at the controls to the actions pilots want to take. The author learned to appreciate this last point as a passenger in a C-130 during an emergency landing when the pilots successfully put the plane down on a much too short runway on a moonless night during a storm.

Profiting from the Trend Toward the Ideal and the Optimal

The technology evolution trend toward the ideal and optimal creates an important point for the strategist to consider. Places where technology is evolving at an exponential rate represent a sweet spot for new applications, so you will want to seek patent protection on the enablers of those future applications.

Where the performance change is exponential, as was the case for the first 50 years of aircraft evolution, a sweet spot of opportunity for new applications will appear. Within 50 years of the first powered flight, we had transports, fighters, bombers, reconnaissance planes, crop dusters, aerobatic planes, airliners, private general aviation planes, sailplanes, amphibious aircraft, unmanned aircraft—and the list goes on. Along with all of the different planes, we also had associated innovations such as the system of airports, aircraft carriers, air traffic control, radar, VHF Omni-Directional Radio (VOR)—and again the list goes on. As performance improvements became more linear toward the 50-year mark and beyond, the creation of new applications has diminished. Arguably, the only major new airplane applications to have developed after the 50-year mark are Vertical/Short Take-Off and Landing (V/STOL) aircraft such as the Harrier and the space plane such as the Space Shuttle orbiter, although the Space Shuttle could be considered more of a first representation of reusable spacecraft than an extension of the airplane. Equipment has modernized, yes, but fast-forward to the present someone from the 1920s, the first quarter of aircraft existence, and he or she would still recognize a modern airplane as just an airplane.

So a sweet spot of opportunity for new applications, and the associated profits businesses can gain from them, will exist anywhere technological evolution occurs at an exponential rate while improvements still matter to enough people. For example, data storage performance continues to improve at exponential rates and has driven new video and digital imaging applications possibilities; the choice whether to shoot high-resolution still photography or lower-resolution video could become moot as each video frame will have the resolution to clearly print poster-sized photos as is now only possible using a traditional dSLR camera.

In comparison, pharmaceutical advances during the last half of the previous century occurred at exponential rates with discoveries such as penicillin, but they have leveled off in most areas, thus causing significant challenges for that industry. It could seem that the "good-enough" state has hit the pharmaceutical industry for many of its products. Will people pay four or more times the cost for new pain relievers that work only marginally better than generic ibuprofen or aspirin? This may be one of the reasons pharmaceutical advertising to the public has increased in some therapeutic areas. The advertising creates a psychological necessity in the minds of prospective patients perhaps beyond the physical necessity for some new pharmaceuticals, in a sense the same way advertising may seek to make it a psychological necessity for people to own cars capable of traveling 160 mph.

Matters of Perspective

A *New York Times* article published on July 6, 2008, discussed the cost and efficacy of Genentech's drug Avastin.[53] Treatments involving this drug for incurable but manageable cancers can cost $100,000 per year, a figure that is both expensive for insurers and can bankrupt people who have to pay for all or part of the treatment from their own funds. For that figure, the patient might survive four months longer than otherwise possible, as some trials have shown.

Avastin raises the question of how much an improvement on a technology that is not yet good enough is worth. To the patient, the four months could mean everything, maybe the opportunity to see a graduation he or she otherwise would not have seen, and to the family as well. To Genentech, which invested $2.25 billion in Avistar and continues to work on something better, the revenue is also important to continue as a business and perhaps develop an even better treatment. To insurers and the body of people who pay into insurance pools, however, Avastin raises a major question, since the drug perhaps only delays the inevitable and often not by that long. To families bankrupted by paying for the drug in whole or part, it can also have major long-term financial consequences across generations, made all the more burdensome by the moral dilemma that can occur when thinking about financial considerations in such a time of personal crisis.

So how much is an average of four months worth, and to whose perspective do we give the most weight? This is an environment that a patent strategist may need to navigate, first because of the uncertainty at the outset of whether any patented drug will work at all, and second because of the importance of showing a return on that investment dependent on how the drug actually works. The strategy chosen will need to consider physical, psychological, and moral implications of the situation.

Places where technology is evolving at a linear pace will produce mostly incremental improvements. Where technology takes a more linear course, new applications will generally be evolutionary rather than revolutionary. Once the technology reaches a level of "good enough" for most buyers, technical advancement may prove to be commercially meaningless. This does not mean that manufacturing products in a mature market are meaningless ventures—earlier we mentioned the importance of sanctuary and the important of profiting from past investments. Mature markets can offer both sanctuary and profits to an organization. Rather, the sweet spot trend as an opportunity for exponential growth is something for the patent strategist to consider when prioritizing resources for future growth opportunities that can build from an existing base. It is also an opportunity for those without or separating from an existing base to seek the most potentially profitable new technology and patent positions.

Places where you have exponential growth can lead to an explosion of technical and market applications, but predicting which technical and market applications will develop may prove to be a challenge. Understanding technical evolution, however, can allow you to acquire patents on the enablers that will allow those applications to develop. Staying close to emergent technologies and maintaining a portfolio of patents on emergent technologies may also help you to create the future rather than just trying to predict it. Technology will evolve toward the ideal, and commercially important technology will reside at the optimal until there is a material change in the environment that changes what is optimal. Accordingly, you can create the future by changing the technology when it is not good enough or by changing the environment so that the technology is no longer good enough, with the understanding that the former can sometimes cause the latter.

Keep in mind also that the ideal solution toward which all technology evolves will typically not be in the same solution quadrant as existing technology. Your ideal airplane will not be an airplane; it will be some other way to achieve the benefits for which you currently use the airplane. Part of the reason we use an airplane to transport cargo is that it can do so faster than a ship, provided it is a comparatively small amount of cargo. However if that cargo already exists where and when it is needed, then you no longer require the aircraft or the ship to make the delivery, nor could you find any other method to get a cargo to a location faster than it already being there the moment when it is needed. Likewise, the ideal way to treat a disease is not to need to treat the disease; this could be accomplished through a vaccine, the eradication of the disease itself, or the absence of exposure to the disease. The patent and invention on the vaccine could obviate much of the value of the patent and invention for the treatment, and any method to eradicate the disease or otherwise isolate it from human contact will ultimately obviate the need for the vaccine. If you own an enabler, such as one from which to create such a vaccine and do not depend on the corresponding pharmaceutical as a sanctuary, your decision to pursue this more ideal solution for the application of the vaccine becomes all the easier to make. If your sanctuary is in the pharmaceutical, your decision becomes more difficult, since it could affect your own revenue stream, but it needs to be made in the context that if a more ideal solution can exist at a valuable point of entry, it will exist at some point.

From Inventions to Solutions and the Technology Life Cycle

Innovation is about more than inventing; it is also about applying existing inventions in new ways. This becomes an important distinction, particularly when a company's products reach the optimal "good-enough" threshold. At the optimal threshold, a change in innovation focus is often prudent. For example, now that consumer priced dSLRs can shoot images with the quality of film, meaning that they offer good-enough image resolution for most people, it makes sense to focus on other advantages inherent with dSLRs, such as the capacity to adjust shots right on the camera. Innovation can also involve creating new business models from which to profit from inventions—for example, a print shop's providing tools for customers to manage their digital photos that link directly to the print shop's printers.

Another important point to appreciate is that product evolution can go in less intuitive directions than what most people would consider as advancement. Crafting or emulating the ideal solution to a problem does not necessarily involve using the latest technology and may actually involve the way existing technology is repackaged or deployed. If you use C-130s for the rapid deployment of military equipment, you might create an even more ideal solution, as has been done, by prepositioning equipment in advance so it is already there when needed. Prepositioning equipment when you are not in a rush could obviate the need to use a C-130 at all in your solution. You could move the equipment on a barge, something that has been around for thousands of years. Newness of technology and the ideal solution are independent quantities, and should your customer have such solutions that obviate a need for your technology, you should expect them to discover such solutions and be prepared for the ramifications. The drive toward the ideal seeks ever to make existing solutions extinct or nearly so, and this is an important factor in a product life cycle.

In appreciating that newness of technology and the ideal solution are independent quantities, note that only in rare instances is an invention ever the first of its kind from a solutions perspective. Gordon Gould's invention of the laser is a case in point. No invention like the working laser had ever existed before, although the concept had been thought about decades earlier.[54] Much effort went into the invention of the laser in order to be the first to succeed in making one, almost irrespective of what anyone might actually do with a laser. However, even new-to-the-world creations like the laser, once applied as products, generally replace or supplement existing solutions, and then only if the new solution is more ideal, optimal, or both. Among the solutions lasers provide are alternatives to a scalpel for surgery, a ruler for creating straight lines, radar for detecting speed, wires for communication, and a pair of binoculars, map, and smoke for missile guidance.

Inventions approved for development will therefore do to other inventions, and eventually have done to them, the following:

- Inventions will evolve existing solutions.
- Inventions will displace existing solutions.
- Inventions will provide a solution to new or otherwise underserved markets.

The organization that develops an invention will address one or more of these three solution paths until it chooses to exit the initiative, and the patent strategist will craft the patent strategy accordingly throughout that life cycle. Patent protection will be globally oriented around what the invention will do in the marketplace, how to keep competitors out, and how to establish profitable interactions with facilitators for the life cycle of the invention. If you can displace an existing solution, you want to have and enforce the patents that make it difficult for other people to copy your initiative. If someone can displace your existing solution, you want to prepare for that eventuality, up to and including bringing about the displacement yourself.

Each invention associated with a core solution and its applications creates new challenges. Those new challenges make a development plan imperative, not only so you will know where you want to go, but so you will know you have arrived when you get there. Lasers took decades to perfect until they could truly evolve or displace existing solutions or serve underserved markets. Since current solutions may become obsolete to new inventions, two tracks of a development plan can exist. One is for how to profit from the existing solution while it is still viable and where it may continue to have value even after alternative solutions exist. The second development plan exists for the alternative technology. For example, although lasers currently take an increasing role in surgery, surgeons continue to need traditional scalpels to perform their services. A company that can offer both innovative advances in traditional scalpel technology and alternative solutions in laser technology could hold a strong position in that market as an overall solutions provider. Likewise, a significant market continues to exist for videotape technology despite the success of the DVD. For an organization to completely turn its back on one solution and completely embrace the new technology may be a hasty move, particularly if it already holds a position in the older technology. Although being ready for the DVD technology was wise for consumer electronics product makers, not all new technologies are an optimal solution for every situation.

So to conclude with the Innovation section, through innovation, internal to the organization, external to the organization, or both, you have a product, service, or portfolio of products and services that your company sells, the means to sell them, and patents and other intellectual property to protect them. The lines of innovation that led to these products and services are reasonably predictable. It is important to seek patents on the enablers that drive the evolution and a plan to manage the technology associated with the patent strategy through its full life cycle. It is correspondingly important to have a way to market the inventions.

Advancement

The next Center of Excellence is Advancement—the overall process by which a company puts its products and services into the hands of consumers. In business, Advancement is traditionally led by sales and marketing forces; however, all members of a company participate in the process in some way. Sales and marketing cannot function without support.

Regardless of an individual's position within a company, Advancement ultimately involves selling. Anyone who intends to advance anywhere needs to sell sometimes, even if only internally and behind the scenes, in an effort to have important tasks done. It is a critical skill to know how to sell.

Selling is a key part of interacting. Selling is how we persuade people to help us, to let us help them, or to at least not get in the way. We will focus, therefore, on the sales aspect of Advancement as it relates to patent strategy and discuss marketing as it is important.

The Sales Advantage

The ability to sell is a skill useful for anyone. In patent strategy, it becomes an important skill for research and development professionals in particular, who need both to conceive inventions and to sell them to people inside and outside their company.

Research and development professionals who understand the fundamentals of sales have an advantage in conceiving and producing more saleable inventions over those without a sales background or education. From the ranks of sales-savvy engineers sprang some of the most successful entrepreneurs in the world. As examples, consider Bill Gates (Microsoft), Steve Jobs (Apple Computer), Larry Ellison (Oracle), and Larry Page (Google). Such individuals have both the capacity to create and the capacity to sell at the level of top peers in each respective art. In a sense, they build personal Centers of Excellence in innovation and advancement wholly within themselves. The addition of appropriate associates and counsel can enhance the innovation and advancement centers while bringing in security to protect that value. As a part of any patent strategy, it makes good sense to give research and development professionals some background on the skills needed to sell their ideas, even if they will not do the actual selling to customers.

> ### The Sales Strategy Fundamentals
> *The Sales Strategy Fundamentals* is a card set of 54 winning sales strategies designed to sharpen the skill of any professional with a product or idea to sell. It is also a playing card deck made from casino grade card stock.
>
> *The Sales Strategy Fundamentals* has been peer reviewed and acclaimed by sales professionals, including founders of the vaunted IBM Sales Training School where the author received his original sales training.
>
> The ability to sell is the most important business skill in any profession that involves person-to-person interaction. As such, it has universal applications inside and outside of the sales profession.

Saleable Benefits

From the sales perspective, an invention exists to provide benefits for both customers and stakeholders in the invention. Stakeholders invest in an invention to gain a profitable return on their investment. Customers purchase the invention to provide an advantage in their business pursuits or their personal lives. Their purchases follow the pattern of problem identification outlined in this book in the sense that the buyer has a current situation "A" and a desired situation "B," and the purchase of your invention should help your customers get partially or all the way to their "B." In other words, the invention is usually purchased to help solve a problem or satisfy a need. For example, if a customer's desired situation is to have a sealed can opened and you sell a can opener, you provide a tool that gives your customer a better way to open that can than perhaps otherwise available. A description of the delivered advantage will often appear in the specification of a patent application to cover the usefulness requirements that patent examiners consider when reviewing patent applications. Still, research and development professionals often do not talk about their technology in a sales-oriented way.

Research and development professionals often only communicate information about an invention in terms that salespeople would consider features. Features focus on what the invention physically is—for example, a bigger can opener with a rubber grip. A further description of the invention's benefits by research and development professionals and other stakeholders will help to give the invention context with respect to the patent strategy and the advancement of the business—for example, a can opener that can accommodate a wide variety of container sizes with a rubber grip that better prevents the user's hands from slipping, meaning that it is both safe and easy to use. From the perspective of customers, the description of benefits should always include one or more aspects of the following, thought about broadly in context with the given solution:

- Sustainability benefit
- Speed benefit
- Effectiveness benefit
- Efficiency benefit
- Durability benefit
- Convenience benefit
- Cost benefit
- Reduced harmful impact benefit
- Appeal benefit

This list of nine benefits broadly encapsulates the benefits consumers would expect from a product from their point of view. For example, Energizer® battery advertisements declare that they last longer than other comparable batteries, which would offer a sustainability benefit. It could possibly offer other benefits, such as cost benefits, if the advertised longer battery life is accurate and the cost of the better Energizer® batteries is not overly higher than the cost of competitive batteries. In the example of the can opener, the rubber grip could improve efficiency, since the user wastes less energy keeping his or her hand from slipping that could otherwise be focused on actually opening the can.

Sometimes though, an advancement in benefits might have trade-offs. For example, steamships ultimately made it faster to cross the ocean, certainly a benefit to those needing a speedier delivery of goods and passengers overseas. Steam power also improved efficiency, since shipping companies could better predict the time of arrival of vessels that no longer depended on variable winds. That meant better planning for unloading shipments at the docks and loading a new shipment. Steamships, however, had high fuel costs compared to sailing ships that fundamentally did not have any fuel costs. Steamships also needed to devote a large amount of space for fuel, which reduced different aspects of efficiency. Due to such trade-offs as the high fuel costs and limited cargo capacity, steamships could not replace sailing ships for many customers until better-designed engines and vessels satisfactorily addressed these drawbacks.[55] A key driver of invention, from the business perspective, is to improve one aspect of a technology without causing an unacceptable drawback in another aspect of the technology.

The first eight benefits in the foregoing list represent practical considerations for customers. The ninth benefit, appeal, allows for the introduction of psychological and moral elements of the customers' decisions. Certain offshoots from the perceived benefit of appeal often appear that take inventions away from the physically ideal or optimal. If an appeal factor did not exist and all technology evolved linearly toward the ideal, then we would all likely wear the same color clothes and drive the same type of car so as to eliminate the inefficiency associated with too many variances.

An invention might psychologically or morally appeal to a buyer because of its practical benefits in the other benefit categories of sustainability, speed, effectiveness, efficiency, durability, convenience, cost, or reduced harmful impact. But just as likely, the concept of appeal will be represented for other reasons, such as a brand identification or because one invention is, for whatever reason, more fun to use than the alternative. This latter explains the continued existence of standard (manual) transmissions in high-priced sports cars despite the availability of automatic transmissions, as well as the continued existence of luxury ocean liners despite the availability of airplanes. With today's high-end technology, automatic transmissions have negligible drawbacks in shifting performance and gas mileage reduction compared to the manual transmission alternative, yet some people still enjoy shifting gears when they drive. Even though automatic transmissions are more practically closer to the ideal in that drivers no longer need to think about shifting, many drivers prefer the added control of manual shifting. Ocean liners, now in the guise of cruise ships, continue to transport people long after airplanes have displaced ocean liners for general travel because they are enjoyable.

Even though airplanes are more practically closer to the ideal way to get from A to B than a ship for a passenger, if the journey itself is part of the experience, then the ship offers that added appeal. When determining descriptive benefits for your customer, never discount the appeal factor. Within their patents, for example, many Japanese golf club manufacturers note such advantages in their golf club heads as the creation of a pleasing sound on impact with a golf ball.

Megapixel Envy

The core of inventing, from the sales perspective, involves increasing benefits and decreasing drawbacks associated with the features that most interest prospective customers. For example, when digital cameras first appeared on the market, the pictures they took were grainy and fuzzy, and most people considered the technology a novelty instead of a viable alternative for traditional film cameras. Higher megapixel cameras existed, but cost thousands of dollars more than most customers were willing to pay—a drawback in monetary costs. A significant inventive effort took place to deliver higher resolution cameras at a lower cost. The process of doing so has pushed inventors to evolve digital cameras closer to the ideal, meaning more megapixels in lighter and less expensive cameras. The eventual success of this endeavor was never an issue, although who would succeed and when remained uncertain.

The most competitive cameras in this evolution seem to have found their optimal or "good-enough" image capture range at around 8 to 12 megapixels, because that megapixel range provides resolution comparable to that of traditional film cameras. As consumer digital cameras have reached this threshold, additional megapixels have had less significance; in fact, the corresponding larger file sizes of higher-resolution photography can make managing images more difficult, at least for the moment. Consequently, camera makers have had to rely increasingly on other benefits to sell their cameras, such as durability of components and shells, ease of photo management and printing, image stabilization, and a host of other possible improvements.

> For the patent strategist, a given patent will tend to have more value when the invention described by it offers a meaningful benefit to the consumer beyond what he or she already has. A patented technology that does not appreciably improve the benefit will usually be less valuable by comparison.

Advantages

Benefits produce advantages for buyers. Whether you sell a technical solution or a strategic solution, you sell the benefits, and therefore the advantages of your idea to buyers. In either case, you typically offer up to three solutions to the buyer: the premium solution, the best-fit solution, or the lowest-cost solution. The sweet spot is generally the best-fit solution. Related to these three solutions is the degree of specialty or generality associated with the invention, or as we may describe it more colorfully, whether your invention is a goose or a horse.

An old fable argues about whether the goose or the horse is the superior animal. The goose says it is superior because it can walk on land, swim in water, and fly in the air. The horse says it is the superior animal because it has been perfected to move across the land with grace, whereas the goose waddles more than walks, cannot swim like a fish, and when compared to an eagle, shows no grace in the sky. The horse would rather be an expert at one thing and forsake others, whereas the goose would rather do all things well enough and forsake expertise. Which is better? It depends.

The iPhone is a goose in the communications space, since it has inferiorities compared with a dedicated cell phone, a dedicated Internet workstation, or a dedicated MP3 player. However, like the goose, the iPhone will perform each of its functions well enough for most buyers. "Horse" inventions tend to prevail more when the best is not good enough. The memory chip within the iPhone is an example of a "horse" product, since storing more and more data on less space continues to make a meaningful difference to consumers.

Why is the distinction between goose and horse important to the patent strategist? Because it helps you to focus on where inventions need the most protection. For the horse, you need to protect the intellectual property associated with improving performance. Even a little better performance "running across the land" can make a difference to a horse. With the goose, you need to add interconnectivity, and you will also likely find yourself comparatively more involved with licensing, since you can bring in preexisting and "good-enough" solutions instead of inventing them. It does not matter that you are the best flyer in the sky, as long as you can fly well enough for your purpose. When you can find "good-enough" inventions from an outside source, your inventors can focus their attention on areas in which you have no available alternatives. When you cannot find "good-enough" inventions from outside sources, your inventors can focus on areas for improving performance.

A Goose With a Horse's Brain

In accord with Altshuller's laws of technical evolution, as a system reaches the threshold of "good enough" it will become a part of other systems; an invention that starts out as a horse, and focuses on doing one thing really well, frequently evolves into a goose once it performs well enough for most users. At a certain point in the early 1990s, the digital PBX, or digital office telephone switch, reached a level of performance that was good enough for most buyers. ROLM Telecommunications, however, continued to market and price its PBXs as if they were still horses, even though ROLM engineers had transitioned to a "goose" phase of linking PBXs to other systems such as mainframe computers and specialty software. PBXs were being linked to improved auto-mated call distribution software for call centers, direct data feed and retrieval on computer networks, performance-measuring software, video, and a host of other new applications.

From the sales perspective, ROLM suffered from the dis-connection between its marketing force, firmly in a "horse" mindset, and engineering that was evolving into a goose mind-set, particularly with accounts outside of its installed base. A key rival, Northern Telecom, offered digital PBX systems that could, on the broadest of estimation, perform to 80% of the ROLM system's level for half the price. That 80% of comparative performance on the Northern Telecom systems was more than ample performance for what most buyers actually needed. Being the best could no longer justify the premium price that ROLM had enjoyed throughout the 1980s, and ROLM's new business sales suffered as a result.

A Degree of Separation

When considering the advantages that inventions will support, it is important to understand your place in the market. Do you plan to have the premium, best-fit, or lowest-cost position, and how will you make the distinction? Also, at what scale do you make the distinction? Both BMW and Select Comfort offer technologically advanced products to their customers and, on the company level, are firmly entrenched in the "premium" category. An examination of their patents will show a number of inventions that technologically help them to maintain and grow that position. Within their own product lines, however, they have a premium, best-fit, and low-cost option. For Select Comfort, this is their models 5000, 4000, and 3000 beds respectively. For BMW, this has been an M-class car for each model and then two models below it, with the best-fit model having a larger engine and more options than the low-end model. Since the low-end 3000 bed and low-end BMW car outperform many standard beds and cars respectively, you can see that the nature of the advantageous position needs to be put into perspective with both the competition and the company's own product line.

Intel provides an interesting example of a company that has products oriented to the premium and best fit positions. The Intel Pentium® processor, and associated research, competes for the premium technology position in consumer-based microprocessors. The Intel Celeron® processor, and associated technology, competes for the best-fit technology position. Intel keeps a degree of internal separation between these products, including physically separate research and development locations. Separation avoids confusion within the market and within Intel. The Celeron® chip performs well enough for most buyers, but there is still a significant percentage of buyers for whom the best microprocessors are still not fast enough.

This example of Intel products presents a good opportunity to bring up that in strategy there are no absolutes, and everything needs to be analyzed in context with the respective situation. We have said that interaction tends to lead to growth, and isolation tends to lead to decline, but we have to clarify that concept with the word "tends," as exceptions always exist. Intel's separation of its Pentium® and Celeron® research and development efforts is a case where deliberate isolation has served a useful purpose. The isolation allows disparate product groups to evolve in accord with their unique environments. Isolation leads to the elimination of commonality, which is fine if that is what you want to have happen, especially if it helps you to better differentiate in the market. The underlying dynamic is the same from which new species evolve such as Darwin's finches on the remote Galapagos islands. Diversity in a product set depends on some level of isolation from related products.

Depending on the position taken, the patent strategist needs to understand why his or her company has a premium, best-fit, or cheapest position and assure that the company gains and maintains protections on the technical aspects of those reasons. Once an organization understands its product category, technologies in that product category and often technologies associated with their production need security.

---

iPod as Premium, Best Fit, and Low Cost

Positioning as the premium product has strength when the current state of the art physically, psychologically, or morally underperforms. Positioning as the best-fit product has strength when the current state of the art physically, psychologically, or morally performs satisfactorily. Positioning as the cheapest product has strength at any time the stakeholders have advantages that make it difficult for competitors to copy the reason for their product being the cheapest. An invention that simultaneously has the cheapest solution as well as the premium or best-fit solution has the potential to generate a solid return on investment for its stakeholders. Inventions associated with MP3 players have created this position for some stakeholders, in particular the shareholders of Apple with its iPod® and iTunes®. These products in combination offer a cheaper way, per desired song, to collect music than through the previous and existing avenue of purchasing a compact disk (CD). Purchasing music on a CD or other fixed medium traditionally forced buyers to pay for the less-desired songs as well as the most-desired songs on a given album. iPods also offer the premium and best-fit ways to listen to that music while on the move without the bulk of the portable CD player and associated CDs.

Security

"Everything you do is evil to someone." Your very success will be an "evil" to those who covet that success and cannot participate in it. If you create value and people think they can take some of that value for themselves, then you will have competition. This means you need security. Security involves all manner of how we protect the value of the business inclusive of, but certainly not limited to, patents. It includes, for example, the literal locks and keys that keep unauthorized people out of sensitive research and development facilities as well as softer security measures, such as coaching salespeople and engineers about what information they may share outside of the company and what information is for internal use only. Considering the Centers of Excellence and patent strategy, you create or acquire important inventions, advance them into the market, and once you have a good thing going or have a reasonable potential for success, you secure that value with patents and by other means. Security, therefore, is the next part of our discussion on crafting a patent strategy using the three Centers of Excellence.

The Primary Utility of a Patent

We have talked about competitive strategy being an interplay between interaction and isolation. A patent as a strategic tool serves as both an isolating tool (it provides a means to keep competitors away) and a tool for interaction (it provides a mechanism and a reason to set up relationships). This interplay of selective interaction and isolation is the primary strategic utility of a patent employed by the patent strategist with both interplays built around the rights a patent grants to enforce exclusivity of the patent's claims. This is important to consider when deciding whether to patent and how to prepare the patent documentation. Ask how a patent and an associated invention will be used as an isolating tool to keep others out. Ask how a patent and an associated invention will be used as a tool for interactivity to draw others into positive relationships. You should know the answers to these questions before you prepare patent documents and put those answers into context with your patent budget and other priorities for that budget.

The Ultimate Security Advantage

The ultimate security advantage for any organization or individual is invulnerability. Invulnerability is traditionally described in terms of having impenetrable defenses, but it can also come in the form of an absence from threats. The Ace of Hearts from the *Art of War: Sun Tzu Strategy Card Deck* describes invulnerability as "Let the Tiger Find No Place to Sink Its Claws," meaning to make the hostile intents and capabilities of your adversary irrelevant. To visualize this in practice, think about how an ancient warrior might have protected himself from an enemy arrow in flight. He had three obvious options: He could raise his shield and block the arrow, he could step aside so that the arrow misses him, or in some way he could be out of that arrow's range altogether.

Like a shield, a well-written patent with superior supporting documentation can prove practically invulnerable to competitive action if well-placed within other aspects of the organization's power. Its weakness as a component of a security plan is that you can never know for sure whether your shield is strong enough until after the figurative arrow hits it. Not infringing (the absence of wrongdoing) should also leave the organization invulnerable to infringement rulings. This is equivalent to stepping aside so that the arrow misses, or not stepping onto the field of combat at all. Its weakness as a component of a security plan, assuming that you have chosen to compete and are on the field of contest, is that you might not know that a figurative arrow threatens you until it actually hits you, leaving no opportunity to block it or step aside. So these concepts of carrying a shield or stepping aside run up against the reality of the patent environment very quickly; it is almost impossible to draft an invulnerable patent, and not infringing, particularly relating to those patents applications filed but not yet published, could also prove difficult to impossible. As we have explored, when conducting a prior art search, you can never be sure that you have found everything; intellectual property information is vast not always easily accessible, and time is always limited. So you need to take another approach when seeking to emulate the ideal of invulnerability, beyond the patent equivalent of raising a shield, stepping aside, or avoiding the competition altogether.

Vulnerability and Invulnerability

In 1997, biotech company MedImmune licensed technology from Genentech to make a drug used to prevent respiratory illness in children, but it did so under protest, claiming that Genentech's patent was invalid. On January 9, 2007, the U.S. Supreme Court ruled to allow MedImmune to continue to seek to invalidate Genentech's patent, via patent infringement proceedings, without requiring it to terminate the license first.[56] This allowed MedImmune to take legal action without risking damages for patent infringement. Looked at from Genentech's perspective, the Court's decision considerably increased the vulnerability of Genentech's patent position, since part of the deterrence of an infringement lawsuit to the alleged infringer is the possibility of paying treble damages should they lose. Often the threat of losing the case is enough to make another organization, such as MedImmune, settle for a reasonable licensing fee without further contest, thus keeping the patent valid and enforceable against other competitors. Allowing the patent infringement lawsuit to move forward for MedImmune on the claim of patent invalidity, while licensing the challenged patent, put Genentech into a more vulnerable position.

Design Around

One useful tool in a patent infringement lawsuit, mostly in electrical and mechanical areas, is to design around the infringed or potentially infringed patent claims. This cannot always be done, but when it can, it creates less vulnerability from injunction and mitigates the continued damages of patent infringement made into the future. That will isolate any infringement action damage to what has thus far occurred. Designing around typically starts with engineers creating alternative solutions; a simple example is the Barnes & Noble solution to use a two-click purchase system to design around Amazon.com's one-click patent while that case was contested. It also involves attorneys who can render legal opinions on whether the design-around solution is sufficiently different from the infringed invention or whether the design-around will have an issue with the doctrine of equivalents. A subtlety to note, however, is that whereas a design-around can diminish a technical vulnerability, it can in tandem create a vulnerability in the willfulness of an infringement ruling, because the act of designing around a competitor's patent claims could become your implicit acknowledgment that there were patent claims to infringe on and that your current technology did indeed infringe on them.

Of further note on invulnerability, physically, invulnerability tends to increase the capacity for interaction, since the invulnerable cannot be harmed, and vulnerability tends to be an isolating force, since isolation can keep the vulnerable safe from harm. Psychologically, however, the two states may drive opposite actions. The invulnerable feel safe and isolate themselves, thereby ultimately becoming vulnerable as conditions outside change, whereas the vulnerable interact to create the means to reduce vulnerability and, provided they survive the interaction, become less vulnerable or invulnerable. This relates to our earlier discussion of equilibrium and disequilibrium, and as with that, balance is important.

The Ideal Patent

Thinking about invulnerability leads us to a counterintuitive consideration useful for developing a better patent strategy. It begins with considering what the ideal patent would look like in accord with Altshuller's definition of ideal, since the ideal patent, by the nature of its nonexistence, would be invulnerable. The ideal patent would provide the stakeholders in an invention with all the benefits desired from a patent without introducing any of the drawbacks associated with a patent. The need to prepare, file, maintain, and enforce patents, with all their associated costs, is a drawback to applying for and owning patents. Excluding others from making, using, or selling an invention, or licensing the manufacture, use, or sale of an invention to others, bestows a major benefit on the patent owner. The ideal patent would theoretically afford all those benefits desired from a patent, but without the patent. That is, you would get 100% of the benefit you seek from a patent, but with 0% of the drawbacks associated with preparing, filing, maintaining, defending, and the like, because the patent does not exist. Of course, patents do exist and have an important utility. Still, the best patent strategy will emulate this ideal for its inventions to the extent that it can.

To accept the logic of this conclusion, consider that the need to rely on a patent for an organization intent on implementing the invention is actually a sign of weakness in the owning organization, not a sign of strength, as might normally be associated with patent ownership. This is easy to prove. If a hypothetical organization spent $10 million to create an invention that a competing organization could easily, in the absence of the patent, copy and sell without that $10 million expense, then the creating organization would have $10 million in expenses to price into the invention when it reaches the market that the competitor would not have to price into its copied version of the same invention. All things being otherwise equal, the competitor that copied the invention could sell it for a lower price than its creator and still make a profit. Of course, this inherent weakness, which can arise from investing in the creation of new inventions, is one of the reasons Thomas Jefferson founded the patent system in the United States, and other countries have likewise adopted patent systems of their own—to foster investment in innovation by providing a reasonable opportunity for stakeholders to recover their investment and receive a reasonable profit from the effort and risk taken. Still, those preparing a patent strategy should prefer to minimize this weakness by other means than just the patent. When those other means, which we will discuss, become powerful enough, the need to have an actual patent diminishes, and you can start to emulate the ideal of attaining all the benefits of a patent without necessarily needing the patent.

A key to minimizing weakness in a patent position is to make competition *not* otherwise equal to competitors in favor of the stakeholders you support. Start by asking how the stakeholders' organization can still succeed in the market in the absence of the patent or patents. One way to do this, for example, is to establish a first-mover advantage where it was found that even easy-to-copy pharmaceutical products could, certainly with many exceptions, maintain a 30% market share and premium price over later entrants.[57] Another way may be to establish support and service around the product made possible in whole or part by the invention that is more valuable than the sale of the product itself. Incorporate answers to that question into your patent strategy. These answers will generally reside outside the domain of patents, such as the presence of established marketing channels, which is another reason why a patent strategy needs to go beyond just patents.

The closer a patent strategy evolves toward the ideal of no patents, the better that strategy will likely be. Again, this does not mean don't patent. You do want to get patents most of the time. But when you can succeed in profiting from a technology without having patent protection, then the selected patents around that technology become a bonus to the overall strength of the organization and not a crutch to address some other competitive weakness. Further to that, where you find you can rely on secrecy and a present leadership position in the market and perhaps want to limit the amount of technology you disclose, you may actually not need or want a patent at all on certain inventions.

Motrin® Brand Name

Even though the patents for ibuprofen have expired, McNeil Consumer Healthcare can still charge a premium for the compound over generic producers because of the brand name Motrin®. Although McNeil has certainly lost some benefits of pricing power by no longer having active patents for Motrin®, the power of the brand, as well as the McNeil name, its distribution system, its marketing power, and so on allows it to charge a premium for ibuprofen even in the face of lower-priced generic competition. In short, McNeil still gets much of the benefit it received from its patents on ibuprofen without the patents because it has built such a strong brand around the formerly patented product. Put another way, the original patents helped to establish the brand, and the established brand then helps to keep the value built around those patents even after the associated patents have expired. The brand allows McNeil to continue to charge some premium over generic producers after patent expiration, and because being able to charge a premium is one of the benefits of a patent, McNeil still gets a portion of that benefit, but without the overhead of the patents.

A Counterintuitive Result

Although it might seem that adopting the approach to emulate the ideal patent as a policy would cause a reduction in the number of new patents entering a company's patent portfolio, stakeholders will likely see the opposite result. Certainly by seeking to emulate the ideal of succeeding with no patents, you are likely to identify patentable invention candidates for which you do not want or need patents, but you are also actually likely to increase the strength and number of new patents entering the patent portfolio. Why? The patents actually pursued by an organization that seeks to emulate ideal patents will tend to have more value than otherwise and will encourage more investment in the process since they will have, with deliberation, more sources of the organization's power supporting them. Also, in the cases where you cannot emulate the ideal patent, you will better appreciate specific weaknesses that make a given patent essential for commercial success with the invention, again resulting in stronger and more valuable patents to counter those weaknesses.

Fox and Tiger
Another way to think about how you emulate the ideal patent comes from an old fable about a fox and a tiger.

A fox happened on a hungry tiger in the woods. It was too late for the fox to escape the tiger, so he had to think quickly. Fox asked Tiger, "Why aren't you afraid of me?"

Tiger asked, "Why should I be afraid of you?"

Fox answered, "Because I am the lord of the jungle."

"That's ridiculous," Tiger said.

Fox said, "I will prove it to you. Follow me."

So Tiger followed Fox. As all the animals spotted Fox, they also saw Tiger and fled. Fox asked, "Do you believe me now?"

Tiger, perplexed, said, "Yes, I was wrong. You are fearsome."

Then Tiger fled also.

So as someone involved with patent strategy, think of Fox as your patent and Tiger as anything else that gives your company power. Then ask what can walk behind your patent like Tiger that gives your patent more strength than the patent alone.

Links within Claims

The ideal patent is just that, an ideal, not a reason to say "don't patent." We seek to emulate the ideal as much as possible so that your patents are more often a bonus to your strength and less often a crutch to mask weakness. You can start this by linking together patents and important elements within patents. This represents another variation of isolation versus interaction. An isolated claim, like an isolated patent, is easier to attack than one that is integrated with other claims. Broad, intermediate, and narrow claims need to work together. A narrow claim, for example a "fastener," could be used to prevent a broader claim on the associated object from being interpreted as meaning only a "button."

Further to linking claims, you should examine natural lines of technology evolution that you could claim immediately on the current patent application or within subsequent patents. So you start with your individual patent or patent disclosure. You ask, as the invention in this patent document evolves, what will happen to it in the future? As discussed previously, we saw that technology takes very predictable lines of evolution, and it does so through a limited set of inventive operators. There are anywhere from 40 to just over 100 inventive operators in innovation that universally apply across industries, depending on the system of inventive operators you use. For example, "remove unnecessary parts" is an inventive operator that represents a common way to improve technology within industries. This operator has been applied to industries as widely separated as scuba gear manufacturers with the evolution from twin to single stage regulators and wireless telephones with the removal of telephone lines by wireless.

You can quite literally go item by item with a patent or specific set of patent claims and ask whether the idea represented by your collection of inventive operators could be relevant to a given invention. If so, describe it, include it, or record it for another patent application or an invention disclosure. This creates another link that adds to the defensibility of that claim if for no other reason than it makes it harder for a competitor to "picket fence" that claim. Picket fencing is the act of inventing ahead of the competition, typically in order to force a cross-license. For a basic example, if your competitor patents the wheel and you have the opportunity to patent the axle first, you can force a cross-license of the wheel if your competitor wants access to the axle. Exhibit 4.2 shows how you might develop the theoretical invention of the first chair.

If someone invented the first chair, there are many very predictable lines of evolution that the person could describe even within the first patent. These include, but are certainly not limited to, the idea of segmentation that leads to reclining and folding, the idea of spheres that leads to rolling on wheels or rotating, the idea of nesting that leads to stackability, the idea of composites that lead to making chairs from varied materials, and the idea of consolidation that suggests attachments such

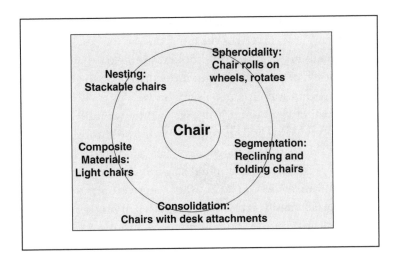

Exhibit 4.2   Predictable Chair Improvements

as cup holders. The theory of inventive problem solving (TRIZ) and other invention sciences have described inventive operators that allow you to systematically review a given invention (e.g., the chair mentioned previously) for the applications that someone, if not you, will otherwise invent in the future. Systematic review of these inventive operators allows you to record ideas in advance, like adding a cup holder to your chair, that may otherwise appear obvious only in hindsight.

If you do not describe and claim a line of technical evolution and the patented invention has value, it is a fair bet your competitor will. In fact, running this exercise of extending claims on competitive patents is a very good way to start isolating competitive patents and therefore reduce your competitor's freedom of action in areas of your interest. The degree by which you run this exercise on your inventions and those of competitors is proportional to the importance of the technical art to you and your competitors, since the exercise demands some commitment of time and money. IBM, as a related example, has for many years published IBM Technical Disclosure Bulletins that often disclose without patent protection all the other less favorable ways to solve given problems so that competitors do not establish proprietary patent positions from solutions alternative or in substitute to those on which IBM has focused. In intellectual property circles, such disclosures are often called "defensive publications."

Universal Inventive Operators

The theory of inventive problem solving (TRIZ) that is available within the public domain provides 40 universal inventive operators. The analysis of any invention in any industry would show, at its core, that all inventions use one or a combination of these inventive operators to solve one or a combination of 39 problems also defined by TRIZ.[58]

The *Innovation Planner Card Deck* is a proprietary 170-card set of innovation strategies and solutions that gives easy access to the unique I-TRIZ knowledge-based inventive problem-solving methodology. The deck has 85 refined inventive operators that relate to each of the three Centers of Excellence discussed in this section: Innovation, Advancement, and Security, along with another 81 cards associated with other aspects of invention and innovation.

The *Innovation Planner Card Deck* may also be combined with *The Sales Strategy Fundamentals* and the *Art of War: Sun Tzu Strategy Card Deck* as a powerful tool to develop breakthrough strategies. The *Innovation Planner Card Deck* focuses on the innovation Center of Excellence. *The Sales Strategy Fundamentals* focuses on the advancement Center of Excellence. The *Art of War: Sun Tzu Strategy Card Deck* focuses on the security Center of Excellence. Each provides the core fundamental operators of each respective Center of Excellence. Excellence can be achieved by mastering these fundamentals.

Beyond the Claim

Make your claims strong and comprehensive, but also consider the rest of the patent document. A court case, *Phillips v. AWH*, set a precedent that if the court sees a claim as being too broad, it can move to the disclosure of the patent specification to look for details about what a patent's claims actually cover.[59] In a related case with a technology easy to understand, *Nystrom v.*

(Continued)

Trex, the court interpreted the word "board" within the patent specification to mean wood and not synthetic material, because the disclosure discussed scrap from a board cut from a log. The claim itself was broader, but the disclosure was used to limit the claim.[60] This means the patent drafter needs to take care when using narrowing terms anywhere within the written patent document.

Links to Other Patents

The next level up is to see how patents link and relate to each other. The actual product sold to a customer usually contains technology described in many individual patents. A typical system structure involves inputs, outputs, an engine, a transmission, a working body, an instrument of control, and a system interface. So a patent network might have elements of the entire system within it, keeping in mind that a patent network could include patents from partners or even competitors. The key part of this exercise is to determine whether the utility of one patent depends on access to other patents, and if so, which of these other patents you have access to, and sometimes more importantly, which of the other patents your competitors do not have access to. In the latter case, even if a competitor invalidates one patent and can make use of that specific technology, the other patents remain and continue to inhibit that competitor from competing in the market or invalidating the best use of the technology. Even though a patent might be invalidated, if other linking patents block the competition, your position as a whole is minimally affected.

Analyzing a patent network will show that some patents have more importance than others in maintaining the integrity of the whole system. These are often called "control point" patents. When you identify these patents, you should run the previously shown exercise of systematically exploring inventive operators and natural lines of technology evolution to make them as strong and as broad as possible within their own network of claims. As you undertake this exercise, keep in mind the idea of emulating the ideal patent and understanding when and why, for a given patent, you cannot emulate the ideal. For example, a new pharmaceutical compound may work only in the form of a very specific molecule; therefore, a patent on that specific molecule and its method of use is essential. When you know this, you can put added effort into ensuring that you have "all your t's crossed and i's dotted" in a way that you may not economically be able to afford with every patent that you seek.

Links to Other Resources

Of course we do not stop at just the patents. Next, we want to link the patent network to the other resources of the organization, considering that these resources are another aspect of power. We showed earlier that tying an invention to a brand, a domain of marketing, can allow you to emulate the ideal patent by allowing you to charge a premium for the branded technology, even in the absence of owning an active patent on that technology. In the presence of an active and defendable patent, the patent and the brand together are more powerful than either the patent or brand separately. So in a way, the patent and brand create a sum greater than the individual parts: $1 + 1 > 2$. Likewise, think about how the power of an invention often rests with the people in the organization who can make, use, develop, and sell it. Manpower is a powerful resource to link to a patent network. Capital is another powerful resource to support the integrity of an invention, if for no other reason than you can often buy yourself out of a poor situation and into a better one. A solid network of competent patent attorneys is yet another important resource to support the integrity of a patent. Lawyers who understand how to draft claims well and for the best coverage possible raise the chance that any given patent will stand up to scrutiny, which in turn will leave those who might like to challenge the patent less likely to do so and less likely to succeed if they try. Ultimately, any aspect of your organization can enhance the power of your patents—be the tiger (power) that walks behind your patents—and help you to emulate the ideal patent if combined properly. Conversely, the patent can be the tiger (power) that walks behind those other sources of power—for example, that fledgling new brand that could otherwise be defeated by competitors until it is better established. Everything is mutually supportive.

The network of resources within your organization that are useful to effectively create additional barriers for your competition can be classified into seven broad categories:

1. Know-how
2. Legal
3. Financial
4. Relationships
5. Location
6. Technical
7. Timing

An invention, even if did not arise from within your organization, takes people and ideas to implement. Even if you seek to make money solely by licensing the patent, its value as a licensed patent still depends on having people and ideas to implement it at the licensing organization. People and ideas (know-how) provide another tiger (power) that can walk behind your patent and that your patent can support in turn.

As a barrier to competition, a patent falls into a category of legal devices that includes patents, trade secrets, trademarks, brands, copyrights, contracts, and regulations. All can afford additional advantages for using the invention to advance business. For example, people do pay more for products with specific premium brand names regardless of patent protection status. This is demonstrated by the continued success that many over-the-counter brand name drugs, such as Motrin® discussed earlier, have had in capturing a premium price over otherwise identical generic versions. So if the patent and brand combination is the most powerful defense in a given situation and the stakeholder loses the right to exclusivity afforded by the patent, as was the case with expired patents associated with McNeil Consumer Healthcare's Motrin®, then the brand may continue to provide a base for charging some premium over other options. In contrast, if McNeil Consumer Healthcare did not have a solid brand position with Motrin®, the loss of patent protection could have effectively ended its opportunity to profit any more than the generic drug competitors that entered the market.

A trade secret, the legal element of know-how, might be another legal device that could walk behind your patent and that your patent can support in turn. In fact, often the best licensing combination for a patent is to license a patent and trade secret at the same time. If you patent a new type of valve, but have as a trade secret the optimal means to maintain it, then anyone who may want to copy that invention may find it best to purchase it from you to gain the know-how under contract on how best to use it. The associated trade secret might keep you profitably involved with the licensee even after the patent behind the original license expires. So in short, legal vehicles in their various forms become another tiger (power).

Other advantages to consider include financial advantages and barriers to competition associated with finance. If it costs a lot for competitors to come up to speed or tool up to manufacture or use an invention, then that could prove to be an additional line of defense to protect an invention, even in the absence of a patent. Combine a financial advantage with a solid brand position, an associated trade secret, and a body of people able to make best use of the invention, and the organization has five lines of defense: the people, the patent, the brand, the trade secret, and a high cost of entry. Each line of defense supports the others.

Relationships provide another line of defense. Established relationships that facilitate the advancement of an invention in the market can prove to be difficult for a competitor to overcome, even one with free access to an invention. These relationships involve customers, facilitators, complementors, competitors, regulators, students, and any other people who may positively or negatively affect your business.

Good relationships lead to cooperation (interaction) instead of conflict or apathy (isolation). Good relationships can specifically lead to beneficially exclusive or open licensing agreements. Good relationships can also lower the risk of litigation if any toes accidentally get stepped on during the evolution of products and services in the market. Even among staunch competitors, there is always a place for treating others as you would like to be treated. Your competitors, after all, do share an interest in maintaining a viable and competitive market in which to compete. So now the given patent becomes even stronger since it is supported by and supports good people, a strong brand, sound financial positioning, a trade secret, and good relationships.

Relationships are very often also linked to location and how presence or absence in a market affects the use of an invention. Location is not always constrained to geographic locations, but it can be. An obvious advantage in business is to have local access to an important market that competitors do not have, or do not have as well developed, which can be facilitated by having a physical presence there. Other advantages also exist, some of them psychological. Detroit, Michigan provides an example. Detroit is well known in the United States for the automobile, and the collection of people and suppliers in the region can provide a significant advantage to those seeking to operate in that location. The automotive manufacturers, even with their long history of aggressive competition against each other, have a strong desire to unite when it comes to fending off overseas competition. This becomes the concept of "us against them," and if your location puts you in the "us" category, you will be in a stronger position if people care. Assuming enough people do care, or that you otherwise have market presence–based advantages, seven integrated lines of defense become possible: the people, the patent, the brand, the trade secret, cost, relationships, and location. Possibilities do not stop there.

Technical advantages may come into play. You may have other technology, aside from or including your trade secrets, that complements an invention and is not as readily accessible or useable for competitors. If competitors find it difficult to leverage an invention without this technology, even in the absence of that given patent, you will be in a strong position. Furthermore, protection in numbers can develop here through links to other patents. A network of related patents, covering all or part of an entire system, can reinforce the strength of other members in the system and mitigate risk in the absence of patent protection from any one part of the system. Such a network of patents proves better at protecting an invention than an isolated patent in almost every case. However, competitors can isolate even a large network of patents in fundamentally the same way that they can isolate a single patent if given the opportunity to do so. Effective links, such as to brand, cost, relationship, and location advantages previously discussed, help to reduce this risk. Put another way, it is even better to have multiple tigers (sources of power) if they are also coordinated with each other.

Finally, timing also comes into play as a potential barrier to be used against the competition and provide another tiger (power). In the absence of a patent, it could still take too long for competitors to use an invention in a significant way to impact the market. It could take too long for researchers and developers at competing organizations to duplicate the invention to make it worth their while. Although competitors have been known to find accelerators to make up lost time, and such worst-case scenarios should generally be planned for, you should recognize that timing and tempo can provide critical sources of potential advantage. Tempo is discussed in Chapter 5, Act.

To conclude here, if you review the Centers of Excellence illustration and the graying of corporate boundaries, the beneficial resources to which you link your patents—your tigers (sources of power)—will be found both inside and outside of your organization. To reuse a phrase, the possible combinations are limited only by your imagination. Also, remember this idea of linking sources of power in context with strategy being an interplay between interaction and isolation. Interaction is generally the position for growth, and selective interaction with the right entities is likely to produce growth and therefore strength. As well, you may want to selectively isolate competitors and some would-be facilitators from you so as not to weaken your position. Regardless of the desire, you should prefer to be the one deciding whom to interact with or isolate and you do not want other people and organizations, through their actions, to make those decisions for you.

The Master Does Nothing, Yet He Leaves Nothing Undone

"The master does nothing, yet he leaves nothing undone," from the *Tao Te Ching*, written in China around 500 B.C., may be the most insightful strategic observation of all time. In the ideal strategy, you accomplish everything you want without any mechanism. This is important because you have a limited amount of resources to dedicate to given tasks. So if you were to create the conditions whereby people fear launching a lawsuit against you, you can achieve all the benefits of not being sued for infringement without even knowing that someone was considering it. You have done nothing regarding that someone, yet nothing is left undone regarding that same someone. In doing nothing, you use no resources, which means the resources you did not use can be used elsewhere.

(Continued)

A patent strategy that uses this principle is to not patent every technology you invent and use. Since U.S. patent applications are not published for 18 months, you can receive 18 months worth of psychological protection for unpatented technology while competitors wait to confirm the absence of corresponding patent applications. By that time, especially in very fast moving industries, you might be on to the next thing anyway. The key to this strategy is to patent enough and enforce enough to create fear, uncertainty, and doubt in your competition about how you would respond to an infringement—just enough enforcement so that the competition will not take the risk of infringing.

Parallel Lines of Competition and Security

In building on your network of links to other sources of power, one of the most important aspects of strategy is to leverage your strengths in areas where competitors have comparative weaknesses. On the product level, strengths and weaknesses are often readily apparent. As a case in point from a company we previously visited, in the 1990s ROLM Telecommunications executives decided to launch a sales initiative to put ROLM's Model 10 PBX (telephone switch) into hospitals. The Model 10 PBX, however, had a critical weakness in this market that distributors selling a competing Northern Telecom Meridian system easily exploited. If a CPU failed in a PBX, the phone system would shut off until it was repaired. The ROLM CPU was extraordinarily reliable and almost never failed, but because of this reliability, it had no redundancy in the Model 10 PBX. The Model 10 PBX had only one CPU. The comparable Northern Telecom Meridian system had a backup CPU, meaning that if the primary CPU failed, the other CPU could take over while a repair team was dispatched. In a hospital environment that needed the phone system to be up and running 100% of the time, the ROLM sales initiative did not go very well.

With patent strategy, you can also use strengths against weaknesses. By linking patents to other sources of power, you can craft very powerful asymmetric strategies. Asymmetric strategies, as we have seen, are a classic way to use strength against weakness. In short, if a competitor is strong in one line of competition, you endeavor to compete in another line of competition where it is comparatively weak. In the illustrative game of "rock, paper, scissors," if the competitor plays "rock," you want to play "paper."

When deciding on which lines of competition to focus, there are no less than 12 parallel lines of competition to consider as we discussed in the previous chapter, with patents being one of those 12 lines. The only reason you would ever want to use your patent line of competition, or any other line of competition for that matter, directly against the same line of the competition is if you have an overwhelming advantage in that line of competition or truly have no other choice. In patents, overwhelming advantage would be any or all of the strength of a given patent, the sheer volume of good-enough patents, and the quality of the people behind the competitive effort. Otherwise, you want to leverage an advantage that you have elsewhere to support the patent position. Your decisions are rarely singular. In almost any case, your selection of parallel lines of competition will involve several parallel lines of competition working in tandem with each other.

Charles Ferguson, the founder of Vermeer Technologies, which created the Web browser product acquired by Microsoft and named Microsoft Frontpage®, recognized the importance of patents early on in the development of his company when he considered how to succeed in a Web browser market where Microsoft and Netscape had overwhelming marketing and innovation advantages. After searching the Lotus Notes® patent database available at the time in the mid-1990s, he noted that Microsoft, Netscape, and other companies of concern had not and were not establishing patent positions in browser-oriented technologies. In review with his attorneys, Ferguson learned that Vermeer's own technology in the area was patentable. Ferguson recognized that this absence of competitive patents could present Vermeer with an important advantage if he had patents and the other competitors did not.[61] This is an example of an asymmetrical advantage, although Ferguson did not use that term.

During the development of Ferguson's company, and to further justify his decision to focus on patents, Microsoft faced the patent infringement lawsuit from the Stac software company. Stac would win a $110 million patent infringement judgment against Microsoft and an equity investment by the same. This event helped Ferguson to leverage his own patent position and Microsoft's newfound respect for patents to make his $133 million sale of Vermeer Technologies to Microsoft. He succeeded at a time when Microsoft had more potential innovative and marketing power to bring to bear than Vermeer could possibly have matched on its own.[62]

The 12 parallel lines of competition are rewritten here for your convenience. Depending on the specifics of your environment, you may be able to add more lines, subdivide others, or take some away. The important thing is to identify and use parallel lines of competition as they exist and work in your industry and internal culture.

1. *Leadership.* The competition for initiative and access to initiative
2. *Human resources.* The competition for talent and access to talent
3. *Branding.* The competition for identity and access to identity
4. *Patents.* The competition for inventions and access to inventions
5. *Sales.* The competition for customers and access to customers
6. *Marketing.* The competition for markets and access to markets
7. *Finance.* The competition for capital and access to capital
8. *Research.* The competition for ideas and access to ideas
9. *Development.* The competition for innovation and access to innovation
10. *Supply.* The competition for materials and access to materials
11. *Logistics.* The competition for distribution and access to distribution
12. *Manufacturing.* The competition for production and access to production

As someone involved with patent strategy, you want to look at each line of competition as it relates to given competitors, and then, to the extent possible, focus your competitive strategic actions on those lines of competition where you are strong and your competitors are comparatively weak. Add or subdivide lines of competition if it makes sense for your organization, industry, and the situation. Then pay close attention to one other important subtlety about how parallel lines of competition actually work much of the time.

In our previous illustration, Microsoft and Netscape had strong market positions but poor patent positions, which Vermeer Technologies was able to exploit. It was a clear case of using strength against weakness. In many if not most cases, a situation will present a less clear strength-and-weakness profile. You will need to go a little further to understand why a condition of strength or weakness exists to fully appreciate it as a strength or weakness and, because conditions can change, decide which signals (actions your competitors can observe) you need to manage to optimize those conditions.

Physical conditions of strength and weakness in business often have an underlying psychological root. So when examining the parallel lines of competition, examine the psychological conditions under which they exist as well as the physical. Part of what gave Ferguson at Vermeer an opportunity to leverage patents was the prevailing opinion by most other industry players that patents had minimal importance in the software industry.[63] So while Vermeer applied for its patents on Web browser software, it did not advertise its decision to patent until those patents became important for negotiations. Otherwise, its competitors might have responded to shore up their weaknesses in the patent area. This is an example of signals management, which means to manage what people outside and in some cases inside your organization see. Sometimes you need to be stealthy.

Under Armour®, a rising star in the sports apparel industry, which we previously showed had succeeded as a start-up without patents, established a brand position right under the nose of brand powerhouses such as Nike, Adidas, and Reebok. It gained a first-mover advantage by introducing a new product class of compression fabric sports shirts that the major brands did not offer. This invention, a product of Under Armour®'s research and development lines of competition, provides its wearers in intense sports activities with a fabric that absorbs sweat instead of containing it in a soggy T-shirt. Coupled with this, Under Armour® created a clever brand name for itself. On paper, Under Armour® lacked superior strength in branding, research, or development compared to the major sports apparel brands, as well as no patents. Any of the major brands could have produced compression fabric sports shirts that absorbed sweat, along with the added advantage that the major brand logos and names themselves already had worldwide recognition that Under Armour® did not have. Strength, however, does not matter if its holder, for whatever reason, does not respond to an opportunity or threat. So what happened?

Under Armour® succeeded because the major brands did not act on the signals that Under Armour® provided them once its products entered the marketplace. Under Armour® became, by luck or design, stealthy. Stealth, caused by astute signals management, inattention on the part of the opponent, or both, can make up for otherwise significant weaknesses and magnify strengths as well, through the previously discussed advantage of surprise. So any time you make a decision, you want to consider how you will manage who sees the results of your decision and when. You can often, for example, obtain a base of new customers without overtly signaling to the market your grander intent, such as Under Armour® did when it first signed a handful of football teams to establish its marketing base. On patents, you need to consider the message you send by what you patent and where, along with any related materials you disclose, such as published research papers. Always think about what you are telling your competitors as well as your friends.

In the case of Under Armour®, by the time the major brands responded with competitive garments and fabrics of their own, the Under Armour® brand was strong enough to stand on its own. The company could also afford to start building a patent portfolio. This last can perhaps compensate for the diminishing power of its first-mover advantage, because Under Armour® now has the attention of the major brands.

Parallel Lines of Competition for Watchmakers

The Swiss watch companies provide an additional illustration of company dispositions in the parallel lines of competition. They compete as a part of an industry that had gone through tough times when challenged by digital watches. They survived by repositioning their technology as an element of style as well as a timepiece. Faced with competition from established Swiss watchmakers for high-end watches, a hypothetical new competitor interested in entering the high-end watch market would have a number of considerations to address. As a strategist for that hypothetical competitor, consider the following:

1. *Leadership.* Talented people need leadership to get the most out of their skills. As the hypothetical new competitor, how

does your leadership compare with that of the competition? Does your leadership have the drive and experience necessary to succeed? Which leadership has a greater stake in the success of its operation? Who has strong and who has weak leadership?

2. *Human resources.* There is competition for a limited number of skilled watchmakers worldwide. How does your company attract and develop skilled employees who may already be employed by the Swiss watchmakers? How does your company retain skilled employees? How are other Swiss watchmakers attracting and retaining employees? Who is strong and who is weak in this line of competition?

3. *Patents.* The Swiss watchmakers do patent new inventions along with refining the actual know-how craftsmanship of the watchmaking trade. It is perhaps not their most important line of competition in most instances, but it is a factor. The Swiss watch companies typically have a few dozen to a few hundred patents in their patent portfolio. How does your patent portfolio match up to the patent portfolios of other Swiss watchmakers? Can you leverage a patent position in an important area? Who is strong and who is weak in this line?

4. *Branding.* Branding, on the other hand, is a critical line of competition for Swiss watchmakers considering that "Swiss watch" itself is effectively a brand that works in conjunction with the brand name of the individual watches themselves. The Swiss watchmaking trade has many famous brands that all carry somewhat different meanings to prospective watch buyers. Rolex is best known for its overall high prestige, Omega is prestigious for ocean-oriented activities, and Breitling is prestigious for aeronautically orientated activities. What is your brand image? What brand image might you create? Who is strong and who is weak in this line of competition?

(Continued)

5. *Sales.* Nothing happens to advance a business until somebody sells something. Who are the people directly responsible for selling the product to customers and distributors? How active or passive is the process? Who are the buyers and how loyal are they? What type of existing contracts might you need to overcome? Is there a sales approach you could use that others are not using? Who is strong and who is weak in the sales arena?

6. *Marketing.* Marketing is a broader line of competition inclusive of sales and branding that encompasses how Swiss watchmakers actually sell their products. As a broader set of branding, how do you fit into the overall market? What is your niche positioning? Which segments are open, and which contested? How strong are your marketing abilities? Who is strong and who is weak in this line of competition?

7. *Finance.* Every business needs money to operate. How is your company financed? Many Swiss watchmakers have privately oriented finance. How can this be considered a strength or weakness, and should you use the same or a different approach? Who has a large cash reserve and who does not?

8. *Supply.* There is competition for expensive metals and jewels in the watch industry and from organizations outside the watch industry. How do you manage your supply chain in light of this competition? How do other Swiss watchmakers manage their supply chain? Who is weak and who is strong in this line of competition?

9. *Research.* Swiss watchmaking is a mix of centuries-old craftsmanship and cutting-edge mechanical and materials sciences. Who has the strongest research efforts and on what are they focusing? How might watches be meaningfully improved physically and psychologically, and who is pushing in that direction? Are there any avenues relatively unexplored? Who is strong and who is weak in the research area? An analysis of competitive patents may help to answer some of these questions.

10. *Development.* Innovation within Swiss watchmakers is ongoing, and there are challenges from digital watchmakers, more traditionally styled watches from Japanese brands such as Seiko and Citizen, the American brand Timex, cell phone clocks, and more. How innovative is your organization and how do you compare to others? Who is or has been the strongest, and who is or has been the weakest at innovation?

11. *Logistics.* The Swiss watch market is global. How are Swiss watches distributed, and can you get into the network? The ability to find quality distribution is often more difficult than selling to actual customers once you have that distribution. Who has comparable strengths and weaknesses in distribution and where?

12. *Manufacturing.* Swiss watches are made in factories. Where are your production facilities and how do they compare with those of competitors? How might they have an advantage? Who has the stronger or weaker manufacturing position?

So if you were the hypothetical new watchmaker entrant, you may look at these lines of competition and see that access to skilled craftsmen constrains the Swiss watchmakers even as it may constrain you. The Swiss watch industry has patents, but the total numbers are fairly low and so could be investigated in some detail; however, Japanese and United States–based competitors do have a more significant body of patents that you would need to include in an analysis. If you can create and patent unique ways to produce the same or better watches as those from Switzerland, perhaps by using a unique micro-automated manufacturing technique that reduced or eliminated the need for craftsmen, you could technically have a way to enter the market using the patent line of competition as a foundation. Those patents might also be the basis for attracting investment that you will need to succeed against your well-funded competitors. But then you consider branding.

(Continued)

All Swiss watchmakers have had, for over a century, a collective interest in fending off rival watchmakers that are not Swiss based and, as noted, support two brands: one, that they are individually a Rolex, Omega, Breitling or other watch type, and two, that they are genuine Swiss watches.[64,65] Furthermore, the tight relationships and cooperation that exists in the present Swiss watch industry may make it difficult for a newcomer to enter and set up shop in Switzerland; and watches made in, say, Cleveland, Ohio, with no history in watchmaking, would not carry much market appeal. That branding power could prove strong enough to make your patents fundamentally meaningless.

The strategy operator, "Raise an Icon from the Past," the Seven of Hearts from the *Art of War: Sun Tzu Strategy Card Deck*, could open a hypothetical solution to that branding line of competition, now made credible by your patents. If it was possible, for example, to gain access to market your watches under the Elgin Watch name, you could own a credible brand. Elgin is still known for watches that have high appeal with collectors. Under that Elgin banner, you could also set up shop in Illinois instead of Switzerland. With the overwhelming power of the Swiss marketing appeal perhaps put in check with an appealing brand of your own, you might now have a position where your patents in micro-automated manufacturing can create a decisive advantage and you could find a place in the high-end watch market.

A Final Word on Asymmetry for Planning

As we have seen, in the absence of an overwhelming advantage, using a resource against a like resource is an inefficient and expensive way to compete. In the absence of an overwhelming advantage, you should endeavor to use resources against unlike resources and make your plans accordingly. This is the bottom line on reviewing parallel lines of competition for patent strategy. A patent means little unless the owner has a viable avenue to exploit it, enforce it, and defend it, and that very much depends on the other lines of competition with which it is associated.

Launching and litigating a patent lawsuit more often than not involves the commitment of millions of dollars to the effort. Such a commitment, while necessary sometimes and while a reason to have solid patents to better the chance of winning in such an event, is also the antithesis of doing nothing yet leaving nothing undone. So you should prefer, therefore, to find an "unfair" advantage along another line of competition and exploit it whenever possible to reach your goals. Unless your infringement case is overwhelmingly strong, or your patent position overwhelmingly powerful from some other standpoint, you can often find a more efficient way to develop a strategy outside the domain of patents. Perhaps, for example, you can hire the best and brightest engineers in the contested technical discipline and know that over time they will simply out-innovate the competitor into the next generation of products while leaving that competitor behind. If patents are your "paper," look for the competitive equivalent of "scissors" to defeat those patents.

Fear and Benefit

Nicolo Machiavelli, the author of the famous 16th-century political text, *The Prince*, noted that fear is a greater driver of action than the prospect for gain. While you want to drive interaction and positive relationships, you never want to do so by being a pushover. You will spend much less in the way of resources defending yourself when people fear the consequences of doing "evil" to you above any prospect for gain. Think about how the best parents raise their kids, and carry the idea over to patent relationships. Good parents are highly interactive and positive, and yet at the same time serious about discipline. They are highly interactive, positive, and fair; yet at the same time the kids know there will be severe consequences if they step out of line. Therefore, most of the time they do not. You can also develop this dynamic for patents: being fair, open, and interactive on one hand, yet firm with those who attempt to take advantage of you on the other hand. When you are firm, people will be less likely to take advantage of you, meaning that you will not actually have to fight them, thus better emulating the idea that "the master does nothing, yet he leaves nothing undone."

Reciprocal Response

Following the "rock, paper, scissor" analogy, sometimes your "paper" will meet head to head with a competitor's "paper." Although asymmetric action is often the most efficient action, the capacity to respond in kind and win where feasible further creates the option to keep the peace. Being able to respond to a patent infringement allegation with your own potentially infringed patents opens the door to cross-licensing or may prevent a competitor from launching an infringement lawsuit in the first place. Building the capacity to do this can be a reason to seek a merger or acquisition to acquire patents that read on key patents in a competitor's portfolio.

Aggressive action by a competitor may stem from the perception that something of value that belongs to you is open for the taking, and strategic deterrents can convince people that it may not be so easy to take that something of value after all. You may even choose to pursue a perceived wrong by a competitor in excess of the value actually put into jeopardy in order to warn other would-be transgressors that you are serious about your threats. In the *Art of War: Sun Tzu Strategy Card Deck*, this is called "Make an Example Out of Another," and appears on the Four of Spades card. Precedents for action make threats believable.

To protect the integrity of a patent, it should have the capacity to stand up to similar patents. They exist in the same competitive universe and will run into each other. You may want to move a patent-oriented competition toward innovation or human resources competition, but you may at some point be called to the table by a competitor in the patent area. A well-written patent, integrated with other sources of organizational power, will prove essential.

Patent Quality

Regardless of the situation, and the direction chosen as a result, it pays in patent strategy to have high-quality patents. "High-quality" pertains to the quality of the invention as well as the patent document itself. You need to create a reasonable expectation that any patent you use to enforce exclusivity will stand up to scrutiny in court, and that a patent fully covers the inventive concepts you wish to protect within its claims. Again, even though we have seen that the most efficient way to deal with competitive patents is often through means other than patents, your patents may be called to task on review; the stronger the patents, the stronger your company's position during negotiations or trial.

One way to test the strength of a patent is through a concept known as "Red Teaming." Red Teaming patents means that you try on your own to find weaknesses in an invention and its associated patent claims and documentation before applying for the patent to avoid permitting competitors to design around the invention or invalidate the patent later. The term "Red Teaming" is taken from the military practice of having a portion of its force during war games play the role of the enemy (the "Red Team") in exercises against friendly forces (the "Blue Team"). You test your position and capabilities yourself with a Red Team instead of waiting for competitors to test them for you so that you can make adjustments to discovered weaknesses in advance of a real challenge. Red Teaming provides you with an opportunity to resolve shortcomings in your patent documentation before they cause real-world failures. For example, if your Red Team creates alternative or substitute solutions to your inventions, you can draft patent applications on those creations or publish invention disclosures so that represented competitors cannot establish their own proprietary positions.

To conduct a Red Team exercise, challenge selected people inside your organization to design around the invention of concern or to invalidate the prepared patent documentation. Consider expanding this activity further to perhaps challenge the business model you intend to use to advance inventions into the marketplace. You may find that one, the other, or both the patent documentation and the business model may be improved to be more mutually supportive.

Depending on the abilities and availability of your staff, you can expand your pool of Red Teamers to include the services of an outside search firm that specializes in invalidation, outside engineers who specialize in deconstructing inventions, and should you expand the scope further, business people associated with advancing patented inventions into the marketplace. Some organizations, for example, may task an outside design firm to reverse-engineer a prototype product and develop objective work-arounds outside of the influence of the parent corporation. If any of these efforts initiated by you succeed, your competitors will most likely succeed also. Modify your plans, the invention, and the patent documents accordingly. Include the design–around concepts in the claims and specification of the patent document or in additional patent documentation or technical disclosures. Determine with the advice of patent counsel the truly novel aspect of your inventions and draft your claims to cover it. Doing your homework upfront will not only create a stronger patent in the end; it will also save on prosecution costs and delays in getting the patent approved by the Patent and Trademark Office. As a side benefit, your Red Team will gain additional skills in challenging patents that you can then apply to troublesome patent positions belonging to competitors.

Since patents are an ongoing legal concern, you will want to control the flow of information during Red Team exercises. Work only with external organizations, whether conducting invalidity searches or reverse engineering, that understand how to handle sensitive material. Red Teaming in the military is considered highly confidential, and Red Teaming activities in business should be treated the same way. You also need to account for discovery issues, and discovery alone may cause resistance to performing a Red Team exercise on a new invention and its patent documentation. The argument for doing a Red Team exercise despite this drawback is simple. If you can design around your inventions or successfully challenge the validity of your patents, then so can your competitors. The capacity of other organizations to design around and invalidate patents is getting better, not worse, as techniques for inventing on demand improve and more and more information becomes increasingly accessible in public sources. Aside from your wanting better patents, you also want to develop your skills in this area of invalidation and designing around that Red Teaming can build.

Drafting a Strong Patent

This book is not about drafting patents themselves; however, we can examine one technique to help the patent become more useful for patent strategy. It follows a mathematically proven concept that you cannot describe a system in context with itself, as put forward by Kurt Gödel's incompleteness theorem in 1931.[66] Strong patents account for other aspects of the system of which a patented invention is a part.

Well-written patents with full, rich disclosures and mutually supporting broad, intermediate, and narrow claims better support future strategic options.

To draft the strongest patent possible, consider the invention described by the patent as only one element within a hierarchy of systems, and then include within your patent both the higher and lower systems. It is difficult to effectively describe a patented invention only in context with itself. That would be equivalent to attempting to explain the written word without putting the written word into context with the letters that make up the written word and the sentences that use written words. So we have a hierarchy of systems that is useful when preparing patent documentation. Include the following in the patent:

1. Describe the system of which the invention is a part (super-system).
2. Break the invention down and describe its sub-systems.
3. Put the description of the invention itself in context with the systems in items 1 and 2.

As an exercise, write a patent for the invention called the written word. See and compare what you and your colleagues come up with. In fact, this exercise could be used when interviewing to hire new patent attorneys. Examine the approaches they use for the effort, given that they will likely be the same underlying approaches they will use when working for you.

Position Survivability

There is a saying in classical strategy that over time, not losing can create the same results as winning. The *Art of War: Sun Tzu Strategy Card Deck* defines the Two of Clubs, "Prolong the Fight," in this way. The following guidelines provide steps to take to make a patent position survivable so that first, you do not lose, and second, you retain the potential to win. A high quality patent or group of patents provides a greater margin of error should those executing the patent strategy violate one of these guidelines, but generally speaking, you will improve your chances for success if you do not violate any of them. Included here are the general concepts for singular patent positions and additional considerations to use when you have hundreds or thousands of patents to manage.

Guidelines for Patent Position Survivability

1. *Address a threat before it becomes a problem.* Identify the threat and eliminate, isolate, interact with, or negate that threat (the four key effects) through the use of competitive strategy.

   Commentary: Proficiently eliminate, isolate, interact with, or negate a threat in accord with the circumstances, and it will not become a problem.

   Macro considerations: When a patent portfolio becomes large, it can become exceedingly difficult to address individual threats based on the sheer number of those threats. In such a situation, you can consider using the strategic operator "Let the Tiger Find No Place to Sink Its Claws" as a guiding principle. This strategic operator means to make the hostile intents of your adversary irrelevant. You can accomplish this most effectively by creating partnerships that people will not want to risk damaging with a patent infringement lawsuit. You can further enhance your position if you create a reputation for responding aggressively to patent infringement lawsuits or patent infringement on your own products that do occur. You want to create the conditions where you avoid providing a worthwhile opportunity for your opponent to take advantage of a misstep. Your intent is to cause people to prefer not to tangle with you in patent-related matters in the first place, even if you do provide such an opportunity for them. You accomplish this by making yourself a poor target or non-target from the perspective of your potential opponent and threat to the extent that you can.

2. *Minimize exposure.* Take steps to reduce vulnerabilities, such as accidental or intentional infringements, that leave the organization open to damage.

   Commentary: The greater the exposure to a threat, the higher the odds that the threat will harm the organization.

   Macro considerations: As the number of applied inventions in your portfolio increases, the probability that you will infringe on patent claims belonging to other people or organizations also increases, and to check every infringement possibility could actually cost more in delayed or deferred action than the value of the infringements avoided. So while you should generally take steps to minimize your exposure to patent infringement on a micro scale through a reasonable prior art search plan, you can also minimize your exposure on a macro scale by maximizing the exposure of your competitors to potential counteraction. Your own portfolio of patents can provide your base for counteraction as well as any positive interaction you may have with the potential opponent that the potential opponent will wish to preserve. Any value that your potential opponent may lose in a confrontation with you will tend to diminish that opponent's desire to attack or infringe on one of your vulnerabilities. By supporting all of these principles, your own policing efforts can reinforce the credibility of your threat as an organization able and willing to assert its own patents.

3. *Do not become distracted.* Appreciate vulnerabilities that leave your organization exposed, and continually monitor competitive actions intended to exploit those vulnerabilities. In the patent field, this typically involves, at a minimum, a review of new inventions, patents, products, and research papers that appear in the field and an assessment of how they will impact your plans.

Commentary: Lapses of attention expose the organization to threats from which it could otherwise protect itself.

Macro considerations: By attempting to protect everything, you can effectively end up protecting nothing. Patent portfolios can simply become too large and too complex to address every possible vulnerability. To deal with this, it is important to first identify those elements of your own patent portfolio that are more critical than others so that they can receive special and individual attention. Second, as per the previous statements, you want to create the conditions to the extent reasonably possible whereby your potential opponents view that taking advantage of a distraction on your part is not worth the risk to them.

4. *Know what the threat is and will be.* Understand specific threats, present and future, on each line and angle of competition. Appreciate who you are "evil" to from their perspective so you understand who might attack your position and why. Study who might have reason to change an established equilibrium and how they might do so.

Commentary: Addressing a threat requires its recognition as a threat. This holds true for both active and passive defenses.

Macro considerations: Certainly you will pay attention to the major and recognized threats to your present and future core business. You also want to know what else could happen to you that is important but less immediately apparent. You can accomplish this by using a Red Team exercise whereby your own people become your competitors and attempt to poke holes in your strategy and patent positions. Based on the identification of what could happen, you can then focus on who might make the "could" into a reality and take appropriate action. To do this effectively, your Red Team must go beyond just playing the potential opposition; it needs to psychologically become the opposition (your competitor) for the period of the exercise.

5. *Build a network of patents and other defenses that has ample size and connectivity; do not become isolated.* Set up a portfolio of patents on related topics, such as the other key elements of a technical system—engine, transmission, working body, instrument of control, inputs, and outputs—and link patents to other aspects of the organization's power, such as brand, people, market position, and the patents and power of associated organizations. The progression of links and parallel lines of competition discussed in this chapter provide guidelines for building this network.

Commentary: Your competitors may otherwise seek to isolate your position if it has value to them, since this is a natural step in defeating your position.

Macro considerations: It is important to remember that all the intellectual property in the world is potentially a source of intellectual property to advance your business. As you build beneficial links to foster interaction and reduce isolation, remember that many of the links that can keep you from becoming isolated will be with organizations outside the home organization. For example, a brand that walks behind your patents to make you patents stronger could actually belong to another organization that licensed your patents. Generally speaking, increased interactivity is better than less interactivity, provided you are driving the interactivity and getting more benefit out of each link than it costs.

6. *Avoid infringement.* This means preferably not to infringe. The first step toward accomplishing this is to learn about prior inventions

through patent and literature searches and through a reasonable study of competitive products. This recommendation can, however, run into an anomaly of the intellectual property legal system in the United States that suggests that in certain circumstances it may make sense not to look at prior art in order to avoid the treble damages risk of willful infringement. Because understanding a situation is the first key in classical strategy to crafting an effective strategy, any decision not to review prior art should therefore be made with deliberation and with an appreciation of its potential risks and benefits. Patent pools, patent commons, and licenses provide other tools to avoid infringement, or at least its more onerous consequences. So does being a leader at technology's cutting edge where you can invent a cycle ahead of your competitors into areas where people have not yet been.

Commentary: The best defense against patent infringement is not to infringe. This is in keeping with the guiding principle to "Let the Tiger Find No Place to Sink Its Claws," discussed in guideline number 1.

Macro considerations: As your portfolio of inventions and patents increases, your risk of patent infringement tends to increase. So in tandem with avoiding infringement, you should consider ways to mitigate infringement risks if infringement occurs. This means that you should have at your disposal the means to defend yourself and the means to design around or invalidate potentially threatening patents if that is possible and makes sense. As stated previously, it can also mean building valuable relationships through cross-licenses or business partnerships, or perhaps turning potential opponents into customers. It can also mean showing that you are a less than desirable organization to target for patent assertion because of your propensity to fight back. More than one major organization the author has met with, based on the track record for infringement in its own experiences, budgets in advance the expected money needed to address inevitable infringement challenges that, considering the size of its research and development operations and the interlinked nature of products, is all but unavoidable. This latter idea is more common when the dominant strategy among competitors is to stockpile patents (typical of high-tech industries) because of the sheer volume of patents that might require analysis for each given product to clear it of infringement risk.

7. *Have a way out.* Have a contingency plan in case a patent infringement or other harmful incident occurs. Contingency plans include alternative technical solutions, value to trade, preestablished cross-licensing terms, or a business position that can absorb the cost of enforced royalty payments, infringement settlements, or invalidity rulings.

   Commentary: Alternatives provide a measure of power and recourse even in difficult situations.

   Macro considerations: You should have resources, such as money and alternative plans of action, to address any level of accepted risk such that a loss associated with a patent infringement dispute, even if improbable, does not become a catastrophic, "game over" event. If you cannot do this, you need to accept the "game over" risk and be prepared for how you will accept that possibility as your final way out.

8. *Do not force an action.* Do not take the expedient solution regarding an opportunity or threat without due consideration of its consequences or your alternative possibilities. Do not seek to obtain a desired outcome that has become improbable because you refuse to accept that improbability.

   Commentary: Forced actions cause unnecessary exposure because they are often based on emotion rather than logic and therefore may not take full account of the real risks. Emotional decisions do poorly against logical decisions when comparing the odds for success.

   Macro considerations: Remember that everything you do has consequences throughout the entire organization. So while it may make sense, for example, to settle a case from the perspective of one of your divisions, it may make no sense if that settlement would materially damage the credibility that your organization as a whole will defend itself in the patent space. Conversely, a fight, even if you know you would win and especially if the evidence shows you will lose, may not be worth the cost in time and the damaged relationships that could result. Therefore, any action you take should make sense for the good of the whole organization ahead of whether it makes sense for the specific position or state of mind of those people responsible.

9. *Avoid occupying the same place where another has run into a problem.* If another organization runs into difficulty on similar ground to that of an existing position that your own organization holds, expect the same difficulties to occur, and either change your position or improve your position to better address the threat.

Commentary: If a threat continues to exist, a place where that threat has already manifested will likely deliver more problems. For example, if a company successfully enforces a patent against one competitor in an area, others in that area can expect to hear from that enforcing company. If your ends can be achieved by avoiding such problematic space or you can otherwise change the conditions that cause the threat (e.g., by seeking a license in advance) you will tend to improve your chances for success overall. Otherwise, it may be prudent to enhance your defenses of the position.

Macro consideration: You will need to operate in contested space if you hope to succeed in patent strategy because any technical space of value tends to draw competitors. Therefore, it is almost impossible, as your patent portfolio grows, not to occupy "dangerous ground." The key to addressing this with large patent portfolios is to ensure that you have an ample network of patents and other sources of power such that you could lose a patent position and still succeed as an organization. Where a single patent position becomes highly critical to the business, you can concentrate your resources on its defense. In tandem to that, you can build your deterrents by improving your capacity to fight back.

Murphy's Military Law of Security
When you have secured the area, make sure the enemy knows it too
Since we are talking about strategy, military analogies can be useful from time to time, appreciating that business strategy tends to be more complex because of the multiple number of parties involved and the greatly increased forms of possible interaction.

(Continued)

One useful military analogy, however, is Murphy's Military Law of Security: "When you have secured the area, make sure the enemy knows it too."[67] When reading Murphy's Military Law of Security, consider that even with as strong a patent position as you can create, the lesson behind the law can still apply to your patent position. Your competitor, just as the enemy in the quote above, has a deciding vote in determining how well you have actually secured a patent position.

The capacity of competitors to design around patent claims, invalidate patents in whole or part, challenge patents on obviousness, or otherwise find a means to defeat patents is increasing. You should, therefore, be reluctant to rely solely on the strength of a patent position. You should prepare countermeasures to scenarios in which the patent or patents do not stand up in court and in which engineers from other organizations succeed at designing around your patent claims. These potential actions of your competitors provide another reason to explore how to emulate the ideal patent to make a patent position more secure. If you can still succeed without a patent, your patent becomes a bonus to the strength of your organization, instead of a crutch that would lead to defeat if it does not prove to be as secure as you had hoped.

Secure Today, Insecure Tomorrow

A recent ruling by the U.S. Supreme Court on *KSR International Co. v. Teleflex, Inc.* threatened all existing patent holders with new litigation over obviousness, because it lowered the threshold for proving the obviousness of an invention. Teleflex filed and held its patent under the former standard for finding obviousness used by the U.S. Court of Appeals for the Federal Circuit. The Court, in its ruling against Teleflex, effectively relaxed the standard. The ruling gave judges greater latitude to use their own opinions and common sense above objective evidence or testimony and set a tone that the patent that held up in court yesterday might not hold up tomorrow.[68]

KSR v. Teleflex brings into issue what a person of reasonable skill in the art might consider obvious when determining patent validity. This assessment, which focuses on combinations of technology, could actually go further if it took into account the obvious combination of ideas. When this author showed theory of inventive problem solving (TRIZ) charts to the chief counsel at a multibillion-dollar high tech company, the initial reaction of the chief counsel was that if all patents are composed of one or a combination of 40 inventive principles, then nothing would be patentable. This gut reaction is not true, given further reflection. Novel, useful, and unobvious inventions that use common inventive principles are still patentable. However, there is certainly a list of ideas developed in TRIZ and other like sciences that one could consider obvious. For example, someone could argue that it should never be patentable to add wheels to anything you wish to move without carrying, since that is a known and obvious idea. Adding wheels in such circumstances could be put into a universal checklist of ideas known to be obvious, and improving an invention by making it round or adding spheres (wheels) is one of the TRIZ inventive principles. TRIZ offers a way to invent on demand instead of depending on inspiration or any other less systematic approach. TRIZ, computer assisted design, and automatic screening of pharmaceutical compounds are all examples of tools whereby creative and experimental activities can be systematized and possibly challenged on obviousness. It is very possible in the not-too-distant future that computers themselves may create important inventions on their own as they encounter, assess, and solve their own problems.

For a patent strategist, the main point to draw from this is that a secure position today may not be a secure position tomorrow as the professions and laws associated with patents change. Even if written laws themselves do not change, changes in the interpretation of the law could make a secure position today insecure tomorrow.

Doctrine of Equivalents

The competitive angles discussed earlier in this book included a competitor that we called the "alternative use" competitor. From a marketing standpoint, this describes a competitor that could make its presence known in a doctrine-of-equivalents challenge. The doctrine of equivalents comes into play when a technology performs essentially the same function in the same way as a prior technology with the same underlying result, even though it may not provide that benefit to the exact same industry or system as described by the prior patent document. For example, if you could patent the headlight for a car, could someone then turn around and patent a headlight for a motorcycle even if you did not specifically claim motorcycles in your patent?

From the court records of *Royal Typewriter Co. v. Remington Rand*, the doctrine of equivalents is intended to "temper unsparing logic and prevent an infringer from stealing the benefit of the invention." It is important, therefore, that the patent practitioner understand how people outside their normal scope of focus use related technologies so that they may be addressed as creators of prior art in advance of a contest. Also, for those defending against a doctrine-of-equivalents challenge and in danger of losing freedom to operate, knowledge of inventive theories such as TRIZ can provide a means to argue that a convergence of functions and methods that provide fundamentally the same benefit but in disparate industries are from solutions obvious enough that no party should have a patent, in order to maintain that freedom of operation.

The Dominant Patent Strategy

The backlog of patent applications at the United States Patent and Trademark Office (USPTO), along with a perceived decline in the quality of patents granted by the USPTO, has led, through the 2000s, to calls for patent law reforms. The intent of these reforms is to raise the tempo and proficiency by which the USPTO can grant patents for inventions that truly meet the patentability requirements used by patent examiners to assesses the merit of a patent application. The success or failure of these reforms has a global impact following from the importance of the USPTO to world intellectual property protection, and to a greater or lesser extent, its efforts at reforms are paralleled by reforms and improvements in patent authorities outside the United States.

One of the reasons that patent law reform is difficult to achieve is the existence of two different dominant patent strategies in industry, each of which suggests the need for different and possibly conflicting refinements. One of these, patent stockpiling, is most strongly realized in the high-technology industries where systems interconnectivity is especially important, where there are typically many patents associated with each product, and where the research and development cost per patent filed is comparatively low. This dominant strategy is further driven by the fact that many products involve patents from several different organizations, which can lead to multiple points of contention when those organizations are competitive. For example, the MPEG-2 standard for digital video compression contains inventions claimed in an estimated 1,000 patents belonging to 22 companies.[69]

Patent thickets, as they are sometimes called, can arise from complex technologies such as MPEG-2 when many disparate organizations hold patents related to one overall solution. In the absence of suitable agreements between these organizations, many of which may be direct competitors, these patent thickets can be tricky to navigate. Patent researchers may need to review thousands of patents and patent applications, as well as associated nonpatent literature, to comprehensively identify the inventions within a patent thicket that may be an infringement threat to their own efforts. This can make innovating without infringing on someone else's patent claims difficult to practically impossible.

To deal with patent thickets, companies have made efforts to create cross-licensing arrangements, patent pools, patent commons, industry and standard licensing conventions, and to set technology standards. These efforts to address patent thickets generally improve for a company involved in the process when it has an ample body of valuable patents related to the technology in question. That body of patents offers leverage in setting up the most suitable cooperative arrangements for that company with entities that will want access to those valuable patents.

When dealing with patent thickets, gaining and maintaining freedom to operate in a given technology field often takes precedence as an end result over gaining the value of the right to exclude others from making, using, or selling the many potentially enforceable patent claims found within a large patent portfolio. A freedom-to-operate focus develops due to the presence of multiple potential rights to exclude among the multiple different parties that hold patents within a given technical system. The very presence of these multiple potential rights to exclude within the same given technology becomes the underlying driver of the invitation to the parties involved to participate in a joint and cooperative solution to a patent thicket issue, rather than to sue and countersue each other.

The other dominant strategy, that of seeking a blockbuster patent, is most strongly realized in the pharmaceutical industry, where technical systems tend to be more self-contained—that is, a Merck drug does not necessarily depend on an interface with a Pfizer drug to provide a solution to a patient. In the pharmaceutical industry, there is often a one-patent-to-one-product ratio, and the research and development cost per patent filed is comparatively high. This latter point on cost per patent is irrespective of the total research and development expenditure, which can be comparable to similar-sized high-tech or pharmaceutical companies. That pharmaceutical leader Pfizer obtains less than one U.S. patent for every 10 U.S. patents high-tech leader IBM obtains, for example, does not mean that the IBM research and development effort is 10 times greater than Pfizer's. It only reflects that the total research and development expenses in the pharmaceutical industry are typically divided among comparatively fewer patents and that in the blockbuster strategy, the pharmaceutical company seeks for one or a handful of those patents to produce a very high return on the investment made to own it.

A dominant strategy is defined as the best strategy to take, no matter what a competitor does. To illustrate, the dominant strategy for a sprinter in a 100-meter dash is to run as fast as possible from start to finish after hearing the sound of the starter gun. Although not every competition is as straightforward as a foot race, comparable dominant strategies can still develop even in complex environments. A dominant strategy for high-tech companies in general is to stockpile patents within their capacity to afford it, whereas a dominant strategy for pharmaceutical companies is to seek the blockbuster patent. Other industries, likewise, usually fall in one camp or the other. For example, mechanical inventions tend toward the strategy of patent stockpiling, and chemical inventions tend toward the blockbuster strategy, although the pressures that drive a dominant strategy may differ in strength between given industries. These dominant strategies are executed in accordance with the rules of the governments at hand, keeping in mind the precedents of government intervention, such as in 1956 when the U.S. government required IBM and AT&T to license their patent portfolios. The U.S. government viewed that IBM and AT&T had done too good a job of locking up key technologies within their patent portfolios and that to avoid a break-up of the companies, it required them to license their patent portfolios at reasonable terms to outside companies. Bottom line: You would aim to execute dominant strategies within the limits of affordability and the legally acceptable practices of business as they pertain to your own particular industry and situation.

Let's examine the stockpile and blockbuster strategies using the four rules of patent strategy introduced at the beginning of this book: use patents to isolate, threaten to use patents to isolate, use patents to interact, and leverage the possibility of interaction. In examining the four rules of patent strategy, you will see that a high-tech company with the means to do so will achieve its best results in all four rules by stockpiling a large quantity of relevant patents, and that a pharmaceutical company will achieve its best results in all four rules by selectively investing in a few key patents that have blockbuster potential, with its patent portfolio growing only to match the number of opportunities it can reasonably afford to pursue.

High-Tech Dominant Strategy: Stockpile Starting with the high-tech companies, the dominant strategy of patent stockpiling in relation to the four rules plays out as follows:

Rule 1: Use Patents to Isolate For assertions and counter-assertions, a large patent portfolio in high tech tends to provide more potential options than a small patent portfolio for patent enforcement actions that will isolate competitors. The more patents you have in a technical area, the greater the likelihood that you will have at least one patent in your portfolio to assert or counter-assert against a competitor. Pursuant to this, high-tech innovation generally moves quickly, often with many fast followers eager to copy or improve new and existing technology, particularly if it is both valuable and inadequately protected. High-tech fields also often allow for easier design around opportunities as inventive technologies develop and evolve when compared with pharmaceutical inventions. In cases where pharmaceutical design-around is comparatively as easy, high-tech fields do not need to undergo expensive and time-consuming clinical trials. So owning a larger number of patents in a relevant area burdens a competitor in that it will have more potential patent claims to avoid or defeat in order to proceed without infringing on those patent claims, or it will proceed without such evaluation and expose itself to patent infringement lawsuits.

Related to using patents to isolate is the converse, by which a patenting entity avoids being isolated by competitive patents. Because major innovative companies continually and inventively evolve their products, and because in most patent authorities outside the United States the first inventor to file for a patent receives the granted patent if it issues, avoiding isolation caused by competitive patenting activity frequently necessitates filing many patent applications sooner in the invention cycle rather than later. This can often mean that a patenting entity will file patent applications before it has had the time to evaluate the corresponding inventions' complete commercial potentials simply to prevent a competitor from obtaining a priority on that invention. But this effort is worthwhile on the whole. A high-tech company would not want to find itself barred from using its own technology because of another organization's granted patent; therefore, the tendency is to file patent applications as soon as reasonably possible. Bottom line: The more patents of relevance a high-tech company has within its patent portfolio, the easier it will likely be to isolate other competitors as well as to prevent its own isolation.

Rule 2: Threaten to Use Patents to Isolate All things being equal, the more patents a high-tech company has in its portfolio within a relevant technical area, the greater the likelihood that someone will infringe on one or more of those patents, and the more credible a threat to assert or counter-assert a patent position will be. If you have few patents as a high-tech company, your threat will have less credibility in aggregate, will be easier for competitors to study, and often will be easier to work around. Patent analyses help to explain why this is so. Many patent analyses that high-tech companies commission to explore patent-based opportunities and threats in the high-tech arena overwhelm patent practitioners simply because of the sheer volume of patents they must study to address a strategic issue, such as a patent assertion threat. It can easily take a full day to analyze the details of one patent, and several high-tech companies file more than six patent applications per day. This can be turned to an advantage when someone else investigates you.

With the issue of patent quantity in mind, indicating to a competitor that you believe it is infringing on any number of your patent claims can prove more threatening to that competitor than otherwise when you have a large number of patents in your portfolio that your competitor would need to analyze to assess that threat. A patent portfolio of ample size makes it hard for others to assess the full extent of your threat and therefore raises their uncertainty about the actual seriousness of your threat. You can take further advantage of this uncertainty by leveraging the psychological tendency in people to magnify the seriousness of a threat beyond what it really is.

On the counter-assertion side, having a large number of patents in your patent portfolio creates an implied threat that if a competitor should chose to assert a patent against you, you may respond with a battery of potential counter-assertions. This threat is made more credible by a having a large patent portfolio, because it raises the odds that you will have patents to use in the counter-assertion and because it is more difficult for that competitor to assess the counter-assertion threat of many patents versus few patents.

Rule 3: Use Patents to Interact Licensing and cross-licensing requires a company to have patents important to others to license or cross-license. Having more relevant patents within a patent portfolio leads to more possibilities to have important patents through which to create useful interactions with others. A large number of relevant patents also creates a pool from which to offer broader cross-licensing arrangements of major sections of a patent portfolio. Having fewer patents means having less potential technology to trade, which can correspond with a greater likelihood that you will have to pay royalties, if even given the opportunity to access another company's technology at all. Therefore, the culture within high-tech companies is to patent new inventions often and, if given more thought, to create tight networks of patents that competitors will find hard to design around or invalidate in whole. A company with many strong patents will typically be most interested in interacting with another organization that can bring comparable value to the negotiation table, or to any patent pools or cross-licensing arrangements. The more patents a high-tech company has in a relevant area, the more able it is to interact with others and to be an insider, not an outsider, to patent-based relationships that develop.

Rule 4: Leverage the Possibility of Interaction Having a large patent portfolio in a relevant high-tech area can serve as a draw to make other people and organizations want access to that portfolio. High-tech companies often study patent landscapes on new technologies. These landscapes reveal who the lead patent holders and who the predominant inventors are within the explored technology. The larger the patent portfolio in a relevant area, the greater the likelihood that it will spur useful interaction. If you have comparatively few patents in your patent portfolio on a technology of interest, on aggregate, you will have fewer reasons for other companies to want to work with you. The dynamic is the same as that which determines whether a person going shopping would prefer to shop in a department store with lots of products or a specialty store with just a few. In the high-tech world, all things being otherwise equal, the larger the patent portfolio, the more options it creates and the more attractive the company becomes.

Pharmaceutical Dominant Strategy: Seek the Blockbuster With pharmaceutical companies and the four patent rules, the dominant block-buster strategy plays out as follows:

Rule 1: Use Patents to Isolate The fortunes of a pharmaceutical company are often anchored on just a few patents since there is most often a one-to-one or a one-to-a-few ratio of patents to products. A pharmaceutical company can extend this ratio somewhat by patenting similar molecules to those used in the actual associated product as well as other aspects of diagnosis, treatment, delivery, manufacture, or fundamentally any patentable aspect of the drug from inception to use that could strengthen the overall patent position. Still, at its root, there is typically a central patent or handful of patents that comprise the core product. Should such a patent's validity be challenged or should a competitor infringe on that patent's claims, the owning company will more than likely respond to defend the validity and viability of its patent and its role as an enforcement and therefore isolating tool. The infringing competitor will rarely be able to respond with a counter-assertion of another patent in its own portfolio because pharmaceutical products typically work with a significant degree of independence (e.g., a Merck drug does not necessarily need a Pfizer drug to work, and so a benefit to stockpile patents for such a counter-assertion purpose does not exist). In the pharmaceutical environment, the value of a single patent can eclipse the value of hundreds of lesser patents, and patent quality and scope are the most important considerations. In addition, cross-licensing strategies common in high-tech industries do not play out in the pharmaceutical industry, because the presence of even one competitor selling the same pharmaceutical can drop the profit margin of that product severely.

Even in those cases where cross-licensing occurs in combination treatments of related but not directly competitive drugs, it is still fairly focused on a limited number of patents.

Rule 2: Threaten to Use Patents to Isolate In the pharmaceutical industry, the threat of isolation will be focused on specific pharmaceuticals, which unlike in high tech, does not generally depend on interfacing with other inventions. The threat to use a patent to isolate is typically based on a single patent or small handful of patents; while a single or few patents may also be at the crux of a high-tech threat, the viability of that threat in the pharmaceutical industry will remain relatively the same regardless of the number of patents you or the competitor have in the respective patent portfolios. The quality and scope of the central patent or patents will rule in this environment, and since counter-assertions rarely enter the equation, often a single strong patent is all that is needed to effectively threaten its use as an enforcement tool and achieve a competitor's isolation.

Rule 3: Use Patents to Interact Patent licenses play a major role in the pharmaceutical industry, but these are generally licenses for royalties or equity, not cross-licenses, as often is the case in the high-tech industry. If Hoffman-La Roche, for example, seeks a license from a small pharmaceutical start-up, Hoffman-La Roche's interest will focus on one or a handful of related patents from that pharmaceutical start-up. The size of the respective companies' patent portfolios will have little if any relevance other than to influence, perhaps, the importance of the given licensing transaction to each party. Those other patents held within a patent portfolio of a company that owns a valued patent would become more important primarily if a company seeking access to that valued patent also considered acquiring the entire company. Even in this instance, a few high-quality opportunities from a handful of valuable patents can outweigh any number of lesser opportunities, so patent stockpiling does not make sense.

Rule 4: Leverage the Possibility of Interaction Since patent interactions in the pharmaceutical industry are usually based on one or a few key patents, the quality and scope of those patents is the most important issue. Quantity of patents will have little, if any, relevance. The capacity of a small pharmaceutical start-up to negotiate a lucrative licensing arrangement by putting an exclusive license out to bid to several major pharmaceutical companies can be anchored on a single patent. So, while having several good opportunities may be preferable to having just one, patent stockpiling itself does not make sense. Having one or just a few valuable patents around those opportunities from which the company can defend against an encroachment is key, with the goal being to build one or more of them into blockbusters.

High-Tech vs. Pharmaceutical   To further understand the difference behind the dominant stockpiling strategy for high-tech companies versus the dominant strategy of seeking a blockbuster for pharmaceutical companies, it is useful to compare the dynamics in research and development between the two kinds of companies. High-tech companies typically file one to two patents per $1 million invested in research. Since the dominant strategy, for high-tech companies that can afford it, is to stockpile patents, the total number of patents filed each year will presumably grow. In contrast, pharmaceutical companies can expect to obtain one patent per high tens to hundreds of millions of dollars in research and development spending. This is usually attributed to the large amount of validation and safety testing surrounding pharmaceutical products.[70]

As noted, the foregoing figures do not indicate that high-tech companies spend less on research and development than pharmaceutical companies, since this is definitely not the case. Considering that a typical high-tech product can have many patents associated with it instead of one to a few patents for a pharmaceutical product, the ratio of research and development spending per product will often be less striking. In fact, because a given high-tech product may incorporate several patented inventions, it can cost more in patent office fees and patent prosecution attorney fees to actually gain comprehensive patent protection for a high-tech product at the conclusion of a research and development cycle than it does for a pharmaceutical product. Still, the comparatively lower cost of research and development per patent does lend itself more to a patent stockpiling strategy for high-tech companies than for pharmaceutical companies, and that makes the likelihood of patent stockpiling in high tech even higher.

As we have reviewed, however, to receive global patent protection on an invention, a company can expect to pay in the high tens of thousands of dollars to costs exceeding $100,000 per patent. So although a dominant strategy to stockpile patents exists in high tech, it needs, in practice, to be put into perspective at participating organizations with the actual resources available for patenting and the comparative resources of competitors. This perspective brings us back to the importance of using all aspects of a company's power within the patent strategy. Generally, the less able or willing a company is to match a competitor in a patent arms race, the more important its comparative advantages in other lines of competition become, and even when a company can afford to compete in a patent arms race, it will better leverage its efforts by linking them to other sources of its business power.

In contrast to the foregoing, although larger pharmaceutical companies do tend to have proportionally larger patent portfolios than smaller pharmaceutical companies, their dominant strategy does not involve stockpiling patents. It involves having enough opportunities with enough patents for it to have confidence in the likelihood of producing a blockbuster product. The dominant strategy is to selectively develop those inventions with the most promise to be blockbuster products with the understanding that just one or a few patents can make or break the profit performance of a given company for many years. For example, Merck had dozens of Angiotensin II Inhibitor patents in the early to mid-1990s, but only one of those became the basis for the drug Cozaar®. Whereas a high-technology company like Cisco Systems or Sun Microsystems might find value in an entire block of high-tech patents associated with a key patent that describes a new software product, compared with the compound described in the key Cozaar® patent, the value to Merck of the other related Angiotensin II Inhibitor patents was much less.

Although it is possible to have a high-tech patent or handful of patents that have claims so critical to a product or technology that it exhibits the blockbuster characteristics of a pharmaceutical patent, as might arguably be the case with five NPT patents used in the *NPT,*

Inc. v. RIM case that threatened the BlackBerry®, it is more often the aggregate of patents that go into a given product that delivers value. Anchoring on one or even a few patents to support an otherwise weak high-tech position can be problematic, because, as history has shown in all professions that include patent management, there is almost no such thing as an impregnable defense. Realistic defenses, patent strategy and otherwise, involve building a position that is strong enough to discourage an attack, and then interlocking those individual positions so that the entire defense does not depend on the continued integrity of just one position. Patented products in high tech typically work together in large systems, and the nature of those systems means that inventors can often design around or otherwise circumvent a single patent on its own. In contrast, though design-around in pharmaceuticals is also possible, the key elements of the solution are more singular in that a pharmaceutical will provide its benefit irrespective of the other products the company has; a molecular compound may have a great deal of specificity in order to work as intended, and a billion dollar plus product revenue stream can therefore be anchored with reasonable security on a single well-drafted patent. Even when a potential drug has more viable alternative variations and therefore a higher design-around risk, the considerable time and expense needed by competitors to conduct clinical trials on those variations can have the effect of helping to secure the existing position.

So high-tech patent power is in the aggregate whole of a body of patents, which further fuels the tendency to stockpile patents. High-tech companies that can afford to do so, therefore, stockpile patents. Pharmaceutical patent power is held in the blockbuster patents, so their dominant strategy is to develop and defend a few key patents. In both cases, this ultimate value of the exercise links to the exploitation of the patented product, which often has a short window of opportunity. Technology in the high-tech world evolves quickly, meaning that a patented technology can become obsolete long before the patent expires and sometimes before it even issues. For pharmaceutical companies, the Drug Price Competition and Patent Term Restoration Act of 1984, known as the Hatch-Waxman Act, has made it easier for generic drug makers to enter the market. It requires them only to show bioequivalence studies instead of much more involved clinical data on generic compounds. This has made rapid exploitation of patented products even more important for pharmaceutical companies, because a valuable patent needs to produce its return on investment (ROI) in a window of time that typically leaves no grace period after patent expiration before generic drugs appear in the market and profit margins decline.

As noted in the beginning of this section, while the high-tech industry and the pharmaceutical industry may be on the extremes of dominant patent strategies, other industries fall into one camp or the other with little middle ground. Biotech and chemical industries, for example, typically orient their strategies around the blockbuster model. Industrial engineering gravitates toward patent stockpiling. The key differentiator will be the degree to which a patented invention must interface with other inventions in the system to provide a benefit, how far on the cutting edge of science the technology is, what the ratio of patents to products is, and the relative cost of research and development per patent attained. This, in turn, affects how the patent portfolio is managed and used, with the capacity to use patents to interact having more weight when patent stockpiling is used, and the capacity to use patents to isolate having more weight with blockbuster strategies. In either instance, previous suggestions to leverage other sources of corporate power, such as leveraging the combined value of patents and brand names to get a $1 + 1 > 2$ result, as well as the importance of drafting strong patents to provide and protect strategic opportunities, remain a constant.

Lie in Wait for an Attacking Adversary

In the early 1990s, Microsoft, wanting to use technology invented by Stac Electronics in its operating system, demanded the acceptance by Stac of a one-time flat payment and threatened to move ahead with or without the license. Stac refused, based on its belief in the strength of its patent position. Microsoft acted on its threat and moved forward without a license. Unlike most small companies that brushed up against Microsoft, Stac responded by enforcing its patent rights. In so doing, it enacted a strategic operator described in the *Art of War: Sun Tzu Strategy Card Deck* termed "Lie in Wait for an Attacking Adversary," which means to challenge your adversary's plans with an aggressive defense that is prepared to receive him. A jury found that Microsoft was infringing on Stac's property and awarded $120 million to Stac for patent infringement.[71]

The verdict became a turning point for Microsoft. Prior to the Stac event, Microsoft had applied for only a handful of patents. Afterward, with the personal endorsement of Bill Gates, Microsoft became one of the more prolific patentees of innovative concepts. Stac held its ground and gave Microsoft a bloody nose, but a bloody nose can serve as a great teacher.

Microsoft presently files about 3,000 patent applications per year, which is consistent with the dominant high-tech strategy of patent stockpiling. Its patent portfolio provides Microsoft with a way to be more interactive with other companies, since it can share technology yet still have a vehicle to assert its ownership of that technology. Presumably also, in another Stac-type scenario, Microsoft could either hope to have within its patent stockpile a means to counter a lawsuit with an infringed patent of its own, or perhaps to have earlier established licensing agreements with the allegedly infringed entity valuable enough to the other entity that it would reconsider its interests in actually suing Microsoft in the first place.

Decision Time at RIM

Only those behind closed doors at Research In Motion (RIM) can know the decision process that took place when they faced the patent assertion problem from NTP, Inc. But we can speculate about some of the things they had to consider. Since history shows that most high-tech patents can ultimately be designed around one way or another, this possibility of designing around the NTP, Inc. patents had to come up, as did the possibility of invalidating the NTP, Inc. patents, which would obviate the need to design around at all. In fact, invalidation appeared to be

(Continued)

an approach used by RIM, since at the time of settlement, key NTP, Inc. patents in the case had been preliminarily invalidated by the U.S. Patent and Trademark Office.[72] On February 24, 2006, statements by U.S. District Court Judge James Spencer indicated that he was leaning neither for nor against an injunction against RIM until the case was decided, showing that he was considering an injunction.[73] This raised the uncertainty and risk of RIM's position enormously, since RIM now had a significant catastrophic risk to contend with. Within a week of Spencer's statements, RIM settled the case for $612.5 million. RIM apparently concluded that any other solution outside the $612.5 million settlement would or could, within too high a threshold to risk, cost more than that $612.5 million.[74] When thinking about real-life defense, it is rare that you can build a truly secure position, or, from the perspective of NTP, Inc. with no actual products to defend, an unassailable challenge. What you really seek in practice is a patent position that is more trouble to take apart at the time it becomes relevant, and under the conditions of the moment, than is worth your adversary's effort or risk to counter.

Final Word on Decision

Always consider the consequences of your decisions, as we discussed in the beginning of this book. These include predicted useful and harmful consequences, as well as the unpredicted useful and harmful consequences. Although some elements of a final result will always be unpredictable, seek to manage the circumstances that allow ignorance or poor judgment to keep the otherwise predictable factors within the unpredicted category. You must be informed if you expect to make good decisions.

Always consider the merits of the inverse solution. If your choice is to go somewhere, consider the merits of not going. If your choice is to keep an invention proprietary, consider the merits of licensing the invention or even putting it into the public domain entirely. The inverse solution is yet another way to create valuable asymmetry in your planning. If your competitor has a proprietary patent position, then competing with a comparable proprietary patent position, in the absence of an overwhelming advantage, could prove expensive and difficult. Pitting an open position against the competitor's proprietary position could create asymmetrical advantages in your favor. An asymmetric strategy contest is currently playing out in the competition between Microsoft and the Linux providers. While another proprietary operating system would stand little chance of defeating Microsoft's proprietary operating system in the market, the Linux open operating system creates a more serious threat, because it uses a different business model that Microsoft cannot easily emulate.

Finally, always have an exit strategy in mind with thresholds for making the choice to exit. It is just as important to know when you have won a contest as to know when you have lost. Know in advance what metrics to use to determine when a win or a loss has occurred and what you will do in either case.

An Exit Strategy

March Networks, a provider of Internet Protocol (IP)-based digital video surveillance solutions, announced a settlement in a patent litigation suit launched in April 2005 against E-Watch. The company agreed to pay $2 million to E-Watch, but with no admission regarding validity, enforceability, or infringement of any E-Watch patents.[75] The payment proved to be an acceptable exit strategy when analyzed by March Networks over the other possible outcomes and requirements of continuing a fight. It apparently also proved to be an acceptable exit strategy for E-Watch, which otherwise ran the risk that March Networks might win the case at the expense of E-Watch's patent position.

Section Summary

In this section on Decision we discussed how to define the objective and determined that to reach your objective, you need first to know what your objective is. We also discussed that at its core, all strategy is an interplay between interaction and isolation and that isolation generally leads toward decline and interaction toward growth. We examined four effects of a proficient strategy, which are to eliminate, isolate, interact with, or negate a competitor, and that the best way to succeed against a competitor is to succeed with a customer.

Going into more depth, we discussed competitive equilibrium and disequilibrium. We saw that when you or a competitor accept a current situation, you will both desire to maintain equilibrium in the situation, and that when you or a competitor do not like a current situation, it will create a desire to cause disequilibrium that will accelerate change. Since everything we do is "evil" to someone, there is usually someone out there who will try to change the status quo if allowed to do so. We developed this discussion, seeing how to put presented ideas into practical use with the recommendation to review the IP Strategy Boarding and Scenario Play available in the Appendix of this book. In the Appendix, we discussed a methodology using the *Art of War: Sun Tzu Strategy Card Deck* and *The Sales Strategy Fundamentals* card deck to devise an infinite variety of plans.

In the second half of this section, we explored how to leverage the three Centers of Excellence, first discussed in Chapter 3, Assess of this book, when crafting a patent strategy. Here, we discussed important principles of innovation, sales and marketing, and security as they relate to patent strategy. We revisited how to define a problem and how that definition allows you to identify the opposition. We further examined why opposition must exist based on the idea that everything we do is "evil" to somebody; and in strategizing using the interplay between interaction and isolation as a model, we developed a tool for identifying with whom we should cooperate or compete and why. We further discussed evaluating resources that are at the heart of cooperation and competition assessments.

Included within this section, we discussed the important concepts of the ideal patent, which provides 100% of the intended benefits of a patent with 0% of the drawbacks. This led to our discussion that if you can create the conditions whereby you will succeed in the absence of a patent, patents will become a bonus to your strategic strength and not a crutch to protect a weakness. Although you cannot achieve this position for all patentable inventions, efforts to emulate the ideal patent as closely as possible will lead to stronger positions.

Finally, we put cooperation and competition into context with the three Centers of Excellence that establish how we cooperate or compete. We then put these three Centers of Excellence into context with parallel lines of competition, which we have seen are key in crafting powerful asymmetrical strategies. Next, we assessed where our sanctuaries are and the dominant or contested nature of competition. This provided the means for us to discuss security and the value of having a strong patent position that can stand up to both competitive design-around and invalidity initiatives. Last, we discussed the impact of the dominant patent strategies of patent stockpiling and seeking the blockbuster in order to decide how to handle these driving patent forces. Now that we have covered all of that, we can turn to the third part of the decision cycle, Act.

Chapter 5

Act

Once you have made a decision, you act. During the Act phase of the decision cycle, you take what you assessed and decided on and put it into operation. As this chapter develops, therefore, we will repeat and reemphasize important concepts from the earlier chapters and relate them to four operational tenets from which you can achieve proficient action. We will build on these concepts by discussing additional material, which includes the use and importance of tempo during operations, the appreciation of luck in strategy, and measuring results. Our key learning points for Act are:

1. *Acting on the goal.* Taking action for a specific purpose
2. *Acting competitively.* Acting with the opposition in mind
3. *Making adjustments.* Adjusting your actions accordingly as the opposition adjusts and the situation changes
4. *Applying appropriate resources.* Using no more and no less the amount of resources necessary to achieve your goal
5. *Four operational tenets.* Key conditions for successful operations

6. *Proficiency at operations.* The strategic application of the four operational tenets
7. *Tempo.* Leveraging the time factor
8. *Luck factor.* The hand fortune plays, both good and bad
9. *Qualifying the result.* Knowing whether you have succeeded or failed

When you take action in patent strategy, you bring people, ideas, and tools to bear in the goal to reach "B" from "A." Some of these people, ideas, and tools are internal to your organization, and some are external. You expect your chosen action to deliver the results you intend it to deliver but also prepare for the unexpected.

Acting on the Goal

Acting is the execution of your strategy. Speaking metaphorically, if you (someone involved with patent strategy) had written a symphony, now you have your symphony performed. Action starts by clearly understanding and communicating where you want to go. To use a cliché of merit that relates to a symphony, "everyone needs to be on the same page." As we stated in Chapter 4, Decide, to go from "A" to "B" you need to know what "B" is, and so do the critical people who will execute your plan. What is your desired result "B"? You should have determined what "B" is in the decision phase; you also should have asked:

1. *What is the ideal result?* Is there a way I can achieve my desired result without the use of an underlying mechanism?
2. *What is the optimal (good-enough) result?* When does any added success no longer provide a meaningful benefit?

In your action, you seek to perform at an optimal level whereby you do no more and no less than necessary to succeed. Nature rewards optimization, and so does business. Consider another statement about the wolf.

The wolf emerges from the trees as no more and no less a hunter than necessary to have the effect on the forest intended of the wolf.

In theory, the wolf could be larger and smarter, have claws instead of just paws, and embody a host of other options that other predators can bring to bear, but it does not. It has no more and no less the capabilities than it needs to take its role in the dynamics of the forest ecosystem and to assure that it thrives as a species. Like wolves, you also strive to use your resources optimally, and your expenditure of any resources needs to produce a worthwhile return. Your mindset should be oriented toward optimization, which can but does not necessarily mean being the best. You understand and appreciate your place in the business ecosystem, use your patent strategy to help you thrive in that place, and consider carefully, when you receive new ideas, whether they actually make sense for your business.

Although many people would think that the best patent position affords total invulnerability, the optimal patent strategy actually protects neither too much nor too little to achieve its purpose. Any other position wastes resources that could be used elsewhere. Too much protection of any single invention or a few of them wastes resources that could have been used to protect other inventions or conduct other important operations. Too little protection could result in a loss of inventions and possibly a waste of all the resources used to create and protect those inventions. It is difficult to impossible to predict exactly what the optimal amount of resources needs to be, and if anything it is probably better to err by using too much instead of too little. Still, it is important to keep the idea of optimizing resources in mind as you move forward.

Sailing without Charts
The key legal risk in action regarding patents is infringement. Further at issue in infringement is whether an infringement was willful, possibly subjecting the infringer to willful damages, and to what extent factors such as lost markets, lost profits, and injunctions will come into play. All factors associated with this, including new court precedents for obviousness, willful damages, and injunction thresholds, are continually being monitored by patent professionals as these issues pertain to their respective organizations.

(Continued)

Patent strategists at some organizations continue to restrict access to patent information from their researchers in order to decrease the likelihood that an infringement will be willful, thus creating plausible deniability. It is a strategy being employed by some and warrants a bit of discussion and review. Figuratively sticking inventors' heads in the sand, as we discussed, actually works against one of the stated purposes behind creating the patent system in the first place—the agreement to trade knowledge for the right to exclude people from using an art for a period of time. If researchers are not allowed to look at competitive patents, then the intended teaching does not take place, and the likelihood of infringement rises. However, the strategy of purposeful ignorance could still be made to make sense to some companies considering that if the infringement is not willful, simply because the inventor did not subjectively know about it, then any damages paid would likely be similar to what would have been arranged anyway through a license or purchase. People thinking this way can also add to the bonus the possibility that neither the infringer nor the infringed would ever notice the infringement, thus allowing them to avoid the licensing or acquisition fees. However, this approach needs to be weighed against the higher costs of reinventing what has already been invented and patented, and most importantly in this section on Act, not leveraging the teachings of others for your own inventive efforts. You forfeit all of the advantages found by patent landscapes, data-based reasoning for isolating or interacting with competition, and effective strategies for benchmarking the best technical direction for the company. This can be the patent strategy equivalent of sailing the high seas without the charts that show you where opportunity and danger lie.

Acting Competitively

With the optimal use of resources in mind, you act in accord with the strategic ideas discussed in this book to create a useful interplay between interaction and isolation with people and companies in your market. You want to raise your capacity to interact even as opponents may seek to diminish that capacity. This is achieved by addressing the problems, causes, or effects that interfere with that sought-after interaction. You craft your action following the four rules of patent strategy discussed in the beginning of this book, and leverage all the other aspects of power that can "walk behind" your patents or that your patents can walk behind. To review, here are the four rules:

1. Use the patent to isolate.
2. Threaten to use the patent to isolate.
3. Use the patent to interact.
4. Leverage the possible use of the patent to interact.

To continue in review, in the business strategy in which your patents play a part, you want increase your own capacity to interact with the market and diminish your competitor's capacity to interact with the market when that competitive interaction works against your interests. This is best achieved by winning good customers who might otherwise facilitate your competitor's plans. Patents are an important tool for isolating competitors when they allow you the right to exclude competitors from making, using, or selling inventions you own that customers want. Your patents are tools both for such isolations and for useful interactions such as licensing; your optimal patent portfolio, when linked to other aspects of your organization's power, serves both purposes.

Mentally Prepare to Adjust

Acting brings another reality into the mix. Often, despite our best assessments and decisions, we can find ourselves undertaking the wrong action. This can be for any number of the reasons explored in the Introduction of this book in the section, Reasons for Unpredicted Results. Whatever its causes, the strategic mind needs to be able to adjust when results turn out differently than intended.

Even if you did not actually take the wrong action, your opposition's response to your action might suggest that you should change course. Here again, strategic solutions differ from technical solutions. When you execute a technical solution, it is usually clear whether your solution worked. If you change the starter on a broken-down car and it still does not start, then either the problem was not the starter, there was more to the problem than just the starter, you improperly installed the new starter, or your new starter had its own problems. You can easily test for all of these cases and make appropriate adjustments. A strategic solution, on the other hand, has an added danger over a technical solution, because it can prove to be much more difficult to understand if and when you are right or wrong, let alone convince others about your view on the situation. Even if you can measure success, possibly through revenues earned or customers gained, uncertainties regarding causes and effects in strategy make it easy for people to assign their own causes to effects to justify what they observe. For example, does a drop-off in your competitor's patenting in a technology area signal that your competitor has moved on to other opportunities, or does it signal that their research phase has ended and they plan to develop and launch a product soon? If you act on the wrong interpretation from your assessment phase, then you may have to adjust your strategy down the road.

The challenge in strategy is to understand when you are right or wrong and to do so as soon as possible. If wrong, you need to figure out why and try something better. The simplest way to check the integrity of your solution is to ask the inverse question about an observed result. When you see something positive, stop and ask yourself, "How could this go wrong?" This may seem pessimistic, but it is extremely important. As illustrated earlier, more than one small company has celebrated obtaining an exclusive license for its technology from a larger company, complete with a lucrative royalty agreement to pay a percentage of sales revenue, only to have that larger company deliberately shelve the licensed technology in favor of a competing technology produced from its own labs. The inverse question, "what could go wrong?" allows you to consider such possibilities in advance and either not act on an exclusive agreement such as the one just presented or make sure that you have a way to deal with the negative result in place.

When you see negative results, seek out data and facts that provide some explanation. Ask on a broad scale if your results are improving interaction or increasing isolation, and why? Then drill down to more specifics. Consider, as an example, a case where your company's sales increased because your competitors had exited the segment in favor of a new disruptive technology. Consider further that your management did not recognize the danger of this, and interpreted this withdrawal as a by-product of its own fine marketing. Even though revenues may temporarily increase because of your competitor's withdrawal from the traditional market, your nonparticipation in the disruptive solution will become an isolating action over the long term. That increased isolation, if allowed to continue, will eventually affect your whole operation. Put another way, effects only respect actual causes, not causes misperceived as responsible by people. Your actions should be based on the reality of the situation in order to have a consistent and reliable chance of success.

The Internet Tidal Wave

On May 26, 1995, Bill Gates wrote a memo titled "The Internet Tidal Wave," to signal a major shift in company direction that had previously focused on PC-based software and had given the Internet little attention. Netscape held a dominant position in the space and had made its chairman, James Clark, a billionaire in 18 months. It had taken Gates 12 years to reach that mark.[1] Netscape and the Internet threatened to be a serious isolating force against Microsoft if Microsoft stayed on its then current course. Bill Gates refocused his company on the Internet, and the new course would prove to be successful for Microsoft by keeping Microsoft the dominant player in personal computation. Bill Gates wrote, "There will be a lot of uncertainty as we first embrace the Internet and then extend it. Since the Internet is changing so rapidly we will have to revise our strategies from time to time and have better inter-group communication than ever before."[2] Netscape, with minimal intellectual property protection and therefore no sanctuary from Microsoft's competitive inroads, would cease to be the dominant player on the Internet and become a company with much less influence and presence.

Categorize and Track Resources

So bearing in mind that you have made your assessment, made a decision, and are taking action, replete with active monitoring for the viability of that action, you come to the issue of resources and their employment. Within your decision to take action, you have determined how you will employ and leverage the resources of your company. For the purpose of your strategy, you should categorize your resources by a method that makes sense to you and other people within the organization. You should then track your resources to make sure you do not overextend yourself in one area or leave available resources on the table in another area. A list of ten major resource categories follows that you can use, in whole or in part, along with categories used at your organization:

1. People—human resources internal to the organization and external
2. Time—any limitations that another entity has the power to impose
3. Money—any source of finance that can keep an operation running
4. Space—all aspects of where to put and move elements of the operation
5. Material—all components necessary for the operation
6. Energy—the power source that pushes the operation forward
7. Information—the data and intelligence from which to take action
8. Function—necessary tasks and tools needed within the operation
9. Security—all aspects of protecting the integrity of the operation
10. Appeal—all psychological aspects of a situation that drive people toward producing the desired result

When a competitor is strong in one resource and you are strong in another, try to create the conditions whereby you can leverage your strength and take advantage of the comparative weakness of your competitor. If a competitor builds a strategy that leverages a large reserve of cash, you might leverage your more experienced people or superior ideas to remain competitive. Consider the foregoing list or one of your own creation each time you act.

Without an advantage in some aspect of resources, you will likely follow a difficult competitive road. Measuring such resources is one of the important functions of a competitive intelligence professional inasmuch as such assessments often need to be inferred or investigated. As an example, more than one organization has estimated the size of another by counting the average number of cars that show up in a parking lot each day.

Many endeavors fail when the people involved run out of an important resource, with money and time being highly important from this standpoint. Money can buy just about any other resource, and while time can often provide the window to accumulate necessary money, time can also be the one limited resource that even money cannot buy. Prudent organizations, therefore, find a position related to resources from which they can win or recognize that they cannot win on the present course; this provides a way to end or adjust the endeavor before consuming too many resources.

Four Operational Tenets

Four Operational Tenets Defined

This leads us to four operational tenets that provide guidelines for how to use the resources you have. The four operational tenets, and a simple example of each, follow:

1. Concentration of effort—for example, which research and development opportunities should stakeholders fund?
2. Economy of resources—for example, what could be bought off the shelf instead of making it?
3. Freedom of action—for example, how can we gain and maintain our freedom to operate in the face of competitive patent positions?
4. Safety—for example, how can we mitigate the risk of choosing the wrong technical standard?[3]

Concentration of Effort The four operational tenets make a lot of sense when you look at the physics behind them. To advance a business into a market, you need to create a certain amount of force. You need to concentrate enough effort to break through resistance put up by prospective customers, suppliers, competitors, the government—in short, anyone who is not immediately predisposed to support you. Part of the force associated with this effort involves selling products people want to buy, which means you will need to concentrate enough resources in performing or acquiring research and development in order to have products or services that people want to buy. The amount of force or effort needed to accomplish this is directly related to the strength of the opposing pressure from those who would rather that you fail or would otherwise show indifference. The optimal result is to concentrate just enough effort (force) to overcome resistance while not overconcentrating and wasting resources that could be applied elsewhere, which leads us to the next operational tenet.

Economy of Resources   Economy of resources directly links to concentration of effort, because resources have limits. You need to concentrate enough of your effort to succeed, but ideally no more effort to succeed than necessary. This is in keeping with our discussion of optimization. You want to use no more and no less of the resources needed to achieve your goal. Further, if you can leverage resources belonging to others, you will have more resources of your own available to advance your business elsewhere. Think about it this way. If you have 10 researchers who can give you 8 solid hours of productive research a day and you can acquire 70% of the research you need from outside sources, then you can have all 10 researchers working on the missing 30% instead of spending their time reinventing existing work. This allows you to concentrate more effort on the most critical point of your research and development effort—the missing 30%—and can also serve to speed the tempo of the whole project, meaning that you finish faster and get to market faster. Looking at the physics of operational tenets again, you need to introduce greater force than that presented by the opposition; however, you also keep the ideal in mind, meaning that in the ideal solution, the sum of forces generated at your own expense of resources falls to zero. In short, just as a falcon uses gravity to accelerate in a strike, you should prefer to use only the limited resources of your own that you need and prudently seek to leverage all other resources from the outside as your "gravity." You want to economize your resources so you do not use them unnecessarily and make them unavailable for other opportunities.

Freedom of Action   Freedom of action relates to both concentration of effort and economy of resources as a measure of your capacity to succeed on your own terms. Active opposition from others, along with inefficiency in your own efforts, contributes to frictions that restrict your freedom to act. For example, paying royalties for an asserted patent that otherwise contributes no additional value to your efforts beside allowing you to continue is a burden that will require added resources to overcome. After all, you could use the monetary amount being paid in the form of royalties elsewhere. This can lead, for example, to the question of how you can invalidate a blocking patent. Your overall objective is to reduce or eliminate any factors that adversely restrict your freedom of action and do not bring with them compensating benefits. If you pay royalties for a license, you want the technology licensed to bring more value to your operational success than it costs.

Safety   Safety is applied in terms of the probability that you will achieve success, experience failure, or experience catastrophic failure. All three measures should come into your calculation and should be balanced accordingly. For example, a 50% chance of success and a 50% chance of failure, but with a 0% chance of that failure being catastrophic, could be deemed a better situation than a 80% chance of success and a 20% chance of catastrophic failure for many people, given that the latter introduces the possibility of a "game over" event.

Patent-related questions concern risks of infringement and lawsuits, but they go beyond that. Patent-related questions include how you can mitigate the risk of committing to the wrong standard or how you mitigate the strategic risk associated with how you concentrate effort. Patenting implies commitment, but it can also serve as a hedge. A patent can reserve your space to compete in an alternative market if written broadly enough to cover a technology used in different markets, and this can be useful should a present endeavor prove to be the wrong course of action or succeed so well that you want to expand on that success. This is particularly so when you patent an enabler, such as a catalyst, instead of just an application, such as one particular product that the catalyst can produce. The patents of others, provided you obtain a stake in them, can also serve as vehicles to give you a defendable stake in another direction should a previous initiative fail.

Operational Tenets: A Summary

All four operational tenets are highly important in how you enact your strategy. In the author's experience in patent analysis and strategy, every project, at its core, has involved answering one or more of the following questions:

1. Where should we focus our effort?
2. How can we best leverage our resources?
3. How can we gain or maintain freedom of operation?
4. Where is our infringement or strategic risk, and what should we do about it?

Have you ever asked these questions? They all relate to the four operational tenets. If you do not have solid answers for these questions, then you have not completed your assessment, and you will take action with a correspondingly higher risk for error.

Words or Actions?

On its Web page in 2007, British Petroleum stated, "BP has transformed: growing from a local oil company into a global energy group; employing over 96,000 people and operating in over 100 countries worldwide."[4] While BP still shows that it is involved in alternative energy sources, it has since, and effectively always has, focused its effort on its oil and gas core. To truly act in accord with the previous statement would have an enormous impact on its strategy, because "oil company" implies only a focus on oil and petroleum-based products and "global energy group" could mean just about anything energy related. While it makes sense for BP to plan and act for a world not dominated by oil in the future, BP cannot do everything in energy and will have to make decisions for the present about where to concentrate its effort, how to economize its resources, how to gain and maintain freedom of operation in its chosen fields, and how to mitigate risks. Its patent strategy should tie directly to these plans, since each course will support and be supported by the body of patents that BP owns or licenses. An analysis of BP patents and published applications from past to present shows that the company continues to concentrate its efforts on petroleum.

Multidimensional Considerations

The four operational tenets have multidimensional considerations to think about. Concentrating effort on a research and development project should include all physical, psychological, and even moral concentrations of effort. People who think only of the future or other matters cannot focus on what they are doing now, and so any given research or development team needs to have a mental focus that matches its direction. Likewise, having the freedom of action to do something physically may give rise to considerable psychological and moral frictions if these dimensions are not aligned; just because you can physically borrow technology from someone else without their detection of infringement, for example, does not necessarily mean you have the psychological or moral freedom to do so.

This latter point is a matter of orientation, given that people think differently about the psychological and moral implications of certain actions. Orientation is your viewpoint of the world and is based on your present situation, your past experiences, and your predictions about the future. Some organizations, as a matter of policy, will do everything they reasonably can to not infringe on the patents belonging to others. Others treat the risk of infringement detection as just another business decision to consider and will proceed with a known infringement if they think they can get away with it. In this latter scenario, people seem to have a greater willingness to infringe on patent claims for an invention they developed independently and then subsequently found to be infringing than to steal an invention outright from the active patent files. It can be easier to justify in the mind that one is not really stealing when one has come up with an idea independently, and so it presents a lower moral hurdle. It all depends on orientation.

The China Question

It is a well-known principle of strategy that while force can produce results, it has limited utility compared to having people do what you want them to do because they also want to. If you use force to create change but the conditions that require

(Continued)

force do not also change, you will have to continue with your application of force so that things do not revert back to the way they were. China's conforming to World Trade Organization standards of intellectual property law presents a scenario in which to investigate this idea.

As one of the conditions for China to join the World Trade Organization in 2001, it was required to develop a better intellectual property system. It made reforms to comply with the Agreement on Trade-Related Aspects of Intellectual Property Rights (TRIPS). Enforcement issues of that reform remained, however, since the conditions that caused China to comply with laws it might otherwise have ignored had not changed. There is little doubt that China in the first decade of the 21st century continues to be a difficult market in terms of intellectual property protection. The Business Software Alliance estimates that 90% of business software used in China is pirated, and that perhaps 20% of branded products are counterfeit. Enforcement continues to be inadequate in China, and penalties for infringement rare.[5]

A number of conditions exist in China that make minimal intellectual property protections in China's own self-interest at the moment. Among these is that more intellectual property enters the Chinese economy from outside China's borders than emerges from within its borders, meaning that Chinese businesses as a whole have a lot to gain by having comparatively easier access to intellectual property than they might otherwise have in the presence of stronger intellectual property enforcement. Corruption can also be an issue any time local authorities have a personal interest in overlooking the production of counterfeit goods. Add to this the low cost of labor, and you have yet another potential issue that works against enforcement.

Many businesses in China, even after making significant research and development investments of their own, have a low-cost manufacturing base from which they could still compete successfully on the world stage even in the absence of their own patents. While these companies may themselves be damaged by infringement, that can be an acceptable trade-off, considering the greater obstacles they themselves may also face under tighter intellectual property laws. Research and development is rising in China as Chinese companies catch up to and match the innovative prowess of their counterparts in other countries. Wages in manufacturing are also on the rise. But at the moment, piracy appears to be less of an issue to Chinese business as a whole than it is to businesses in most other industrial countries.

What changes over time is the incentives that Chinese companies have to want stronger intellectual property protection for themselves comparable to that in most developed countries. To illustrate in principle, since the majority of global and high-value brands originate from companies outside China, the impact of trademark infringement on the Chinese economy is not as great as it might otherwise be. We saw, however, that with the arrival of the Beijing Olympic Games in 2008, the Beijing Administration for Industry and Commerce had the incentive to severely crack down on those violating the exclusive rights to use the Olympic logo, the copying of which was having a direct impact on China itself.[6] This is and will likely be the way with patents also, particularly as Chinese research and development efforts continue to rise, which they will. When any weakness in either the patent law or its enforcement appreciably damages Chinese industry, the incentive to crack down will rise accordingly.

In the meantime, organizations need to approach Chinese markets with care, especially concerning high-value intellectual property. Managers should acknowledge that, despite their best efforts, it may be difficult to impossible to keep intellectual property that is exposed through the manufacture, use, or sale of products out of the hands of pirates. This may require creative enforcement techniques, such as litigating against distributors in countries with comparatively strong patent laws and enforcement instead of against producers in China with comparatively weak patent laws or enforcement. It could involve a

(Continued)

more long-term approach to thinking, as shown by Bill Gates when he told a University of Washington audience, "And as long as they're going to steal it, we want them to steal ours. They'll get sort of addicted, and then we'll somehow figure out how to collect sometime in the next decade."[7] The idea here is not to truly accept the stealing. Microsoft has a global multimillion dollar anti-piracy effort to combat losses that exceed $10 billion a year.[8] The idea is to accept the conditions as they are at the moment, and in Microsoft's case, to build market share in anticipation that conditions for better enforcement will arise. The evidence of improving conditions is present, including a 28.5% increase in patent filings at the Chinese Patent Office of 345,569 patent filings in the first half of 2008 as compared with the same period in 2007.[9]

Orientation also applies to insight, which is one of four key faculties needed to optimize the operational tenets. Col. John Boyd, the father of the highly innovative F-16 fighter, developer of the energy-maneuverability (E-M) theory to maximize fighter performance on which the F-16 was conceived, and one of the most important but relatively unknown American strategists, noted that orientation is influenced by genetic heritage, cultural tradition, previous experience, and unfolding circumstances.[10] Translated into patent strategy, it is important to understand the nature of your company as well as that of your competitors. Organizations from other cultures will have people with whom you interact who have orientations about intellectual property different from your own. You need to be willing and able to step into their shoes to keep communications clear, because they may not be willing or able to step into your shoes.

Think about dealings with China, for example. China has a heritage and cultural tradition of sharing community resources, because everything belonged to the State. Scientists had free rights to use and make improvements to any existing invention. Intellectual property rights are a new concept in China, and because of this, the inclination and incentive to ignore these rights is higher than it might otherwise be.[11] Stealing will only create moral hurdles when people truly view stealing as stealing. As a Japanese businessman the author knows put it, what most people in the West would call "copying," many people in East may call "applied engineering."

So while active opposition is typically the most difficult security threat to deal with in patent strategy, it is easier to deal with opposition when you can appreciate the orientation of that opposition. Aside from defending against outright stealing, an act which most major corporations do try to avoid perpetrating on others, it is important to deny adversaries the opportunity to discern your patterns of action. If they understand your patterns of action too well, they may develop ways to oppose your plans through their own actions in the market. In short, you need good standards of confidentiality.

At the operational level, confidentiality means that you should train people, such as your engineers and sales people, on how to speak about new projects to investors and customers without giving away critical competitive information. To start, teach that typically investors and customers, the people with whom you want to communicate, want to know about the benefits of a new invention, product, or service. Competitors want to know how an invention, product, or service works. People at your organization should therefore show more openness with the former and less with the latter.

Create in your organization clear policies on what is shareable information and what is not. Even the most technologically curious customer, when asking details about how a technology works, will understand when you respond by saying, "I am sorry, but that information is proprietary." Any issues involving patents that do not specifically and deliberately advance or secure the business, such as the need to explore a joint venture with another party, should stay confidential. As a rule, competitive trade secrets and not-yet published patent technologies should also stay confidential, and anyone inside and outside the organization should be given access to that information only under enforceable nondisclosure agreements. Published patented technology, general concepts well known in the field, and innovations that are beneficial to your organization when used by others need not be kept confidential, nor need they be advertised if you would rather keep a lower profile. The practice of using general titles on patents and disclosing technology in obscure places is alive and well for organizations that do not necessarily want to make a given new invention easy to find.

Balance

Action in patent strategy on the whole is about balance. Even in your interplay between interaction and isolation, there is such a thing as too much interaction and too little isolation. Sometimes you need to isolate yourself temporarily to regroup and reconstitute. Sometimes, if you interact too much, relationships become confused. All advice in this book is not to be taken as absolute; anything that is absolute starts to become less about strategy and more about an operational "how to."

Every strategic tool almost always has an inverse application that can produce a desirable result. For example, we can talk about elimination from a situation as being something to avoid, yet at times your elimination may be the only way to reach your goal. The word "sacrifice" applies to this type of inverse thinking, as was illustrated by IBM's decision to offer (sacrifice) 500 patents on which it could otherwise seek royalties to the open-source community in order to build its standing within that community and encourage people to use IBM inventions.

The First 500

When Thomas J. Watson, Jr. was the CEO of IBM, IBM made a shift from calculating machines to computers that anticipated, and then created, the future of data processing and analysis. Now one of the world's patent leaders, IBM continues to benefit from the current patent environment in interesting ways. In January 2005 John Kelly, the senior vice president for technology and intellectual property at IBM, announced the release of 500 IBM patents for use by open-source programmers. Kelly stated that "this is not a one-time event," indicating that IBM might repeat this action with other patents in its portfolio.[12] This is an inverse solution to the traditional route of using patents to gain royalties or technical cross-licenses or to keep competitors out that recognizes, given changing conditions, that IBM could receive more value from the interactions gained by allowing open-source programmers ready and free access to selected inventions that they could otherwise access or create elsewhere.

We have also discussed the choice between doing and not doing. Within these choices are errors of doing too much or doing too little. Between either end is the optimal point of doing and not doing just enough. In the four operational tenets, this balance plays out as follows:

1. Concentration of effort must be balanced against the risk of applying too much or too little effort, both of which cause waste, and against the associated risk of not diversifying. Patent strategy calls for a balance between focusing your activity on the main effort and having some diversity within the patent portfolio to be able to redirect if needed.

2. Economy of resources similarly needs to be balanced against the risk of using too many or too few resources, along with the risk of losing control caused by any overreliance on external resources. Some things are better for you to support and do yourself, even if you could use outside resources. In addition, there is a trade-off in creating a highly streamlined operation, a goal often implied by economy of resources, because such streamlining tends to create inflexibilities. Many companies have introduced processes that greatly reduce the need to think and even the quality of people needed to perform given tasks. Just think about Henry Ford's original assembly line, where one individual needed to learn only one task in auto assembly as contrasted with the craftsman who might need to know how to assemble the entire car. The Henry Ford assembly line could produce more cars faster and cheaper than building them individually by hand, but throw something unusual in front of Ford's assembly line worker and the whole system could suffer. Today, most assembly line workers are cross-trained on multiple stations and take additional training on understanding how to assemble the entire vehicle. It is believed by most that a bigger-picture understanding helps to improve job understanding, performance, and an appreciation for the assembly worker's role in the process. Similarly in patent

strategy, even the processes introduced to make patent prosecution more efficient must be weighed against the need to treat each case on its own merit if a given patent is to stand up in court. In patent strategy, keeping an eye on the big picture and remaining flexible will help in effectively minimizing the use of internal resources without cutting back too far.

3. Freedom of action must be balanced against the risk of inefficiency, in some cases making this a polar opposite of economy of resources. For example, a certain level of staffing is required to guarantee availability and a familiarity with the organization's art during critical events; cutting back on staff too far might make the department less able to handle the variations in workload that come up or to turn around important assignments at a fast tempo. On the other hand, many ways exist to handle work flow variability without requiring a large full-time staff. Outsourcing legal work allows the organization to hire and pay for support as needed and to have a greater latitude to seek out specific talent that may be too expensive or used too infrequently to keep in house. Like everything else, this is a balance. You need to consider how you can "turn on the afterburners" if a situation demands more work than necessary in the normal course of business, yet at the same time not support excessive staffing when you do not actually need it. Both cutting back too far or not enough can restrict your freedom of action.

4. Safety must be balanced against the risk of non-achievement. This is the balance between surviving and thriving discussed at the beginning of this book. To thrive, you will likely need to take and accept some risk, and with risk comes the occasional failure. So while you do want to take no more risk than necessary, you also need to take risk as necessary. Balance is important. Risk is itself a matter of orientation, as what may be an acceptable risk to you may be entirely unacceptable to someone else. Many years ago, the author met a lead counsel at a major technology company that made it its practice not to look at the prior art and calculate, based on past years, the resources it would need to address the invariable infringement lawsuits that would arise. He believed his company could do practically nothing without infringing on someone and that most of the organizations his company infringed on would not notice anyway. He appeared to make no appreciable effort to avoid infringement

beyond avoiding outright theft. Not many companies would be willing to take this risk, nor would their management teams likely view the nature of this risk in the same way.

Multidimensional Considerations: Additional Notes

To summarize what we have discussed up to this point in Act and to look at this from a multidimensional perspective, your overriding aim in strategy is to improve your capacity for independent action, which in turn drives your capacity to succeed on your own terms. Patent strategy, through its use of patents as tools for interaction and isolation, improves your capacity for independent action. Your use of patents as tools for interaction and isolation depends on your disposition of resources in terms of the four operational tenets. The availability of resources in turn helps to form what your disposition can and should be. That disposition has physical, psychological, and moral characteristics—for example, your having a lot of patents in an area could discourage a competitor from entering a field psychologically when physically it could do so, and patenting a life-saving technology and enforcing that patent could have moral consequences if it restricts people who could benefit from that technology from accessing it. With all these elements in mind, you strategize by playing each patent in terms of the four rules:

1. Use a patent to isolate.
2. Threaten to use a patent to isolate.
3. Use a patent to interact.
4. Leverage the possible use of a patent to interact.

Now to go further, the interplay between interaction and isolation implied by these four rules ties into a company's freedom of action, making freedom of action a key target for competitors and a key target for defeating a competitor's plans. In short, you want to be free to do things that your competitors are not free to do and ultimately to succeed on your own terms. This idea allows you to create additional advantages. Thinking just a little more deeply, the products and services you sell that are at the core of why a patent strategy exists will also be most successful if they improve aspects of your customers' four operational tenets, with freedom of action being at the forefront. In everything from the cars that move us about, cell phones that allow us to talk to anyone anywhere, and pharmaceuticals that keep us healthy, freedom of action is a top underlying benefit for anyone who wishes to succeed on his or her own terms. You want, therefore, to sell freedom of action or the means to obtain it to others.

Defending the Lab

In 1993, a belief that Hoffman-La Roche was restricting access to patented life-saving drugs in the HIV area necessitated having armed guards at the research site in Nutley, New Jersey to protect the facility from outside protesters. This situation, in effect, necessitated that Hoffman-La Roche link its patent strategy to its public relations efforts in order for it to have the moral freedom of action to profit from its considerable research and development efforts. As a long-time employee of the company told the author, the issue regarding HIV research and public perceptions came up several times thereafter, including at Hoffman-La Roche's Colorado facility in the early 2000s, where much HIV research and development work was done. Hoffman-La Roche, being a private company without a large body of public shareholders to which management needed to answer, had the managerial freedom of action to decide that the HIV line of research was no longer worth the public hassle and so discontinued its HIV research. As with any action, however, there are multiple perspectives to consider, including how successful the Hoffman-La Roche research effort had actually been when related to other opportunities the company could focus on.

Fine or Injunction

On April 13, 2006, a Marshall, Texas jury reached a verdict, deciding that EchoStar had willfully infringed TiVo's patent on its time-warp technology for DVRs, and awarded almost $74 million in damages to be paid to TiVo.[13] Willful infringement had exposed EchoStar to treble damages. TiVo's general counsel, Matthew Zinn, noted after the trial that an injunction would have been even more meaningful to TiVo than the sheer dollar award. An injunction would have limited EchoStar's freedom of action associated with this product, which would ultimately have a more severe impact on the company and created a better position for TiVo than even the expected treble damages award.

Subsequent court proceedings on January 11, 2008 upheld the verdict and did indeed grant the injunction limiting EchoStar's freedom to operate. However, EchoStar, which changed its name to Dish Networks, subsequently released new software with the intent to stay in business without infringing on the TiVo patents.[14]

On the situation, TiVo CEO Tom Rogers said,

> I would say based on our experience with litigation, the costs of litigation are far less than the returns that we are seeing just from the cap side of this equation and I don't think people have seen the end of what the cap side of that equation is, but just on the basis of damage award, what we've spent versus what we've gotten back, it's been a great business move.[15]

Value in litigation comes from a number of sources, including monetary damages, restriction of competition, and the improved possibility of enforcing patents allegedly infringed by other competitors. Any outcome should be reviewed from several angles for its full impact on the parties involved.

Freedom of Action Enhancements

The importance of freedom of action leads to the question of how to enhance freedom of action in the patent space. You can do this by employing:

1. Variety—having adequate intellectual property access, through your own patents and the patents of others, to meet challenges and opportunities that arise

2. Rapidity—having a fast-tempo capacity to create or acquire innovation to address challenges and opportunities
3. Harmony—aligning people, ideas, and tools physically, psychologically, and morally with the direction of the organization
4. Initiative—performing the right actions at the right time in the right place; *innovating where the puck will be, not where it has been*
5. Creativity—having access to great ideas

Any or all of these enhances freedom of action in the patent space, and that freedom of action will give the people you depend on to innovate, advance, and secure great ideas the best chance to succeed. Variety gives you more tools to work with. Rapidity gets you to valuable hills before other people occupy them. Harmony reduces friction that costs resources to overcome. Initiative means people will see and act on the unexpected, such as the opportunity created by the accidental invention of Plexiglas® at a Röhm laboratory in 1935, which opened up a new and valuable product line for Röhm and Haas.[16] Creativity gives people in the organization the capacity to adapt to the opportunities and challenges of their environment, the means to think out of the box or get out of the box, depending on the psychological or physical nature of their problems.

Creative Zen

On August 23, 2006, Steve Jobs at Apple Computer agreed to a $100 million settlement over a patent dispute with Creative Zen. In the settlement, Apple Computer retained the ability to recover some of the settlement if Creative Zen succeeded in enforcing the patent on other MP3 manufacturers.[17] This positioned Apple to benefit from Creative Zen's suing Apple competitors to assert the patent at Creative Zen's own expense with Apple taking a cut from the results. In the *Art of War: Sun Tzu Strategy Card Deck*, this approach would fall under the category of "Strike with a Borrowed Hand," the Six of Clubs, which in review means to bring about a conflict between

> your adversary and a force other than your own. When you
> can achieve a goal with someone else's resources, you retain the
> freedom to use your own resources to achieve other goals.

How to Be Proficient at Operations

The recommendations given thus far in this section on action are not linear. In fact, they create a complex dynamic system in which an adjustment of one factor will impact the disposition of the others. So we need a guideline as to where to target operations to be proficient. Since strategy is a solution, and action is the enactment of a solution, our target once again is the ideal. In mathematical representation, the ideal operation provides 100% of the desired benefits with 0% drawbacks. This is the same ideal described so eloquently in Chinese literature as "The master does nothing, yet he leaves nothing undone," a phrase we have already discussed.

So how do we improve operations by doing nothing, yet leaving nothing undone? Classic ways to accomplish this include:

1. *Doing it the better way.* Emulate, create, improve, or in some cases, challenge the best practices for getting the job done.
2. *Concentrating on the essential.* Streamline by removing unneeded burdens.
3. *Delegating.* Have somebody else do selected work for you so you can concentrate your effort elsewhere.
4. *Borrowing.* Use something that already exists so you can concentrate your creative efforts on things that do not yet exist.

Achieving a proficient operation also involves embracing the concept of strategic nonaction in order to husband essential resources so that you can use those resources when and where absolutely necessary. When you do use your resources, use them with the advantages we have discussed: overwhelming advantage, surprise, asymmetry, and the benefit of a sanctuary. Action for the sake of action rarely produces notable results. Patenting for the sake of patenting is one example of a misguided handling of resources. Every patent should have a purpose and should be managed in accord with that purpose. The costs of patenting and patent management alone that we have discussed make this imperative. The purpose need not be ground-breaking, just a reasonable purpose for future advantage that can be articulated during an invention review and can have an acceptable chance, either alone or within an aggregate of other inventions, of providing an adequate return on the investment. On occasion, it may even make sense to seek a patent as a reward for inventors, provided that reward does bring indirect benefits to the business as a whole.

A Case of Free Value

In operations concerning patents and inventions, one way to do nothing yet leave nothing undone is to take advantage of the opportunity to extract low-cost or free value from the ideas of others. Whereas licensing someone else's patented technology or contracting with people to solve problems and create ideas specific for your product or services can cost a lot, ideas and solutions associated with other technologies are often free.

Take the case of how a diamond-cracking operation found within the bell pepper–stuffing industry a proficient solution to cracking diamonds. To efficiently crack a diamond, people from that industry put the diamonds under high pressure. With a sudden release of that pressure, air trapped in fissures and imperfections within the diamonds expands and cracks the diamonds. Similarly, when bell peppers rapidly go from a high- to a low-pressure environment, air trapped within the bell peppers expands and cleanly pops the tops off of the peppers.[18] The fundamental idea behind bell pepper stuffing, patented in 1968, provided a solution for diamond cracking many years later without any exchange in technology or license from one to the other. The underlying idea for how to solve the problem in this example is the same, although its actual application differs. The people seeking to crack diamonds had the opportunity to extract considerable value from bell pepper–stuffing techniques with little cost. Nothing was done; finding the solution did not require an extensive research and development effort. Nothing was left undone; a solution for proficient diamond cracking came to light.

As a second illustration, what do a book, a wallet, a cell phone, a laptop computer, and a seat at the movie theater all have in common? Answer: Segmentation, so that each device is opened and larger when in use, and closed and compact when not in use and stored. Such inventive principles as segmentation are universal and free to use, yet they provide tremendous value when applied to inventions. What characteristics do your products share with noncompetitive technologies? What information is out there right now that is free to use on your products?

Account for Change

The patents on which you base your future should capture the future: *be where the puck will be.* We have discussed how to see the future using Altshuller's laws—that components in a system will become more efficient over time, particularly with the concept of the ideal and the optimal. Although you cannot always predict the applications that will arise from new technology, you can predict its direction and track areas that show exponential improvements in performance as locations where new applications will arise. Patenting for the future, therefore, often means patenting the enablers from which new applications will arise. It means that although you cannot predict all the new applications that may arise from, for example, faster microprocessor speeds, you do patent faster microprocessor speeds because you know that those yet unknown applications will need faster microprocessors or will arise because faster microprocessors exist. What enabled Amazon.com, from our earlier example, to create an inverse solution to the traditional brick and mortar bookstore was the Internet technology that other inventors and organizations created. The creators of that enabler did not necessarily have any specific thought in mind that one of the applications their enabler would allow was an online bookstore.

Patenting for the future can, however, create some resistance. It can appear to be deviating from the core when, in fact, it is protecting where the core will need to go. Wang, as illustrated earlier, got stuck in word processors in the 1970s. In the 1950s, IBM made the jump from tabulators to computers and all that they enabled because its CEO, Thomas J. Watson, Jr., recognized and influenced where the puck would be. Patenting needs to be at the forefront of observations such as Watson's.

There is significant risk in not keeping up with change. We discussed how, depending on your position, you will often be more inclined to seek equilibrium rather than disequilibrium, particularly if business is going well. Change, by its nature, creates disequilibrium, and disequilibrium creates uncertainty. Regardless of any desire for equilibrium, you will experience change. The main question is whether you cause the change or react to the change. Since change is inevitable, it is generally better to facilitate change instead of just going with it or holding fast against it. When waves appear, such as the Internet tidal wave noted by Bill Gates, you can duck under them, stand fast against them, or surf them.

Act soon when comparative conditions will worsen. If you cannot solve a problem now, how will you solve it later when you are weaker? Show patience when comparative conditions will improve. Prepare and act at the optimal time, and be very careful about making stands with your feet firmly planted in ever-shifting sands.

Tempo

Do you remember the early video game Pong®? If not, think about almost any early video game you might have played. Once you got proficient at playing the game, how did the program make it more difficult for you most of the time? Answer: It raised the tempo of the action.

Likewise, considering the material discussed thus far and all things being otherwise equal, those who proficiently operate at an optimal tempo—which more often than not means a faster tempo—will have a significant advantage over their competitors. Also, since we compete against active and intelligent opposition, the standards for optimal tempo rise all the time. Consider the following quote from Lewis Carroll's *Through the Looking Glass*:

> Now, here, you see, it takes all the running you can do, to keep in the same place. If you want to get somewhere else, you must run at least twice as fast as that![19]

The influence of tempo is a reality in all strategies, including patent strategy. Although occasionally the capacity to move at a slower tempo affords advantages, we will focus here on high-tempo operations from which most advantage is derived.

Decision Cycle and Tempo

All patent strategy is built around a continuing cycle of assessment, decision, and action, on which we have structured the major sections of this book. Companies that can move through these decision cycles at a higher tempo than their rivals gain a significant competitive advantage because they gain control of their situations. The faster you can make accurate assessments of a situation, good enough decisions on what to do, and good enough actions doing it, the more competitive you become. Why is this so?

If you can innovate faster than competitors, then you can create new products and services before they can. That affords the opportunity to gain first-mover advantages, or alternatively to select the right pace for the circumstances by your own choice. With patents themselves, if you are first to invent or first to file you hold advantages simply because someone else, therefore, cannot be first to invent or file. The movie *Talladega Nights*, a parody of NASCAR racing, made light of a philosophy, "If you're not first, you're last."[20] In NASCAR, as in many other things in life, you can actually finish second, third, or some place other than last. But in patent strategy, the literal philosophy of "If you're not first, you're last" often does hold true. If you are not first to file or invent, depending on the importance of either in your respective patent authority, you not only do not get the patent, you can lose much, if not all, of the investment associated with the effort it took to be the second or third. Coming in second in the world of patents could make you fall behind other competitors who never entered that race and used their resources more fruitfully elsewhere. In the race to attain patents, if you're not first, you may very well be last.

The Mind of Minolta

Konica Minolta's exit from the digital camera race illustrates the impact of decision cycle tempo. Konica Minolta apparently exited the digital camera (dSLR) race because it did not have the resources it needed to keep pace with leaders Nikon and Canon in an intensive innovation race for better professional and consumer dSLR cameras. Konica Minolta has

(Continued)

since focused its efforts on other aspects of imaging and printing technology. The Konica Minolta press release that announced the withdrawal stated, "In today's era of digital cameras, where image sensor technologies such as CCD is indispensable, it became difficult to timely provide competitive products even with our top optical, mechanical and electronics technologies."[21] This statement from Konica Minolta indicated that it withdrew because it was not keeping pace with Nikon and Canon, and its future in dSLRs looked dim—at least compared with other opportunities it could pursue. Sony, a company with the capacity to keep pace in dSLRs, picked up much of the Konica Minolta technology as a result of the Konica Minolta decision.

Col. John Boyd

The late Col. John Boyd, the father of the F-16 jet fighter, and the aforementioned relatively unknown but important American strategist showed that, as author Grant Hammond wrote from his discussions with Boyd,

> The ability to operate at a faster tempo or rhythm than an adversary enables one to fold the adversary back inside himself so that he can neither appreciate nor keep up with what is going on.[22]

Boyd went to great lengths to push the General Dynamics F-16 fighter program through Pentagon channels at a time when the McDonald Douglas F-15 was the Air Force's priority fighter project.[23] The foregoing quote, which had its origins in Boyd's observations of aerial combat, encapsulates why many seemingly competent operations fail: they cannot appreciate or keep up with competitors or the changing environment in which they operate.

Time is a major component of any strategy at all levels. You can have an overwhelming advantage in time because you have more of it, or simply because you are already where a competitor would like to be. Time certainly allows us to create surprise, in that we can use its availability to us to be where or show up when competitors do not expect us. Time also has the potential to be an asymmetrical advantage. If you can innovate faster than a competitor, you can consistently create offerings that your competitors do not yet have and protect those offerings with patents and with your capacity to continue to proficiently innovate faster. Your capacity to access or use time, or align it with other resources such as money, can also allow you to wait while pioneers blaze technical trails that you can capitalize on once you see success. Although you cannot actually recover lost time, you can often effectively buy the time of others by investing in their past success.

Any organization that is ahead in its development cycle also has the initiative as far as building its patent portfolio. It is almost always easier to "take a hill" before a competitor arrives to contest it, keeping in mind the importance of choosing the right hill. In the absence of that, you will need some other advantage, such as the capacity to buy that hill from its current occupant before someone else does or the capacity to otherwise outcompete and push your competitor aside. Furthermore, as indicated earlier in this book, time and timing is a measure that you can use to make the ideas presented in this book advantageous for you, even if all your competitors also read this same book. Proficiency plus tempo with a right decision wins competitions.

Oh, What a Feeling!

Tempo is a major theme discussed by Sun Tzu. Col. John Boyd was a student of Sun Tzu's *The Art of War* text and believed rapid tempo to be a major strategic asset. Toyota's management is also one of many Japanese management teams using Sun Tzu's *The Art of War* as a guiding text in its Toyota Production System.[24] Toyota proficiently operates at a higher tempo than rivals from product conception to launch and seeks to do so as a specific part of its corporate philosophy. This has a cumulative effect on its rivals; if Toyota releases a new product six months ahead of a rival, it will also be six months into the development of the next product before competitors even get

(Continued)

started on their response to the first product. If Toyota finishes that next project faster too, then they could be a year ahead. At some point, their competitors lose the capacity to compete, because their solutions are no longer good enough to match the latest Toyota has to offer. News articles over the last decade have been making references to GM, Ford, and Chrysler, stating that they need to "catch up" to the Japanese auto manufacturers. Where North American manufacturers have statistically caught up in reliability, tempo remains an issue in the creation of products that people want to buy when they want to buy them.

Sonshi.com, a website dedicated to Sun Tzu and *The Art of War*, interviewed Dr. Chester Richards on the late Col. John Boyd. Dr. Richards worked with Boyd at the Pentagon and is a retired USAF Reserve colonel. When asked about Col. John Boyd, Dr. Richards responded,

[Col. John Boyd] always believed that his ideas should apply to any form of conflict, not just war, but he had devoted his life to studying war and strategy. So he did not feel that he could produce a business version of *Patterns of Conflict* [an important Boyd paper on competition]. He was fascinated, however, by the Toyota Production System (TPS) and read everything he could find by people like Taiichi Ohno and Shigeo Shingo. In these works, he found many of the same ideas that he had put into his own briefings, particularly the fundamental role of harmony and the use of time as the basis for shaping competition.[25]

Taiichi Ohno and Shigeo Shingo are credited with inventing the world-class Toyota Production System. Sun Tzu, Col. John Boyd, and Toyota's Taiichi Ohno and Shigeo Shingo all used time as a strategic tool for shaping competitive advantages.

Factors of Importance re: Tempo

Raising tempo requires the following:

1. Vision—seeing what is out there: perceiving the opportunity, or threat, as well as which facilitating objectives the organization should pursue is critical for arriving at a right "B." A high tempo does not matter much if you head in the wrong direction.
2. Speed—getting there or getting away first; tempo is about more than speed, but just as in almost any race, raw speed matters.
3. Agility—adapting to changing conditions; strategy deals with uncertainty, and uncertainty produces a number of different possible outcomes and occurrences to which you must be willing to adapt and adjust. If you cannot adjust to change, a high tempo may mean only that you crash sooner, harder, or both.
4. Transition—going from one state to another; the right objective today may not be the right objective tomorrow, and the ability to recognize and transition is highly important. This can mean a complete transition from one mode of competition to another, such as Sega's transition from a vertical video game and console company to a horizontal video game maker for numerous other console maker companies. This can also mean the ease by which you can transition from cash to ideas to patents to some other resource and perhaps back to cash as one or the others become most important to the strategic situation.

To succeed at proficient and high tempo operations, you need to be highly interactive with your environment—not just with your customers and facilitators but with your competitors as well. The aforementioned quote, "Keep your friends close and your enemies closer" from the movie *The Godfather* brings with it a lot of competitive truth. The reasons for interacting with customers and facilitators should be obvious, but with competitors it can seem less so. Isolating a competitor from a technology does not mean you should not interact in any way with that competitor, because doing so isolates you from that competitor's plans and can open you up to some unpleasant surprises. As discussed earlier, even a seal, when faced with a great white shark in open water, finds that its best defense is to "glue" itself to the side of the shark to keep away from its jaws, and in fact this author and many other people have seen seals deliberately swim with sharks in an apparent bid to keep an eye on them. As it is said in shark-diving circles, it's not the shark you can see that you have to worry about. Interact with your environment, respond to your environment, and influence your environment. Consider using selected patents as a way to keep competitors close through licensing. Such interaction makes it much easier to understand their plans, to compete accordingly, and perhaps to become more, not less, cooperative over time.

Levels of Adaptation

In the course of operations, you will be required to adapt. Your strategy impacts or leverages the ability or inability you and your competitors have to adapt at the necessary pace. Tempo, therefore, affects operations from tactical to grand strategic levels. Levels of adaptation include:

1. *Technical adjustment.* This could mean a change in product line that can be made rapidly, such as adding cup holders to a pickup truck so they appeal to SUV buyers and commuters. Fundamental aspects of the business would not require change.
2. Schema adjustment. This includes a behavioral change of conditions that affects the business model, such as the decision to start a robust licensing program when previously the policy was to keep most inventions proprietary.
3. Directed evolution. This includes selective innovation for particular purposes, such as the directed creation of hybrid technology to meet consumer demand for hybrid cars, which will involve problem solving and the time and resources required to solve or acquire solutions to those problems.
4. Evolutionary adaptation. This includes adaptation that requires technical and behavioral change through innovation or acquisition, such as required by oil companies to become energy companies or a tabulating company to become a computer company, as in the case of IBM. Evolutionary adaptation often requires the greatest amount of time to succeed, which is why luck is often a factor in some business success. Companies such as Novozymes that have been in the

alternative fuels business for years, find current conditions of rising oil demand highly favorable for their investments.

As you move down the levels of adaptation list, the time required to implement change grows. Tempo affects each level slightly differently in that, for example, a company could prove very adept at making quick technical adjustments to add new features yet be unable to evolve at the pace of disruptive technologies that will make its product line obsolete. It is important, therefore, to investigate each area within your company and to tie that to the patent strategy. Action in patent strategy needs to match the tempo of the organization, and both need to be optimized for the outside world. A directed evolution effort will generate large volumes of new inventions that the patent department will need to handle, particularly in highly competitive first-to-file environments where delay can mean losing control of an idea.

Adaptation from Film to Digital

Kodak and Fuji are traditional film rivals that had to keep pace with rapid environmental change. Both organizations proved adept at making technical adjustments regarding film. If one rival came out with a new type of film, for example, an ISO 400 film that minimized graininess on the photos, the other would quickly have a rival product to match it. Schema adjustments proved more difficult as traditional film cameras gave way to digital cameras. Film is a consumable, whereas digital cards and cameras are not. This meant building business models around durable assets, such as digital cards and cameras, and developing new consumables, such as paper and printers for home and professional printing of those digital images. To support the schema adjustment, directed evolution took place to develop products, such as printers, papers, cameras, and cards, that would keep the companies vital. This put Kodak and Fuji into direct competition with camera makers and printer companies such as Canon and HP, respectively, that had previously been more complementary than competitive. Evolutionary adjustment is ongoing

(Continued)

> as Kodak and Fuji both develop their version of a total imaging
> company that includes consumable goods, durable goods, and
> services. At any time, if either company had failed to keep pace
> with these changes, it would have gone out of business. As it
> was, Kodak in particular went through some trying times.

The need for speed brings up a nuance that we discussed earlier related to freedom of action. Tempo often implies efficiency in terms of streamlining, but in fact efficiency often opposes the other critical variables in tempo of adaptability and the capacity to make transitions. To illustrate, let's look at camera lenses. The most efficient camera lens has only one focal range. A lens with a single focal length is lighter and cheaper than a zoom lens, has less comparative complexity, and can be completely optimized for that focal length. The zoom lens, however, is considerably more adaptable to changing conditions. The zoom lens allows you to get closer to or farther from a subject when you cannot physically move the camera closer or farther. Because of its superior adaptability, the most popular camera lenses therefore offer some amount of zoom capability.

Operating at a high tempo in the corporate world may likewise mean accepting certain inefficiencies that traditional operations people gear themselves to eliminate. Staffing is a major consideration here, especially since quality staffing comes with a high price tag. Any effort to minimize direct employee staffing requirements should have an accompanying means to deal with work flow volume influxes. Outside counsel and consulting services that you can use as needed, and that may furthermore make expertise available that you may not normally keep in-house, provide a means to keep operational tempo high. Putting certain functions offshore to lower cost has also been a common vehicle of companies for tasks for which physical proximity has less importance. Creative use of retirees, within company guidelines, can also provide a base of knowledgeable people who may be more than happy to contribute on an as-needed basis. Be creative here.

Beyond staffing, other considerations apply in the trade-off between efficiency and flexibility. Having a few more patents in the portfolio than you might otherwise have means you may better react to a competitive lawsuit with a countersuit. Research into a secondary option instead of focusing on just one means you can change over to that option much faster if the primary option falters. Highly competitive organizations, like fighter jets, need to be able to turn on the afterburners at the critical moments that define corporate futures. The balance is to become as efficient and fast as possible while still leaving enough flexibility to adapt and transition as necessary.

The Luck Factor

Any organization may experience the good commercial fortune to have the right products and disposition for the right events at the right time in a given market. When this happens, fortunes bloom. Bayer, for example, could not have predicted the events that made Ciprofloxacin, better known as Cipro, such a hot seller in addressing the anthrax threat of 2001. With only two years left on its patents from which to capitalize before generic manufacturers of the drug could enter the American market, the fear of terrorism, sparked by cases of deliberate anthrax poisonings, significantly increased Cipro sales.

While it may seem odd to put the fear of terrorism and luck into the same case example, it does illustrate an important point to understand about luck and commercializing technology. Bayer, through its own efforts and investment, had a proprietary product that many people, now afraid of the anthrax threat, wanted more than ever. Cipro dealt with a perceived significant problem, namely the mortal harm that untreated anthrax could cause. Bayer could not have foreseen the timing of events that led to the increased demand for Cipro, although it could probably foresee that such events as the anthrax attacks could occur. Had the terrorism attacks occurred two years later, post patent expiration, noting that Bayer did voluntarily halve the price of the drug in response to its perceived level of need, Bayer would not have had the opportunity to do as well commercially. The invention behind Cipro would have been in the public domain. Bayer, without any influence on the events that unfolded, had the right technology at the right time.[26]

This example of Cipro shows a nuance of luck, because luck is almost always a matter of perspective. It is possible for an organization to be lucky in unfortunate times when perhaps individuals even within that organization might also have wished the unfortunate circumstances had not arisen. This is, of course, a conundrum for the pharmaceutical industry as a whole, in that its fortunes depend on the occurrence of unfortunate events it can treat. Even aside from the pharmaceutical industry, an ample portion of the entire product base of almost any industry revolves around solving problems that others might find unfortunate to have. Many of these solutions are patented. That perhaps is the colder nature of luck to those on the other side of good fortune. But unless somehow obligated to have a solution to a problem if it arises, it makes sense that the provider of that solution, which undertook the risk to create that solution, might have some reward for even having a solution to offer. It reflects a key driver of invention. Nothing drives inventions faster than having major problems to solve, and part of making your own luck in business is to anticipate what those problems could be early enough to capitalize on them if they develop.

As with almost all strategic matters, there is a relationship between luck, timing, and choices that also has nuances. Maladaptive systems may have been adaptive systems, but under conditions that no longer prevail in the market. In fact, they probably were adaptive at one time or they would not have existed in the first place. The key here is to make sure that adaptive options remain available over time in order to adjust to changing circumstances destined to be fortunate for some and unfortunate for others. Adaptability is the issue that befell Apple in its general personal computing market and almost killed the company. A proprietary vertical business model for both computer and operating software made sense in the early 1980s for rapid innovation, but it became maladaptive as the 1980s closed and specialist horizontal market companies such as Intel and Microsoft began to prevail. Choices that had made sense for Apple no longer made sense with the new business paradigm. Yet Apple still exists because it ultimately was able to make ample adjustments to survive and then thrive in new ways. It offered more specialized or appealing computer applications and other products showing that luck, over time, can ultimately be about what you actually do in any given circumstance, as well as simply staying in the game.

Mainframes

IBM, with its mainframe computers, was highly adaptive to the computing environment from the 1960s into the 1980s. Its mainframe focus became maladaptive from the late 1980s through the early 1990s, when companies started to displace their mainframes with minicomputers and then LANs. To its good fortune, the mainframe focus became adaptive again in the mid-1990s when mainframes became useful for the growing Internet. A little bit of luck and a little bit of being in the right place at the right time is always a factor in business. Related to this is having an awareness of good fortune when it appears and a willingness to act on it. Luck can make a right decision by all other measures wrong and a wrong decision by all other measures right. That is a reality of life. People and businesses can succeed and fail due to plain dumb luck.

Qualifying the Result

When you take an action, you produce a result. At the end of that action, you assess the result. This assessment leads us to completing the decision cycle. We have a new current situation "A" and will ultimately seek a new future situation "B." Some questions to ask are the following:

1. Did you achieve the intended result?
2. If not, did you achieve a useful result?
3. How close was the strategy to ideal?
4. How close was the strategy to optimal?
5. Was the strategy "good enough"?
6. What were the harmful consequences that arose?
7. How do you improve?

Based on your answers to these and any other questions relevant to your situation, you will make new decisions and take new actions, and the cycle continues. If you can proficiently go through these cycles at a higher tempo than your rivals, then you are likely to gain the initiative and the advantage in the whole competitive environment.

Act: A Summary

This section has discussed taking action, which means deliberately doing something, even when you deliberately decide to do nothing. We now know that you should not take action just for the sake of taking action. Every action should have a purpose. We discussed addressing the identified problem, which relates to the above in that we need to focus on the real issues needed to reach our desired result "B." We also discussed making adjustments when acting, which can be comparatively difficult for strategic solutions versus technical solutions because it is more difficult to establish what the actual causes for observed effects are. Patent strategists need to remain objective to understand when they are wrong or why they are right or how they were just plain lucky in order to consistently improve on their strategies.

We showed that the availability and application of resources determine what an organization can and should do. Patents represent one of those resources, but they link to every other resource an organization has. The disposition of resources in operations focuses on four operational tenets:

1. Concentration of effort
2. Economy of resources
3. Freedom of action
4. Safety

To be proficient in operations, we discussed the usefulness of keeping in mind the ideal that you want to receive 100% of the benefit of acting with 0% of the cost. It is a practically impossible ideal to achieve, but an ideal to aim for. Thinking in this way helps to ensure that you use only those resources available to the company that you absolutely need to use, which is also a key to maintaining freedom of action. A resource, once committed, is not available for use elsewhere, and a resource paid for that does not produce a commensurate benefit for the expense itself becomes a drag on operations and other resources.

In the final part of this section, we examined tempo as a critical factor in strategy since, all other things being equal, the organization that can proficiently operate at a faster, or in some circumstances, slower tempo than a competitor will have a significant advantage over that competitor.

The organization that purposefully and proficiently decides to move at a slower pace can still have a rapid tempo for determining that moving slowly is the best strategic action. We discussed the luck factor, which is always a part of strategy. Sometimes being in the right place at the right time really does make all the difference, but you still must prepare to take advantage of luck and consider foreseeable events by which you can better position yourself to be lucky. With luck in mind, it is important to appreciate that a company that was adaptive in the past may no longer be adaptive in the present, and further that changes in the conditions of business can actually make a company that is maladaptive, like IBM and its mainframes in the later 1980s, adaptive once again, as with the new need for mainframes to power the Internet in the 1990s.

Finally, we discussed qualifying the result. Every action leads to a result, a consequence with elements both predicted and unpredicted. Every distance gained needs to be measured to quantify improvement for future actions. This brings us back to assessment, and the completion of a decision cycle.

The Optimal Leopard

In the miniseries *Shaka Zulu*, aired from 1986, the following dialog appeared between Shaka and his military general Mkobozi after their encounter with the British. Shaka was the famous Zulu chieftain who reigned from 1816 to 1828 in the southern region of Africa. The dialog was in reference to the British and their advanced technology, and the analogy was to a leopard being offered wings to fly.

Shaka: "The leopard is also superior Mkobozi. One day in the proud life of a leopard is worth 100 days in the life of a raven. But if the leopard were offered wings to walk the sky, he would be foolish to refuse them."

Mkobozi: "No Shaka, the leopard's kingdom is the earth. On the earth he is master, in the sky he becomes victim."[27]

(Continued)

This exchange illustrates the need to put all issues pertaining to the creation, acquisition, and maintenance of any opportunity into perspective. It makes sense for a raven to have wings, but it does not make sense for a leopard to have them. For the former, they are an asset; to the latter, a hindrance at best. So as someone involved with patent strategy, it is important to assess whether acting on a promising opportunity is truly valuable or like adding wings to a leopard.

Chapter 6

Connecting the Loop

Q ualifying the result brings us back around the loop of a complete decision cycle, since we can now assess our results. Our intent was to go from "A" to "B," and we have gone from "A" to somewhere. Was it "B"? Was it something less than "B"? Was it something better than "B"? Did we come up short and need to try again, or can we move on to something else?

In the beginning of this book we discussed consequences, both useful and harmful. In speaking of your assessment, we explored how to leverage predicted and unpredicted useful results and how to mitigate the predicted and unpredicted harmful results. Based on the results of your action, we will make a new assessment, a new decision, and then take a new action. Within your grander strategies, there will be many smaller decision cycles that take place in the pursuit of the larger goal. Taking account of everything we have discussed thus far, you will use your patents in accordance with the aforementioned four rules of patent strategy:

1. Use a patent to isolate.
2. Threaten to use a patent to isolate.
3. Use a patent to interact.
4. Leverage the possible use of a patent to interact.

In accord with these four rules, your decision cycle will very much revolve around the creation and processing of new inventions. Without access to inventions, whether created internally or from an accessible outside source, you cannot really have a patent strategy. Although having no patents of your own is a viable patent strategy, you do need access to inventions.

The Invention Review List

This brings us back to the Invention Review List that we introduced at the beginning of the decision cycle. The Invention Review List takes a preeminent position in patent strategy at the link between Act and Assess. The end result of action often delivers new inventions to your attention. The beginning of an assessment often begins with the question of what best to do with the inventions you have, which in turn leads to what inventions you need to create or acquire.

We return to the invention review list toward the end of this book because answering the 10 questions well requires that you use the ideas we have now discussed. They are written particularly for you to do that.

The patent strategist seeks answers for all of the questions on this Invention Review List (see Exhibit 6.1) for every given invention that could serve a useful purpose in a patent and overlying business strategy. If an answer to a question is in the positive for moving ahead, great. If negative, keeping in mind that an invention unsuitable for patenting could be suitable to keep as a trade secret, you should do one of the following:

1. Reject the invention as a patent candidate and consider, based upon your reason for rejecting the patent candidate, publication to prevent others from patenting the invention or keeping the invention as a trade secret.

Exhibit 6.1 Invention Review List

---

1. Is there existing prior art?
2. Does the invention have commercial potential?
3. Is the invention patentable?
4. Can the invention serve our competitive strategic purpose?
5. Will a patent on this invention deliver a business advantage?
6. Do we have other competitive advantages that reduce or enhance the need to patent this invention?
7. Does a patent on this invention support our position in the technical space?
8. Are we willing and able to litigate over a patent on this invention if challenged?
9. Can we detect a patent infringement on this invention if it occurs?
10. Are the business, legal, or technical risks associated with this invention acceptable?

---

2. Provide a solution for addressing the issue that otherwise would cause you to reject patenting.
3. Provide a logical reason to proceed with the patent anyway.

The ability to effectively execute patent strategy depends on the strategist's accurate knowledge of the business and technical environment, as well as his or her appreciation of opportunities and constraints. Any question answered unfavorably requires an adjustment in the invention, the patent plan, or some other aspect of the organization or its operation. For example, if in Question 8 you are not willing or able to litigate over a patent on an invention if challenged, there may not be a point in patenting it, unless you can accept a competitor's calling your bluff with impunity or plan to find someone to litigate for you. This may have been a question that faced the management of Under Armour® when it decided to ramp up its initial business without patents. Maybe luck favored them when Nike and others responded so slowly to the Under Armour® product line. So, in strategy there are no absolutes, just general trends that favor the prepared. It is true that sometimes the smart (intelligently crafted, high probability of success) move loses and the dumb (not well thought out, emotionally initiated) move wins. During your review of past actions you will find that your customers and competitors do not always act in a way that would have best served their interests and yet sometimes they succeed anyway.

Prior Art Search

Be that as it may, you always want to make smart moves; that puts the odds in your favor. We stated early in this book, and several times along the way, that most of the time one of the smartest moves any patent strategist can make before making an important decision is to undertake a prior art search. Although a prior art search is often made at the beginning of a decision cycle involving inventions, it is often made at the end, as well, to assess how conditions may have changed during that time and to investigate new inventions and directions that have developed. A prior art search should accompany any decision to pursue an invention or change the disposition of a patent most of the time, because it provides the very latest information on patent activity associated with that decision. There should be a very specific, understood, and accepted reason not to do so if you choose not to conduct a prior art search.

Unless a line of research is truly on the cutting edge of technology, the prior art search is the most efficient way to help researchers and developers concentrate their efforts on the truly new. Inefficiencies that can otherwise develop may negatively impact every aspect of patent strategy that we have discussed thus far. Tempo itself is enhanced by the cumulative man-hours an organization spends on action useful for the current direction. Conducting prior art searches and making informed strategic decisions from them allows the organization to better focus those cumulative man-hours where they can best advance the organization.

Invention Elicitation

Tied to the invention review process is invention elicitation. Invention elicitation provides the opportunity to consider ideas inherent within the company that you could otherwise miss. Unrecorded intellectual property exists within all organizations, if for no other reason than that people do not usually record everything they know. Recording, categorizing, and protecting intellectual property is important when making the effort to capture the investment made to create it. Recorded intellectual property becomes a transferable, tradable, and saleable asset. Patents and other intellectual property developed from invention elicitation give you the legal leverage of invention ownership.

This means that as someone involved with patent strategy, you or other trained individuals need to sit down with inventors and review their ideas on given initiatives. The categorization of these ideas can be done individually or through group consensus. Brainstorming sessions also serve as an excellent way to generate ideas that can become the basis for new and patentable inventions. A typical brainstorming session, often called an innovation workshop, consists of about 7 to 14 people and takes place over two to three days. It can focus on defining new possibilities for the future as well as evolving existing technologies.

In an innovation workshop conducted by the author that did both, the workshop participants brainstormed potential applications for a new technology affecting electronic information displays. This technology had entered the market in very limited form at that point, but had lots of potential. On identifying the most promising applications, participants backtracked from those applications to the present state of their technology in order to map out the needed technology to enable those applications. That technology map created both research and development targets and licensing targets for the company. A trained facilitator can enhance innovation workshop activities by keeping participants focused and providing objective opinions that can be more difficult for people with a personal stake in the situation to make.

When conducting innovation workshops, it is important to remember that you not only seek to predict future possibilities, you seek to create that future by your own influence on it. If you cannot determine what will happen, but have some say in what will happen, then you ask what future you would like to see and how you can make it happen.

Classifications of Confidentiality

Invention elicitation, when combined with an organization of records such as lab notebooks, allows for the categorization of a company's ideas for security purposes. Categorizing new

(Continued)

innovations helps all members of the organization know what they can and cannot share with outsiders. Well-articulated guidelines on how to handle information with different levels of confidentiality will make the job of salespeople and engineers working with customers and suppliers easier and much less frustrating to them and risky for the organization. Guidelines for the distribution of sensitive information should include people outside the organization who will have access to sensitive information; that way they can appreciate why certain information has been categorized a certain way to protect both organizations involved. If a customer demands full access to certain information, then you may change the categorization of that information, or you may establish an agreement between the two parties to limit disclosure. The following discussion gives a basic overview of the concept of innovation categorization.

You may classify innovations as trade secrets, patentable concepts, or general intellectual property (and some organizations may even choose to break down the general intellectual property into additional levels of sensitivity). As a general rule, you should never divulge trade secrets to anyone outside of the organization, and you should implement additional steps to keep the information truly secret, such as protecting files with passwords on computer hard drives that can be accessed only by designated people.

Once you apply for patent protection, on the other hand, you may share this information because it will become public knowledge once the patent application is published anyway. Keep in mind, though, that the technology will not receive patent protection unless the patent office in a given authority grants the patent, nor might you want to disclose this information before the application publishes. For this reason, most companies continue to treat their patent applications as sensitive documents until that publication date, and even then do not necessarily go out of their way to make newly published patent applications known.

General intellectual property should always be treated as sensitive information, but it does not necessarily require the level of secrecy accorded to a trade secret. General intellectual property may be accessible to everyone within the organization and shared with customers and suppliers as appropriate. However, some kind of nondisclosure agreement, joint venture agreement, or confidentiality clause should exist between yourself and any other organization with which you plan to share sensitive information.

The Invention Audit

Often, it can make sense for a company to step back and assess itself so that it can easily identify the patents it already owns. From a strategic standpoint, the most important thing you can do regarding your own patent portfolio is to set up a classification system in a way that allows you to find things. This often means setting up a proprietary indexing system that classifies your technology in a way that aligns with how your organization views the technical world. It was through such indexing systems that companies such as AT&T and Exxon, which have spoken about classifying intellectual property in public, were and are able to make more effective research, development, divestiture, licensing, and acquisitions decisions. Once you have an effective internal indexing system and a means to keep it updated, you can run analyses on your own patent portfolio. When combined with external views of patent landscapes, these can help you to make decisions in accord with our four operational tenets:

1. Concentration of effort
2. Economy of resources
3. Freedom of action
4. Safety

As a cautionary note, be wary of efforts to mine patent portfolios. Patent mining means trying to actively license your own unused patents to outside organizations. While it can certainly make sense to take a look at what you have and license items of value that you do not need to keep proprietary, only a small fraction of inventions ever have a meaningful commercial value. You can effectively allow prospective customers to do their own patent mining just by making known your openness to patent licensing in general. IBM has taken this to full measure not only by allowing licenses to patents within its vast patent portfolio but by making known in advance the terms people can expect, should they find technology of interest. IBM's approach is comparable to opening a mall and letting people shop for themselves instead of trying to predict what people want to buy.

Chapter 7

Two Imperatives

A s we draw toward the conclusion of this book, we will discuss two imperatives needed to make any patent strategy work. Without these two imperatives in place, you will have a much steeper hill to climb to achieve success. In fact, it might be impossible. These are:

1. CEO involvement in the intellectual property process
2. Mastery of the fundamentals in operational excellence

Imperative 1: CEO Involvement

Patent strategy affects and is affected by many professional disciplines. In order to get the most out of parallel lines of competition, senior management, particularly the CEO, must buy into the creation and implementation of patent strategies. The CEO has the institutional authority to put a patent strategy into effect and can address matters of dueling incentives and silo politics at lower levels of the management hierarchy that may cause an otherwise sound patent strategy to under-perform.

The first reason for CEO involvement is basic fiduciary responsibility. While it will certainly vary by company and industry, based on subtracting the known value of hard assets (e.g., factories and inventory) from the total market cap of companies, no research and development–based company should be surprised that 70% or more of its value is in its intellectual property. A key component of that intellectual property, all of which retains its maximum value as a result of how well each component of a company supports each other, is the patent. That value alone justifies a CEO's spending a substantial portion of his or her time on patent-related matters as both assets and investments. The CEO also needs to ensure that patent management efforts receive the funding needed to produce the best return for the company and to correct any mismanagement of patent assets that occurs. This means that the CEO's role should include the oversight of the people most involved in intellectual property management efforts.

While the person delegated to make things happen in patent strategy could be another corporate officer, such as a Chief Intellectual Property Officer (CIPO), reporting and assessment needs to go to the top. The reason for this is that the typical organization divides itself into departments (silos) that specialize in specific functions. Each department and the person who heads it, typically a vice president–level supervisor, will have different measures of success to account for. This can lead to internal conflict in the form of dueling incentives when the approaches that make one department successful, such as the legal department needing engineers to refrain from looking at patent data so as to avoid the treble damages of willful infringement, work against the success of another, such as research and development needing engineers to look at patent data so as not to have them waste time and money reinventing. When dueling incentives come into play, politics takes an increasing role in decision making as the heads of competing departments seek resolutions that may be at odds with the interests of other departments. While the CEO is not necessarily immune to politics, the CEO's responsibility for the whole operation generally puts him or her in a better position to minimize how politics can negatively impact decision making.

When establishing a patent strategy, the patent strategist needs a high level of cooperation between research and development, business, and legal units, all of which may measure performance differently. Each of the units mentioned have responsibility for the essential Centers of Excellence of the stakeholders' organization. Research and development is a key component of the Center of Excellence for innovation. Business units, such as marketing, sales, finance, and operations, are the key components of the Center of Excellence for business advancement. The legal department is a key component for the Center of Excellence for security. All provide input as to where their respective professions are headed in order to patent effectively for the future.

Although ideally all three Centers of Excellence support each other, and the patent strategy supports and is supported by the Centers of Excellence, the reality is that different measures for success often cause people responsible for different Centers of Excellence to develop different priorities. Research and development may find itself measured by patent output, and it may emphasize the creation of new inventions and the patenting of as many of these inventions as possible, even when a given patent makes minimal business sense. Legal may find itself measured by its ratio of success in prosecuting patents and avoiding infringements, so it may want to steer away from highly contested technology and toward only the most patentable and defendable inventive ideas, even though these could have less potential business value than other opportunities. Business units may find themselves measured primarily by their success in marketing existing product lines, and may find themselves reluctant to push new products, particularly if those products are more difficult to sell than their current products. Even groups within each of these Centers of Excellence may have their own separate and conflicting metrics. For example, a licensing group that measures its success based on license revenue gained may seek to license out inventions that legal and business units would prefer to keep proprietary. End result: conflict. Only an individual with higher-level responsibilities, one above the concerns of dueling incentives and silo politics in respective business units, is in a good position to set and keep in place the strategy that is in the best overall interests of the entire organization despite these conflicts. That individual is most often the CEO. The CEO has the institutional authority to address both dueling incentives and silo politics. He or she can make decisions for the good of the company that an individual heading a specific department may prove reluctant to make.

The CEO and the Patent Line of Competition

A problem that patent strategists run into regarding CEO involvement in patent issues is CEO inattention caused by a common lack of familiarity with the use of patents to gain competitive business advantage. Patent management and patent strategy is generally not taught in business schools, and where it is, it certainly does not take the lead positions of the more traditional finance, marketing, and operations disciplines. In addition, patent management and patent strategy do not represent traditional career paths even within patent legal departments, where so much attention necessarily focuses on traditional patent prosecution and patent litigation. Aside from the educational matters, there also exists a natural and learned tendency among non-attorneys to defer legal matters to the legal department. No one can deny that the patent itself is a legal document, so any decision to have Legal handle patents is entirely understandable; but as good as a patent attorney or entire legal team may be, the education and background of attorneys may be just as lacking in business matters as the CEO's is in patent matters. Put these facts together and you can see how a natural tendency exists to delegate the patent line of competition and give it minimal CEO oversight. However, as this book shows on a number of different levels, the most effective use of patents to improve the bottom line of a business demands that patents be integrated into general business practice. Patents are matters about which business leaders and management need to be concerned, taking advice of patent counsel into consideration in making those decisions. The ultimate employment of patents to best effect is a matter for senior management, namely the CEO, to decide.

So, to become an effective patent strategist, you may need to overcome some frictions in the organization between different departments by involving yourself with the top if you are not already at the top. It is extremely important to succeed here; without buy-in from the top, namely the CEO, all matters discussed in this book could very well prove irrelevant for the innovation-based company.

Bill Gates and Patents

To make the case for CEO involvement in patent strategy, consider once again the attitude of one of the most effective contemporary CEOs, Bill Gates. When the court ordered Microsoft to pay Stac $120 million in 1994 for a patent infringement, Microsoft had only a handful of patents in its portfolio. After that lawsuit, Microsoft's attitude toward patents changed, and this is mostly attributed to the personal involvement of Bill Gates. Microsoft currently has granted an average of eight patents per day, which may be more on a daily basis than Microsoft had in its entire portfolio at the time of the Stac lawsuit. This change in Gates's attitude, and therefore Microsoft's attitude, surprised a colleague of the author's at Thomson Information when, as the story goes, Bill Gates dropped in on that colleague's routine sales visit to ask if he was the guy who had the tool to fix the (Stac) problem. While this author cannot confirm all the details of this story, a directive for change did come from Gates, and it does get to the point that if being directly involved with patents was important enough for a CEO of Gates's stature, it is probably important enough for any CEO of any research and development company on the planet.

Microsoft has now become one of the most patent-savvy companies in the world, which is a reason it has been cited in a number of examples in this book. Its intellectual property department is currently headed by Marshall Phelps, who also headed the world-class intellectual property organization at IBM. Phelps, like other people employed in similar positions, facilitates the need for CEOs to have direct involvement in patent-based activities. Some organizations have seen such an importance in C-level executive involvement on patent matters that they have created a C-level position just for patent strategy and intellectual property protection. They give it such titles as the Chief Innovation Officer (CIO) or the Chief Intellectual Property Officer (CIPO), as noted earlier. Many of the people involved in these initiatives attend conferences, such as the Intellectual Property Owners Association, www.IPO.org, to exchange ideas with colleagues and other people who seek higher levels of executive involvement in patent matters.

Lobbying

All action is driven by incentives. We all take action because we expect to benefit in some way from that action, in terms of either reward or avoidance of harm. François Lévêque and Yann Ménière, in their paper, "Patents and Innovation: Friends or Foes?" note the originally intended purpose of patents as being an incentive to innovate.[1] Incentivizing people to innovate is likewise a desire for most CEOs in their businesses; therefore, most CEOs would prefer that patent laws be written and interpreted to institutionally incentivize innovation. An additional role of the CEO, either directly or through appropriately assigned individuals, is to influence the development of appropriate patent laws suitable to their company, which generally are in the direction in favor of patent laws that do indeed incentivize innovation. This is done through lobbying and other appropriate means that allow the CEO to communicate what he or she would like lawmakers to do.

Imperative 2: Master the Fundamentals

The second imperative is to master the fundamentals of strategy and the operations upon which it is based. This pertains to the world of patents in the sense of both patent drafting and patent strategy. The art and practice of drafting good patents is key to producing quality coverage of innovative ideas. From that art and practice, you can succeed with fundamental strategies, such as with the strategy operators, "Lie in Wait for an Attacking Adversary," or "Strike with a Borrowed Hand," which themselves become a part of the entire strategy you employ. You should have well-drafted patents and employ people who draft patents well, and you should also regularly practice the art of using patents in strategic ways. For example, a way to lie in wait for an attacking adversary is to build a patent picket fence along an important line of research on which your competitor may encroach. Practicing these fundamentals is hard work, but remember our quote from Vince Lombardi, the famous Green Bay Packers football coach: "Excellence is achieved by the mastery of the fundamentals."[2]

Mastering the fundamentals can hardly be overemphasized. Mistakes in the fundamentals are one of the most common reasons patent strategy initiatives fail, perhaps second only to failure to achieve senior management (CEO) support. It is a tendency aggravated by the fact that strategic prowess is difficult to measure, because causes and effects do not always link together easily. As a result, many more people think they have strategic prowess, perhaps based on a string of good luck, than actually do have strategic prowess. They may find themselves inclined to think their training is done, but it is never done. It takes hard and continual work. The reward is the ability to appreciate and respond to situations encountered in ways you may never before have dreamed of.

The execution and success of an exceptional strategy is an exciting thing to watch or to participate in, especially if you are on the winning side. Behind such successes is usually someone who really knew what he or she was doing, backed up by some well-executed fundamentals. After experiencing a strategic success, particularly one that appears out of the ordinary, people naturally want to jump right into advanced strategy material and skip the fundamentals on which it is built. This is putting the cart before the horse, so to speak, both on a personal and corporate level. In strategy, the extraordinary generally arises from the ordinary.

On the corporate level, people at all the three Centers of Excellence need to really understand their roles as supporting units to the whole business before they can be effective in doing so. This starts at the fundamentals of those centers as well. Consider that the value of your patents themselves could depend on whether the people who sell your products really know the fundamentals of sales. So you and the people you work with need to have the very basics down, which, for you as someone involved with patent strategy, are all the different ways to interact and to isolate that we discussed. Even Michael Jordan, one of the greatest basketball players of all time, spent hours just practicing his basic shots.[3] The fanciest of moves on the floor mean nothing unless the ball goes through the hoop; the greatest patent strategy means nothing if the patents you depend upon cannot stand up in court.

AWAKE Cycle™: From Fundamentals to Exceptional Strategy

The strategic mind develops from novice toward master through a continuous cycle of awareness, willingness, ability, knowledge, and experience, which we can term the AWAKE Cycle™. The AWAKE Cycle™ is a framework for developing a strategic mindset that takes you from learning the basics to becoming a master. Regardless of your skill level, the better you know the fundamentals of strategy, the better you can navigate this framework, and the better you will ultimately perform. AWAKE is an acronym for Awareness, Willingness, Ability, Knowledge, and Experience.

To craft a strategy requires you to be aware of opportunities and threats and further aware of the respective strengths and weaknesses of all the participants in the scenario. This awareness should impact your willingness to take action, keeping in mind that even doing nothing requires having the willingness to do nothing. Ability means having the inherent capacity as an individual or organization to act, irrespective of your knowledge of how to do so. Knowledge, therefore, refers to whether you, as the enactor of the strategy, understand how to use the abilities available. Experience refers to the past history of handling the same or related problems, which, in turn, should lead to a higher level of awareness, more proficient choices in connection with the willingness to act, higher abilities, more knowledge, yet more experience, and so on, from novice to master. Through successive loops around the AWAKE Cycle™ you improve your intuitive feel of the circumstances and what needs to be done.

Let's say you become aware that a white space (open) opportunity exists in an area close to your current technology; based on estimates of the resources necessary to develop it, and a lack of corresponding competitive prior art, you have the willingness to pursue those opportunities. Let's further say that technically you have the ability to pursue the opportunity, since you have researchers in the related art, but sensing a weakness in knowledge, you decide to set up a partnership with a university to raise the level of knowledge needed to put that ability to work. By acting, both you and the researchers involved gain added experience, which raises your level of awareness of the opportunity, your willingness to do this and not do that, and so on. In short, your skills in all aspects of assessment, decision, and action improve. A knowledge-based organization will continually refine its AWAKE Cycles™ for those initiatives it considers important, and so will the individual.

So what is the point of the AWAKE Cycle™ model introduced at this point? It is to highlight that even at the base of the fundamentals we have some nuances, and this creates the opportunity to advance the ideas presented in this book even further. One of the exciting and challenging things about strategy is that no matter how deeply you study the topic, there is always another deeper level you can explore. This is the nuance of the AWAKE Cycle™ and the reason you see it here now. As a participant in a strategic contest, you influence the very environment in which you participate and therefore the nature of that contest. Your behavior changes the environment, and your actions have the effect of creating new uncertainties to address and employ. Using the AWAKE Cycle™ as a lens, look at what happens:

1. *Awareness.* Your becoming aware of an environment alters that environment by the fact that it is now known, and elements within the environment may seek to again become unknown.
2. *Willingness.* Any change in your willingness to act or not act alters the environment that would be impacted by your action or inaction.
3. *Ability.* Your abilities, when played out upon the environment, serve to alter the environment and therefore change the relevance and impact of those abilities.
4. *Knowledge.* If knowledge does not create your desired result, you will seek to improve that knowledge, which allows you to both understand and manipulate the environment, thereby altering the environment and invalidating some of the previous knowledge about it.
5. *Experience.* Experience is gained through having some impact on the environment that is therefore changed, possibly invalidating some of the experience gained.

As a master in strategy, you can process these subtle changes without giving them much thought. As a novice, you may not even be able to see them. So the apparent complexity that can arise in strategy furthers the importance of mastering the fundamentals as a base to achieving excellence and mastery in strategy. If you draft good patents that have a reasonable chance of standing up in court and claim inventions in a way that is difficult to design around, then no matter the nuance of strategy involved, you stand on good ground. That well-drafted patent affords the opportunity that you will at least do well enough in a given action to learn something from the experience and better yourself afterward. If you do not do the fundamentals well, then you can not expect to improve, because your more competent opponents will defeat you handily before you can learn anything. When everything with the fundamentals starts to come together for you, which it will, then you will start to influence the nuances, and you will be able to leverage any errors made by your opponents that novices may not even recognize. That recognition, that awareness, combined with the willingness, ability, knowledge, and experience to do something well, is the added opportunity gained both from experience and mastering the fundamentals, and that will lead you to create exceptional strategies.

Chapter 8

High-Tempo Patent Strategy

S ince 1993, the author has had the opportunity to work with more than 100 major patenting organizations on one issue or another. Along the way, a number of interesting patent and innovative practices have come to light. Many of these practices have developed in the high-tech arena where the dominant patent strategy is to stockpile patents, but the lessons learned can also apply to companies that bank on the blockbuster patent strategy, such as pharmaceutical companies.

The following is a composite of a number of best practices found in what we will call a "High-Tempo Patent Strategy." This High-Tempo Patent Strategy has been developed from and reflects many of the most interesting ideas that the author has encountered or helped to create at major patenting organizations, although no one organization seen has used this entire strategy as it is described here. It is likewise not suggested that you do everything described here, but that you consider and pick those ideas most useful to your situation. We will discuss the ideas behind a High-Tempo Patent Strategy as a whole, because the adoption of any idea or group of ideas could enhance the processes and strategies that you already use or plan to use. The strategy has four major parts:

1. Set common viewpoints.
2. Measure the control of technical space.
3. Accelerate innovation.
4. Conduct invention/patent infiltration.

Set Common Viewpoints

The first part of a High-Tempo Patent Strategy is to set common viewpoints for all participants in the strategy. Accomplish this by communicating not only what you want to have done but your intent for doing it. For example, assign the prosecution of patents for a new invention and include with that assignment the reason you want a patent and what you would like to do with it.

The use of intent allows an implicit communication of a task to take precedence over the need for explicit communication. If people know what you want to have accomplished (i.e., your intent), they will implicitly know how to handle issues that may come up without always needing to go back to you. This greatly enhances the speed and flexibility of their performance, or to quote General Patton, "Never tell people how to do things. Tell them what to do, and they will surprise you with their ingenuity."[1]

Implicit communication is equivalent to being able to call a play in American football that intends within that play for a specific player to block a specific linebacker, and knowing that specific player understands the dynamics of the play well enough to block left or right or not at all depending on where that linebacker actually lines up and goes. Similarly, you want people to already appreciate the big picture so that when they draft a patent, it is drafted to that bigger picture without your necessarily having to say how to draft it. You want a well-protected invention, you empower your patent attorney to do that, and you know it will be done in a right way, even if it is not exactly the way that you would do it. The same principle works for litigation, licensing negotiations, and other important patent matters.

Communication through intent improves mental concentration of effort, the psychological side of one of our four operational tenets, because people will take greater ownership of a task when they have a say in how to do it. Those who are empowered to own a task take better care of it and deliver better results than those following explicit guidelines. People often talk about team efforts and the development of implicit communication as being key to this task. In sports, you and your teammates implicitly understand that you want to score and prevent your competitor from scoring. You and your teammates do not care so much how you score, as long as you score. Is the intent of your business or department as clear and flexible as this? Do people appreciate that you want *a* right approach, not *the* right approach, so that you can leverage their ingenuity while also getting things done? If not, consider adding this dimension to your management practices.

Measure the Control of Technical Space

Many patent departments that the author has worked with in the past have benchmarked their success as compared with competitors by comparing the number of patents obtained. Sometimes they normalized the number of patents obtained by using additional numbers, such as patents gained per research and development dollars spent. Although these are easy measures to use, they are not always relevant, in that the total number of patents obtained does not necessarily tell whether an organization actually controls meaningful technical space. A more useful metric, especially in a High-Tempo Patent Strategy, is to measure the organization's control of technical space. By this we mean that if you map the core invention, the elements of the entire product system for which that invention is a part, the present and future enablers that will allow that invention and product system to move down its evolutionary path, and the applications that develop from the invention, product system, and enablers, then you can measure how much of the overall system you actually control.

Control of technical space is actually a hard measurement to make as your competitive benchmark, but at least appreciating the idea when you review the statistics that you have will aid in executing effective patent strategies, more so than traditional patent counts. The concept behind controlling technical space itself is similar in nature to the concept of controlling the high seas by navies, because controlling key points of the system of oceans, such as Gibraltar or the Panama Canal, can influence the freedom of passage for vast areas of the broader oceans. Independent of the size of your actual navy, you seek to deploy it in a way that gives you the most control of the space you desire with the least actual commitment of resources.

In the intellectual property space, however, the oceans as ideas are limitless and the control points both fluid and temporary. A High-Tempo Patent Strategy is a strategy of rapid innovation with this limitless space in mind that uses the decisive control of technical space, a desired strategic effect of a patent strategy, as its strategic measure instead of the comparative number of patents obtained. It involves finding, building, and controlling new intellectual property Gibraltars along the way and discarding old ones that have lost their relevance.

Using a measure based on patent count can produce an over-protected and under-protected body of inventions if technical space is not taken into account as part of the filing process. It is equivalent to measuring the success of a police crackdown on speeders by counting the number of tickets issued, as opposed to measuring whether cars have actually slowed down in an affected area. Would an increase in the number of tickets written mean that the police are having a positive impact on slowing down drivers, or would it mean that more people are speeding or simply that more police officers have been dispatched with the directive to write more tickets? After all, the police could accomplish the stated goal of slowing people down while issuing no tickets at all, perhaps, as some towns have done, by putting life sized mock-ups of police cars at strategic locations along the highway. A metric should therefore be chosen that most accurately measures success toward the desired goal, which here is not the number of patents obtained but the control of technical space that your patents afford.

In a High-Tempo Patent Strategy you use the control of technical space as your measure of success instead of the patent count, even if this measure is a bit foggier on paper, and in so doing you will also consider all physical, psychological, and moral aspects of protecting your inventions, including, but not limited to, the patent itself. The control of technical space metric leverages advanced creativity techniques to increase the quantity as well as the quality of inventions produced and, as a byproduct, the technical space controllable with the right protections. Speed of innovation, combined with a high quantity and quality of new inventions created, becomes the critical factor for business success, not the number of patents held in the portfolio.

With control of technical space as a measure instead of the number of patents awarded, you have some added leverages to use, as discussed in the following text.

Advanced Creativity Techniques

Using advanced creativity techniques, you can both accelerate innovation and direct technical evolution into predicted and predictable open technical space. An example of an advanced creativity technique that you can examine in the public domain is the aforementioned theory of inventive problem solving (TRIZ). In short, you deliberately evolve your inventions—and perhaps selected inventions belonging to your competitors—into the lines of evolution described by Altshuller and in Chapter 4, Decide of this book, or into an open solution quadrant, in order to claim that technical space ahead of your competitors.

You can be pretty exacting with your inventive processes, particularly in the realm of incremental improvements, since you can systematically review inventive operators to see which apply. Through your network of patents, you want to control a technical space. Defensively, you want to control as much relevant technical space as possible with as few resources (i.e., patents) as possible. You accomplish this by systematically evolving your inventions and protecting them not only within patents, but as technical disclosures or as trade secrets. By systematically evolving, we mean simply reviewing the applicability of known inventive principles, such as to execute tasks in parallel, so that you can focus on applying those known principles without also having to remember or reinvent the principles. Such a system greatly increases the comprehensiveness and pace at which you can solve problems and create new inventions.

Offensively, you can infiltrate your competitors' patent protections as necessary by evolving their inventions and seeking patents and technical disclosures around those inventions. By inventing with the technical evolution path shown by Altshuller as a guide, you can get a cycle ahead of your competitors, forcing them to be more interactive with you to access inventions that you have claimed and they want. This creates the cross-licensing scenario derived from a system of blocking patents that many people call a "patent picket fence."

Psychological Protections

In a High-Tempo Patent Strategy, you use psychological protections to supplement physical protections. This is where technical disclosures and trade secrets can come into play to reduce the need to patent while increasing the control of technical space. Just the possibility that a patent may exist can often produce the same result of discouraging competitors from entering a technical space that an actual patent will produce. In fact, it may do even better. The reason a possible patent may prove even more successful at discouraging infringement than an actual patent is that an actual patent can be studied and probed for weaknesses, and a possible patent remains an unknown. People seem to fear the unknown more than the known, a fact used by horror storytellers for years. If you remember the movie *Jaws*, you never really see the shark until well into the movie. Most people think the movie was scarier before they saw the shark on the screen.

To illustrate how this can work in patent strategy, the first example is the use of the "patent pending" notation. "Patent pending" means that you have filed a patent application on the invention. It does not necessarily mean the patent office in question will grant it. Competitors cannot know for 18 full months after you file for the patent the strength or nature of the patent documentation that "patent pending" refers to, or may never know whether you opted out of the publication requirement by forgoing the right to file for a patent outside the United States. That creates uncertainty that will end only when your patent documentation publishes. Uncertainty on the part of competitors is generally an advantage to you, provided they are aware of and respect the potential threat.

Another way you can create uncertainty is with early disclosures and defensive publications. If an organization files for patents on inventions that it discloses to the public often enough and in the past has proven its willingness to enforce patents that it already owns, then any disclosure that organization publishes, from the perspective of competitors, may have a filed patent behind it. Again, it will take 18 months before a given competitive organization can know for certain whether a disclosed invention has a filed patent application behind it, and so it may choose not to risk using even disclosed technology for fear it will infringe on a possible patent in the future. This means the disclosing organization can receive up to 18 months of psychological protection from competitors, even on inventions that have a low probability of achieving patent-granted status. Further pursuant to this, the disclosing organization might have already made progress on the next generation of technology by the time 18 months has passed, particularly for inventions in rapidly developing sectors.

To understand the principle of psychological protection that makes this strategy work, consider how the same principle could play out in a hurdles race for track and field. When hurdlers race, they attempt to stride just barely over each given hurdle so as not to waste energy and lose speed by striding any higher than necessary. In the course of a race, hurdlers often just slightly misjudge and stride a little too low. When this happens, and a knee hits a hurdle, the hurdle gives way by rolling forward so as not to cause injury. The hurdler continues with the race, none the worse for the mistake. Consider how the dynamics of the hurdles race would change if hurdlers knew that race officials had, at random, nailed down even just one hurdle in every race so that the hurdle would not give way if contacted. It is a sure bet that most, if not all, hurdlers would stride a little higher so as not to risk a career-ending injury by hitting the wrong hurdle. From an efficiency standpoint, therefore, an authority so inclined can achieve the same effect that could be achieved by nailing down all of the hurdles by nailing down just one. The key is that the hurdlers must know or believe that one hurdle has indeed been nailed down without knowing which one.

In the case of patents, the patent strategist substitutes normal hurdles with disclosures and nailed-down hurdles with corresponding patent applications, and in so doing realizes three potentially desirable effects.

First, the possibility of pending patents can discourage competitors from infringing on all disclosures for 18 months just as well as any actual patents, no matter whether given disclosures have actual patents filed behind them or not, just as long as the patent owners have a reputation for enforcing patents that do actually issue. Second, carrying the idea a little further, the patent owners may actually receive 18 months of psychological protection on described inventions that have a low probability of reaching patent-granted status, because a competitor wishing to avoid willful patent infringement would always have to consider the possibility that patent claims on disclosed inventions may issue in a granted patent. Third, if a competitor inquires about the patent status of a disclosure, that provides a clear signal to stakeholders in the organization that a given invention is of interest to the market and can actually help to show which inventions they should take all the way through the patenting process.

So what happens when you leverage physical protection with psychological protection? For a given amount of resources, you can protect much more technical space than you can with patents alone. This frees available resources to protect a larger body of inventions and therefore, more technical space.

Is this concept new? Absolutely not. Most people stop at a stop sign, even when they can see their way is clear, because there is a credible threat that a policeman will see them and issue a ticket. The optimal police force strikes a balance in numbers to be ever present in the mind of the community while being mostly absent on the ground. The question is the measure used. If a goal of the police department is to reduce speeding through a crackdown on speeders, should they measure the number of tickets they issue or the average speed of cars that results? How many police cars would be needed to maximize the former versus the latter? We are taking the same base idea here and applying it to patents.

The Game of Go
Three thousand years ago, an inventor in China created the strategy game of Go, discussed previously in this book. The underlying concept of this game is to surround as much territory on the game board as possible with as few pieces as possible while

your opponent from doing the same. Inherent in the strategy are patent strategy–like concepts of controlled space, blocking, surrounding, and linking. Control points develop on an otherwise open board based on previously played pieces.

Go is a good game for a patent strategist to learn because it teaches the mindset needed to master the real life patent strategy profession. Taking this further, Go also develops the psychological aspects of patent strategy, because so many of the threats and opportunities on the board are derived from the absence of pieces as opposed to their presence. Whole sections on the board can remain open because both competitors recognize the superiority and inferiority of their respective positions to contest it. The superior competitor retains implicit control of the space, and both competitors focus their efforts elsewhere on the still-contested areas of the board. Implicit control is an idea to consider when seeking efficient control of technical space. This can be had based on your current patent position plus all other aspects of your business power, to include your reputation in the field.

Accelerated Invention (TRIZ Example)

Accelerated invention techniques are key to making a High-Tempo Patent Strategy work, and, in fact, are part of the reason some companies have employed parts of this strategy. The most effective application of the ideas in a High-Tempo Patent Strategy requires a lot of inventions to make it effective. Accelerated invention techniques produce a lot of inventions, so much so that they can outstrip patent budgets if a company tries to patent all of them. Accelerated invention techniques such as TRIZ recognize that the number of inventive operators and the underlying problems they solve are relatively few, even though their combinations are limitless. Developing an earlier presented analogy, think of inventors as musical composers, and instead of requiring your musical composers to both reinvent their instrument and write their music every time you innovate, you give them the instrument and allow them to concentrate and focus on just writing the music. In a High-Tempo

Patent Strategy, you use proven problem-solving techniques and predictable lines of technical evolution to serve as guidelines to verify that you are headed in the right direction. With accelerated invention, whether through TRIZ or another method of your choice, you practice the fundamentals of innovation and refine them to increasing levels of performance.

To illustrate how accelerated invention works, in 2005 the author undertook an exercise that led to a product idea called the Amber Alert® Cell Phone, the details of which are now in the public domain. This exercise involved putting a cell phone on the table in front of participants, and then randomly drawing a set of inventive operators from the *Innovation Planner Card Deck*, and using the inventive principles drawn with the intent to evolve that cell phone. A brief sequence of the evolution from the participants in the event followed:

1. Based on the inventive operator, "Use the Reverse Action," we sought a reason why a cell phone would call you instead of you calling it. We named one of the ideas generated the "child protection" track.

2. Based on the inventive operator, "Allow Partial Mobility," we decided that we could put a GPS into the cell phone and program it such that the cell phone would call the guardian if the phone left approved places such as home, school grounds, or the school bus route.

3. We developed idea number two further with the inventive operator, "Allow Both Flexibility and Rigidity," so that the cell phone would allow some leeway over where the child was, but it would call if it detected an unusual pattern, such as the GPS detecting large spaces being traveled in short time periods, indicating activities such as a car ride when the child was supposed to be in class. We also determined that a rigid element within the phone should have the capability to call and send a GPS location text message the instant the phone detects it is being crushed or otherwise destroyed.

4. Using the inventive operator, "Move the Other Object," we decided that the phone should also call the guardian if it remained still too long, such as if the child dropped the phone, or worse, if an abductor forced the child to leave the phone behind.

5. Using the inventive operator, "Expand the Range of Options," we came up with the idea to allow the guardian to connect with the phone and receive a GPS signal as to its location—an idea that has since come onto the market independent from us.

6. Based on the inventive operator, "Use Properties to Convey Information," we brainstormed that the cell phone could have the capability to detect biological signals, such as an accelerated heartbeat, that could convey the stress of an abduction or even a medical emergency.

7. Finally, using the inventive operator, "Design for Variable Output," we realized that an Amber Alert® call should create a different ring tone on the guardian's cell phone instead of the regular ring tone to keep the stress level down for the guardian should a child want to call for other than an emergency reason.

You can conduct exercises such as this throughout an entire product line and systematically raise the inventive output of organizations. Exercises such as this are also a key to innovating at a faster tempo than competitors. At one automotive parts manufacturer, the author had the opportunity to see the output of patentable inventions rise from an average of 10 per month to 90 per month through the use of TRIZ techniques. From that, the company could develop many more commercial opportunities than it had before.

Conduct Invention/Patent Infiltration

By applying accelerated invention techniques, such as that illustrated by the Amber Alert® Cell Phone, to competitive patents, you now have the means to infiltrate competitive technical space. Consider if the preceding illustration involved how to evolve a competitor's cell phone. You could patent ideas generated during the exercise to create a "patent picket fence." If your competitor later evolves its technology toward producing an Amber Alert® Cell Phone, your competitor would bump into your patents, giving you the leverage to isolate or seek interaction with that competitor as desired.

Invention/Patent infiltration can be done very efficiently and systematically both to gain space in a market you wish to pursue and to gain patents to counter-assert or trade in hostile patent environments. It is an inverse solution derived from applying steps already discussed, but to competitive inventions instead of your own. It proves extremely effective when a competitor still views innovation as a somewhat random activity of inspiration and discovery instead of the science that it has become.

Necessary Adjustments

Enacting a High-Tempo Patent Strategy does require some adjustments on the part of the patenting organization. It requires your organization to have innovation and market agility comparable to or better than that of your competitors. This means your company must proficiently innovate at a tempo equal to or faster than your competitors' at your key points of inventive activity. Adaptation of accelerated invention and advanced creativity tool sets is a key to making this happen. Standard lines of evolution affect all inventions; technologies get smaller and lighter, parts become dynamic, and associated products deliver benefits more precisely. In short, technologies evolve toward the theoretical ideal state discussed in Chapter 4, Decide, where people receive all the benefit of the invention without the invention existing, and there will come a point where the technology growth slows and resides at a threshold of "good enough" (optimal) without needing to change too much.

Accelerated invention and advanced creativity techniques allow the organization to project evolutionary advances early and to direct the evolution along predictable lines, with the goal of controlling technical space around key inventions ahead of the competition. This should work in concert with input from the market to appreciate what customers are likely to find appealing and how you might shape those markets. Directed evolution in the context of patent strategy means systematically following, describing, and protecting these established and predictable lines of technical evolution ahead of less astute competitors. Putting this against market input will help you keep that evolution in line with prospective customers. You should run such exercises on your own technology and that of your competitors. The former provides a way to beat the competition to market with the latest evolution of existing technology, and the latter provides a way to create patent picket fences, which you could use to leverage cross-licensing for needed technology.

A High-Tempo Patent Strategy also requires an effective competitive intelligence function. This means knowing the progress of rivals in the primary and related fields so as to keep ahead of them. It can also mean inventing into the natural lines of evolution of a competitor's technology to gain assets for future leverage during negotiations and disputes. The counterintelligence side of competitive strategy also matters, because the art of disclosing technology sooner than the organization normally would do so may require an organization to make it difficult for competitors to appreciate the importance of what they see on time. Countermeasures in a High-Tempo Patent Strategy can depend less on technological secrecy and more on speed of innovation and tight interdependent relationships, coupled with the avoidance of signaling to competitors the commercial intent of innovation until it approaches a revenue-generating position. Maintaining an overall corporate policy of a High-Tempo Patent Strategy involves selectively disclosing inventions. Still, some inventions will serve your company best if kept secret for as long as possible. The balance is to figure out which inventions, if disclosed early, will offer an advantage to your position, and which inventions will provide more advantage if not disclosed at all.

High-Tempo Patent Strategy Advantages

Whether or not your organization adopts a High-Tempo Patent Strategy, the conditions that enable it will improve the performance of your patent strategy as a whole. Proficiently operating at a faster tempo than rival organizations provides what many professional strategists consider to be the most significant competitive advantage any organization can have over a competitor. The high-tempo organization seeks to operate inside the decision cycle loop of competitors by making faster assessments of the patent situation, faster decisions that leverage those assessments, and by taking proficient action sooner than rivals can act or react. Proficient use of patent analysis assists assessment, because you need to see where you are and where you can go. A clear and actionable strategy built around sound principles of operation assists decision. The application of inherent and created advantages assists action. Think again about the idea of Col. John Boyd, that highly regarded strategist referred to earlier, who helped to found the F-16 jet fighter program:

> The ability to operate at a faster tempo or rhythm than an adversary enables one to fold the adversary back inside himself so that he can neither appreciate nor keep up with what is going on.

Translated into patent strategy, it means inventing and achieving appropriate protections on inventions at a pace beyond your competitors' capacity to match, and then using that advantage to help you do what you ultimately want to do in business: to sell an ample volume of products that people want to buy for a sufficient enough return on your investment to make it worth your while.

Chapter 9

Conclusion

The late author Ernest Hemingway provides us with some food for thought at our conclusion. He said, "Wars are caused by undefended wealth."[1] This makes a lot of sense when you think about it. If you hold wealth, you become "evil" to someone who would otherwise hold that wealth or seek to take it from you. You yourself may be tempted to pursue wealth that you find relatively undefended. Even if you simply "get to the hill first" instead of pushing someone from it, you now occupy sought-after ground. That means you will need a strategy to defend your hill, and if that hill is not enough for your ambitions, you may need another strategy to seek more. Crafting these strategies is what we have explored here.

As stated at the beginning, this book is not your traditional "how to" book because once this or any other strategy book becomes a "how to" book, it is no longer a strategy book. Although we have examined some "how to" examples, this is a "what to" book. It tells you what to do, not necessarily how to do it. Your situation is unique, and your own ingenuity is required to create your own unique solutions. The strategies you craft, while they will share common and definable ideas, will in their totality be uniquely and entirely your own. All the best in your endeavors.

Appendix

IP Strategy Boarding
and Scenario Play

he *Art of War: Sun Tzu Strategy Card Deck* is a useful tool for
crafting competitive strategy described in Chapter 4, Decide of
this book. The *Art of War: Sun Tzu Strategy Card Deck* shows 54
strategic operators that you can combine in an infinite variety of ways
to craft a strategy. This card deck addresses adversarial relationships and
therefore emphasizes the *isolate* side of our two interplaying elements,
interact and isolate. A complementary card deck, *The Sales Strategy Fundamentals*, describes 54 strategies associated with building relationships
and therefore emphasizes the *interact* side of the two interplaying elements. *The Sales Strategy Fundamentals* card deck has an interaction focus
in the sense that it helps you to win customers and friends. The titles
reflect the initial and independent commercial foci of the products.

Both card decks have no duplicate cards within them, but they link
with the concept on the Ace of Clubs from the *Art of War: Sun Tzu*

Strategy Card Deck, "Create a Center for Advantage," which involves creating a position such that people wish to work with you. Both card decks describe the respective fundamentals of interaction and isolation, and both become powerful comprehensive planning tools when used together. The *Art of War: Sun Tzu Strategy Card Deck*, is derived from an intense application of isolation activity—namely, war. *The Sales Strategy Fundamentals* card deck is derived from an intense application of interaction activity—namely, sales. They therefore find relevance in those named situations and also in all other strategic situations that require interaction and isolation.

All strategy is an interplay between interaction and isolation. Although both the *Art of War: Sun Tzu Strategy Card Deck* and *The Sales Strategy Fundamentals* card decks independently describe this interplay, both describe the fundamentals of interaction and isolation where used intensively, war and sales respectively. They therefore become powerful comprehensive planning tools when used together in those situations and also any other strategic situations. Exhibit A.1 illustrates comprehensive strategy solutions.

The *Art of War: Sun Tzu Strategy Card Deck* and *The Sales Strategy Fundamentals* card decks can be used apart or together when planning strategy. Used together, they provide a way to craft actions that develop

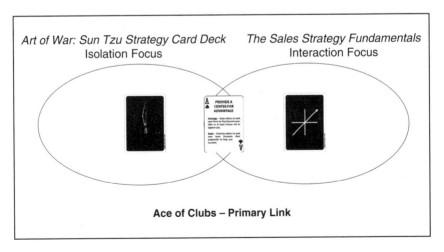

Exhibit A.1 Comprehensive Strategic Solutions

a favorable environment for conducting business. A suggested use takes place as follows:

1. Place the cards on a table or, preferably, on a wall-mounted board. Crafting and framing stores sell wall-mountable baseball card holders ideal for this purpose, as well as plastic sleeve variants that are more portable. Arrange the cards horizontally from left to right in ascending order, starting with the Two and ending with the Ace; and in that arrangement, place the cards on the board by suit with Spades as the top row, followed by Diamonds, then Clubs, and ending with Hearts as the bottom row. Place the two Star cards on the top row to the left of the Two of Spades.

2. Using blue Post-it® Notes and all the cards, detail and number actions you can take and toward whom or what that action is oriented. Your numbers can be a sequence, in order to tell which actions will be linked to others, with parallel actions given the same number, and perhaps a different letter designation such as 1a, 1b, and so on.

3. Using red Post-it® Notes, write what the opposition can or is doing to you, following the same protocol previously stated. (It is often useful to do this step first or to have part of your team do this step independently as a Red Team exercise. Red Teaming means to challenge your plans by stepping into the shoes of your opposition to try to defeat your plans before real opponents have the chance. You adjust your plans based on the weaknesses your Red Team uncovers.)

4. Using yellow Post-it® Notes, develop likely responses to your actions by others.

5. Using green Post-it® Notes, write how you might respond to given actions by your opposition.

6. Now, despite the preceding directions, at no time be overly concerned about the sequence of the steps. For that matter, do not overly concern yourself with any numbering sequence, either, if that adds confusion or interferes with brainstorming. The main thing is to write ideas and thoughts as they come to you and get them on the board. We are after content first, not structure. You can organize later.

7. When you are satisfied with the content, review and record what you and other participants in the exercise have put on the board.

As a "war room" tool, cards from the *Art of War: Sun Tzu Strategy Card Deck* and *The Sales Strategy Fundamentals* can be placed on a strategy board made from baseball card holders available at crafts and framing stores. By using Post-it® Notes of various colors, it is easy to brainstorm and test strategic ideas that will be put into plans for action (see Exhibit A.2).

Upon completion of a strategy board exercise, take your findings and use them within the planning format of your choice. This is where you create structure from your content. Keep in mind that if you like the idea proposed on a card, but are not sure how to make it happen, you will likely find your answer on a different card. For example, the Five of Diamonds card in the *Art of War: Sun Tzu Strategy Card Deck*, "Bolt the Door Behind the Thief," might be the way you execute the Five of Spades card in the *Art of War: Sun Tzu Strategy Card Deck*, "Incapacitate the Leadership." This is a common pairing seen in political maneuverings where, for example, to undermine an undesirable candidate for a top position, you trap him or her in an untenable position, such as presiding over accounting discrepancies. In patent strategy, you might

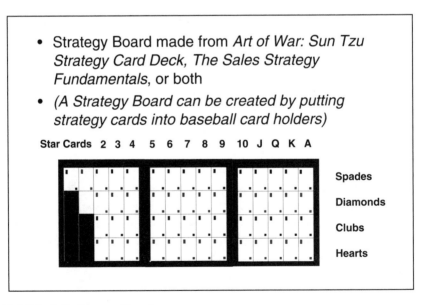

- Strategy Board made from *Art of War: Sun Tzu Strategy Card Deck, The Sales Strategy Fundamentals*, or both
- (A Strategy Board can be created by putting strategy cards into baseball card holders)

Star Cards 2 3 4 5 6 7 8 9 10 J Q K A

Spades

Diamonds

Clubs

Hearts

Exhibit A.2 Strategy Board

trap a small company within an infringement lawsuit, such that fighting the lawsuit effectively occupies so much of the leadership's time that it cannot effectively run the business. The possible combinations of strategic operators are limited only by your imagination, and with practice, the combinations become second nature. They do not convey an implicit message that you should use any one given strategy yourself, but you should certainly be aware of them in case another person or organization seeks to use them against you or your organization.

Some additional information inherent in the card decks will allow you to better appreciate the card deck tools. To start, the rank on each card generally corresponds in usefulness to the situational strength of the user's position. An organization or individual in a strong position will use the higher-ranked cards and an organization or individual in a weaker position will use the lower-ranked cards. The suits are oriented around Hearts as preparation of the self, Clubs as preparation of the field, Diamonds as isolating actions or bridging actions in the two respective decks, and Spades as eliminating or closing actions in the two respective decks. These are merely general guidelines. For example, a master strategist from a start-up company that is overall weaker than established competitors could still use a high-ranked isolating card to leverage a particular situational advantage, such as the Ten of Clubs on the *Art of War: Sun Tzu Strategy Card Deck*, "Lie in Wait for an Attacking Adversary," to create a profitable interaction with one of those established competitors. That would depend on the advantages associated with positions at the specific point of interaction—for example, the ownership by the otherwise weaker company of a particularly powerful patent.

Each of the 54 cards in the *Art of War: Sun Tzu Strategy Card Deck* (see Exhibit A.3) has a:

- Title—name of the strategy
- Strategy—definition of the strategy
- Basis—why the strategy works

Its complementary card deck, *The Sales Strategy Fundamentals*, has a similar layout but with the addition of a sales tip on each card. As you directionally progress through this second deck toward closing on the purpose for interacting, the ranks for the strategies used become higher.

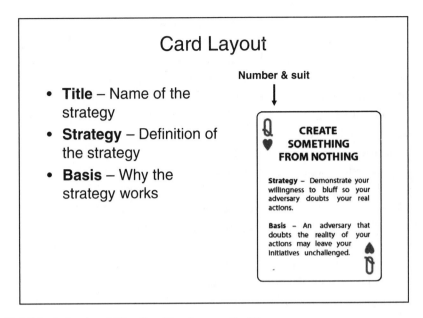

Exhibit A.3 *Art of War: Sun Tzu Strategy Card* Layout

Just as in the *Art of War: Sun Tzu Strategy Card Deck*, the stronger your situational advantage, the higher the rank of the card you will likely use. Each card has a:

- Title—name of the strategy
- Strategy—definition of the strategy
- Basis—why the strategy works
- Sales tip—how to make best use of the strategy

One of the major themes of *The Sales Strategy Fundamentals* is that no matter what your position in business, when you interact with people in a positive way, you are always selling. You sell your ideas on what actions to take, sell your arguments to a jury or judge, or perhaps sell your latest technical initiatives so that you can get money and other resources. Selling is the most fundamental of business skills; nothing happens until somebody sells something. So just as the *Art of War: Sun Tzu Strategy Card Deck* is not for warriors only, *The Sales Strategy Fundamentals* deck is not for salespeople only. Soldiers and salespeople both operate in professions that use the presented ideas intensively. Each of the 54 cards in

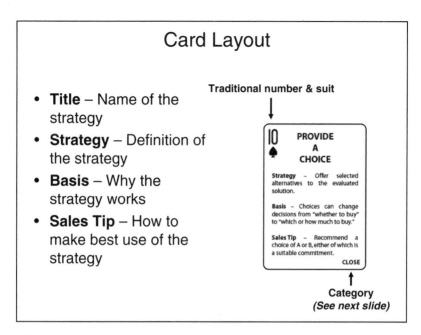

Exhibit A.4 *The Sales Strategy Fundamentals* Card Layout

The Sales Strategy Fundamentals includes a title, a strategy definition, the basis for why the strategy works, and a tip for how to implement it (see Exhibit A.4).

Both card decks work most effectively when synthesized into combinations, just as you might synthesize a musical composition from a given set of musical notes. Synthesis is the creative art of taking known entities and combining them into something unique. To further the analogy, Beethoven, one of the world's greatest composers, assembled each of his symphonies from the exact same musical scale used by Mozart, Bach, and much later by Billy Joel. For this reason, you can play the melodies from any of these musicians on any given piano. Similarly, your strategies will be synthesized from a set of strategic operators that have been known and used, like musical notes, for thousands of years.

Consider the Eight of Hearts card in the *Art of War: Sun Tzu Strategy Card Deck* "Provoke Your Adversary's Reaction." This is used as a way to test how an adversary will react to a real action. "Provoke Your Adversary's Reaction" could appear in a real-life scenario when a company explores how an opponent will react by floating the possibility of seeking a license before actually committing to do so. The opponent's openness or resistance to the idea will give a base from which to plan the actual approach or to seek an alternative course of action.

Another common way to provoke your adversary is to bluff, which may be done in accord with the Queen of Hearts card from the same deck, "Create Something from Nothing." Creating something from nothing means to deliberately show your willingness to bluff so that your adversary doubts all of your future actions, even when you are not bluffing. It is a common operator used by poker players to bluff on a weak hand and purposely lose an affordable pot so as to create the conditions whereby other players will keep upping the ante even in the face of a future strong hand. The player wants to create the conditions whereby the other players will think he or she is bluffing in the future when he or she actually does hold a strong hand. "Create Something from Nothing" might be used in patent strategy by undertaking a patent assertion defense that you are likely to lose in order to signal to others your willingness to defend yourself, even under dubious circumstances. This may make others less willing to assert their patents against you in the future when the stakes are higher.

The Sales Strategy Fundamentals card deck highlights the fundamentals of selling for person-to-person interaction. The strategy on each card of *The Sales Strategy Fundamentals* deck that leads from proposal to acceptance involves synthesizing operators together both to satisfy the needs of customers and to counter the activities of competitors. There is practically no way to achieve success in business in any profession without selling at least some of the time, given that even being hired means you had to sell your skills to somebody in a position to hire you.

To illustrate *The Sales Strategy Fundamentals* further with the cards working together, the Nine of Clubs, "Build a Partnership," means to seek a commitment that benefits both you and your prospect. This could be accomplished using the Ten of Clubs from the deck, "Show a High Return on Investment," which means to offer a financial or emotional gain that your prospect will find attractive. The end result might be to "Dominate the Space," as noted by the King of Hearts from the same deck, which means to fill requirements so well that your competitors offer no meaningful advantage. Thinking competitively again, your domination of space could serve to isolate other competitors from the market that are not in the partnership you just formed, even while you have created a positive bridge to your customer. This strategy is detailed in the Ace of Diamonds card from the *Art of War: Sun Tzu Strategy Card Deck*, "Isolate Your Adversary." The interplay between interaction and isolation ties the two card decks together. Your successful partnership will ideally benefit many people, but it invariably becomes "evil" to those outside that partnership who have a more isolated position because of it.

Together, both card decks provide a strategy crafting and training tool adaptable to be as rigorous as you want your planning to be. This is in keeping with quotes from two famous strategists, one mentioned earlier in this book:

1. "Excellence is achieved by the mastery of the fundamentals." Attributed to the late Vince Lombardi, former coach of the Green Bay Packers[1]
2. "Hard training, easy combat; easy training, hard combat." Attributed to the late Marshal Alexander Suvorov, famous Russian general noted for never losing a battle[2]

No one should expect to be successful in strategy without first mastering the fundamentals of strategy. The combined cards from the two card decks illustrate 108 fundamentals of interaction and isolation that every professional strategist should know as second nature. The only way to know them as second nature is to study, practice, and observe. In his own profession, even Vince Lombardi's championship football teams spent most of their time practicing basic blocking, tackling, and handling the ball. To actually master strategy, you and the people who work for you should do the equivalent. This is the reason for detailing the card decks here.

Endnotes

Orientation

1. Thomas Banks, "A Few Tips to Help Ensure a Win in Patent Litigation," *Boston Business Journal*, June 2, 2006, http://www.bizjournals.com/boston/stories/2006/06/05/focus2.html (accessed August 11, 2008).

Chapter 1 Introduction

1. Niccolò Machiavelli, *Discourses on the First Decade of Titus Livius*, trans. Ninian Hill Thomson (Dodo Press, 2007), Book I, Chapter 10. This is understood to be the first reference to the emperors Nerva, Trajan, Hadrian, Antoninus Pius, and Marcus Aurelius as the "Five Good Emperors."
2. Frans P.B. Osinga, *Science, Strategy, and War: The Strategic Theory of John Boyd* (London and New York: Routledge, 2006), 209. This interpretation of patent strategy is based on an overall interpretation of strategy put forward by John Boyd.
3. Jim Kling, "From hypertension to angina to Viagra," *Modern Drug Discovery*, 1, no. 2 (November/December 1998), 31, 33–34, 36, 38, http://pubs.acs.org/hotartcl/mdd/98/novdec/viagra.html (accessed August 8, 2008).
4. U.S. Food and Drug Administration, "FDA Public Health Advisory: Safety of Vioxx," September 30, 2004, http://www.fda.gov/CDER/Drug/infopage/vioxx/PHA_vioxx.htm.

5. Benjamin Zipursky, "Much Pain, Much Gain: Skeptical Ruminations on the Vioxx Litigation," *Jurist*, January 23, 2006.

6. Nokia Corporation, "Towards Telecommunications," August 2000, www.nokia.com/NOKIA_COM_1/About_Nokia/Sidebars_new_concept/Broschures/TowardsTelecomms.pdf (accessed August 14, 2008).

7. Robert K. Merton, "The Unanticipated Consequences of Purposive Social Action," *American Sociological Review*, 1, no. 6 (Dec. 1936), 894–904, http://www.compilerpress.atfreeweb.com/Anno%20Merton%20Unintended .htm (accessed August 11, 2008).

8. "1996 Ford Taurus and Mercury Sable Wagons Debut in Chicago," *PR Newswire* (February 9, 1995), http://www.highbeam.com/doc/1G1-16437531.html (accessed August 11, 2008).

9. François Coallier and Robert Gérin-Lajoie, "Open Government Architecture: The evolution of *De Jure* Standards, Consortium Standards, and Open Source Software," Treasury Board of Canada Secretariat project report (February 2006), http://www.cirano.qc.ca/pdf/publication/2006RP-02.pdf (accessed August 11, 2008).

10. "Crusader 155mm Self Propelled Howitzer, USA," http://www.army-technology.com/projects/crusader (accessed August 11, 2008).

11. Clayton M. Christensen, *The Innovator's Dilemma* (Boston: Harvard Business School Press, 1997), 108–109.

12. Jon Udell, "Computer Telephony," *Byte*, July 1994, http://www.byte.com/art/9407/sec8/art1.html (accessed August 11, 2008).

13. *Encyclopedia Britannica*, 2008, s.v. "apprenticeship."

14. Morgan, Lewis & Bockius LLP, "Morgan Lewis Trial Team Wins $53.5 Million Patent Infringement Verdict," Nov. 21, 2006, http://www.morganlewis.com/index.cfm/newsID/3DEAA34F-7626-47C8-90E3-1AD90ECEEE58/fuseaction/news.detail (accessed July 7, 2008).

15. William Cole, "Boeing engineers and technologists are constantly developing better ways to design and make products," *Boeing Frontiers Online*, December 2004/January 2005, http://www.boeing.com/news/frontiers/archive/2004/december/ts_sf03.html (accessed August 11, 2008).

16. ACell, Inc., "ACell, Inc. Wins Court Battle Initiated by Cook Biotech and Purdue," August 18, 2006, http://www.acell.com/news/ ACell_Press _Release_082106.pdf (accessed August 11, 2008).

17. Andrea Rothman, "'Airbus' 'big baby' is too big: A380 is still overweight by as much as 4 metric tons, hurting efficiency," *SeattlePI.com*, July 17, 2004, http://seattlepi.nwsource.com/business/182471_airbusproblem17.html (accessed August 11, 2008). *Note:* In order to reduce weight on the A380, Airbus further developed its own use of composite parts in place of parts with more conventional materials.

18. Caleb Carr, "A war of escalating errors," *Los Angeles Times*, August 12, 2006, http://articles.latimes.com/2006/aug/12/opinion/oe-carr12 (accessed August 11, 2008). *Note:* This is one of many sources that have attributed

the quote, "Never interrupt your enemy while he is making a mistake." to Napoleon. It is characteristic of his written maxims. Oftentimes quotes do get attached to famous people even if they did not say them. For example, the quote attributed to George S. Patton, "No bastard ever won a war by dying for his country. He won it by making the other poor dumb bastard die for his country," was actually a creation of Hollywood. It still makes a point, however.

19. "The Wright Brothers: Bicycle Geniuses," http://www.socialstudiesforkids. com/articles/ushistory/wrightbrothersbicycle1.htm (accessed July 8, 2008).

20. Mikel Harry, Ph.D. and Richard Schroeder, *Six Sigma* (New York: Doubleday, 2000).

21. http:// en.wikipedia.org/ wiki / Helmuth_von_Moltke_the_Elder (accessed September 10, 2008). *Note*: This is one of many sources for information about Helmuth von Moltke the Elder.

22. Robert L. Cantrell, *Understanding Sun Tzu on the Art of War* (Arlington: Center for Advantage, 2003), 86, citing Sun Tzu, *The Art of War.*

23. Robert L. Cantrell, *Understanding Sun Tzu on the Art of War* (Arlington: Center for Advantage, 2003), i, citing Sun Tzu, *The Art of War. Note*: There is some controversy, discussed by the author in this book, as to Sun Tzu's actual existence or military role in Chinese history.

24. *Wall Street*, Video, directed by Oliver Stone (20th Century Fox, 1987).

25. "General George S. Patton, Jr. Quotations," http://www.generalpatton. com/quotes.html (accessed July 8, 2008).

26. Wikipedia.org, s.v. "Vince Lombardi," http://en.wikipedia.org/wiki/ Vince_Lombardi (accessed August 12, 2008). *Note*: One of many sources for information about Vince Lombardi.

27. R. Aidan Martin and Anne Martin, "Sociable Killers," *Natural History*, October 2006, http://www.naturalhistorymag.com/master.html?http:// www.naturalhistorymag.com/1006/1006_feature.html (accessed August 12, 2008).

28. Charles H. Ferguson, *High Stakes, No Prisoners* (New York: Times Business, 1999), 36, 62, 245.

29. Michael E. Raynor, *The Strategy Paradox* (New York: Doubleday Business, 2007).

Chapter 2 Decision Cycle

1. Gene Quinn, "Cost of Obtaining a Patent," *IPWatchdog*, 2008, http://www. ipwatchdog.com/patent/patent-cost/(accessed July 9, 2008).

2. "The Cost of a Sample European Patent—New Estimates," European Patent Office, 2005, http://www.3pod.cz/download/cost_analysis_2005_en %5B1%5D.pdf (accessed August 12, 2008).

3. "London Agreement," *Official Journal EPO*, December 2001, http://www. european-patent-office.org/epo/pubs/oj001/12_01/12_5491.pdf (accessed

August 12, 2008). *Note:* This agreement significantly reduced the cost of filing for multiple countries in the EPO by relaxing the requirements to have the patent translated into the languages of the various countries for which patent protection is sought.

4. "Go," The Association for the Advancement of Artificial Intelligence (AAAI), http://www.aaai.org/AITopics/pmwiki/pmwiki.php/AITopics/Go (accessed July 8, 2008).

5. John R. Boyd, "Destruction and Creation" (September 3, 1976), available from http://goalsys.com/books/documents/DESTRUCTION_AND _CREATION.pdf (accessed September 10, 2008). *Note*: This was the central paper for the founding of Effects-Based Operations (EBO) strategic theory in the military. Boyd describes the OODA Loop, comprising Observation, Orientation, Decision, and Action. Many publications have converted this to Assess, Decide, Act (as we have), and have put the critical Orientation aspect into the discussion, given that Orientation plays a part throughout the decision cycle.

Chapter 3 Assess

1. Felicity Barringer and William Yardley, "THE EVERGLADES; Reservation Comes Into Play as Officials Make Water-Management Decisions," *New York Times*, September 12, 2004, http://www.nytimes.com/2004/09/12/national/12water.html?8b1 (accessed August 12, 2008).

2. Arthur Bloch, *Murphy's Law Book Three* (Los Angeles: Price/Stern/Sloan, 1983), 10.

3. Ibid., 20.

4. Jacob Birnbaum, "The Case for the U.S. Patent and Trademark Office's Adoption of an Open-Source 'Bounty' System for Reviewing Business Method and Software Patents, in Light of the Patent Infringement Battles Featuring the U.S. Financial Exchanges that Have Been Waged in Recent Years," 2006 *UCLA J.L. & Tech.* 2, http://www.lawtechjournal.com/articles/2006/02_060707_birnbaum.pdf (accessed July 22, 2008).

5. Joe Barr, "HP memo forecasts MS patent attacks on free software," Linux.com, July 20, 2004, http://www.linux.com/articles/37584 (accessed July 22, 2008).

6. Joseph Campbell and Bill Moyers, *The Power of Myth* (Portland: Audiofile, 2003).

7. Mikael Ricknäs, "Belgian newspapers ask Google for $77.5 million in damages," IDG News Service, May 28, 2008, http://www.pcworld.com/businesscenter/article/1463801 (accessed August 12, 2008).

8. Darren Bibby, John Gantz, and Amie White, "The Impact of Software Piracy and License Misuse on the Channel," IDC, June 2008, http://www.microsoft.com/presspass/events/wwpc/docs/SoftwarePiracyWP.pdf (accessed August 12, 2008).

9. U.S. Department of Justice, "Report of the Department of Justice's Task Force on Intellectual Property," October 2004, http://www.usdoj.gov/criminal/cybercrime/IPTaskForceReport.pdf (accessed August 12, 2008).

10. "Facts on Fakes," International Anti-Counterfeiting Coalition, 2003, 12.

11. Adam M. Brandenburger and Barry J. Nalebuff, *Co-opetition* (New York: Doubleday, 1996).

12. http://www.poemofquotes.com/quotes/military/(accessed July 22, 2008).

13. Arthur Kranish, "IBM to Free Its Patents in Trust Case," *Washington Post*, January, 26, 1956.

14. NBC Encyclopedia Playoff Edition, NBA Media Ventures, LLC, 2008.

15. Paul Raffaele, "Forget *Jaws*, Now it's . . . Brains!", *Smithsonian Magazine*, June 2008.

16. Al Ries and Jack Trout, *The 22 Immutable Laws of Marketing* (HarperBusiness, 1994), 2–9.

17. Sarah Jane Gilbert, "How Can Start Ups Grow?" *Harvard Business School Working Knowledge*, November 14, 2005, http://hbswk.hbs.edu/item/5089.html (accessed September 10, 2008).

18. Lisa Endlich, *Optical Illusions: Lucent and the Crash of Telecom* (New York: Simon & Schuster, 2004).

19. Samuel Zats, "Alcatel-Lucent v. Microsoft," IEOR 190G (April 9, 2008).

20. Stanley Holmes and Aaron Bernstein, "The New Nike," *BusinessWeek*, September 20, 2004, http://biz.yahoo.com/special/nike05_article2.html (accessed August 12, 2008).

21. http://www.fedex.com/us/supplychain/services/cil/index.html (accessed July 23, 2008).

22. http://fedex.p.delivery.net/m/p/fdx/msc/index.html (accessed July 23, 2008).

23. "A Brief History of the Home Video Game Console," http://www.thegameconsole.com/videogames83.htm (accessed July 23, 2008).

24. "A Brief History of the Home Video Game Console," http://www.thegameconsole.com/videogames96.htm (accessed July 23, 2008).

25. "Sega," http://spong.com/company/1212?cb=590 (accessed July 23, 2008).

26. "Inclusion of Windows CE Operating System Creates Platform That Will Deliver Innovations in Next-Generation Games and Entertainment," Microsoft, May 21, 1998, http://www.microsoft.com/presspass/press/1998/May98/Segagmpr.mspx (accessed August 12, 2008).

27. "Qualcomm Business Model," Qualcomm, March 2007.

28. http://www.dell.com/, supplemented by comparative searches from the USPTO that show nearly a 10:1 advantage of computer-based patents for rival Hewlett-Packard over Dell.

29. http://www.gobros.com/under-armour/under-armour-history.php (accessed July 23, 3008) and a review of the USPTO show that the first Under Armour® patent was filed in 2004.

30. http://www.gobros.com/under-armour/under-armour-history.php (accessed July 23, 3008).

31. "Adobe Systems Inc—Early History: Warnock and Geschke," http://ecommerce.hostip.info/pages/4/Adobe-Systems-Inc-EARLY-HISTORY-WARNOCK-GESCHKE.html (accessed July 23, 2008).

32. *Joseph Campbell and the Power of Myth*, Video, Executive Editor, Bill Moyers (Mystic Fire Video: 1998).

33. David Straker, *Rapid Problem Solving with Post-it® Notes* (Da Capo Press: 1997), ix.

34. John Pemberton, "Coca-Cola Syrup and Extract" (1885 advertisement).

35. Kling, 31–38.

36. J. Carlton Gallawa, "Who Invented Microwaves?," http://www.gallawa.com/microtech/history.html (accessed August 13, 2008).

37. http://www.aspartame.net/(accessed July 23, 2008).

38. Lada A. Adamic, "Zipf, Power-laws, and Pareto—A ranking tutorial," Information Dynamics Lab, HP Labs, http://www.hpl.hp.com/research/idl/papers/ranking/ranking.html (accessed August 13, 2008).

39. John Allison, Mark Lemley, Kimberly Moore, and Derek Trunkey, "Valuable Patents," George Mason Law & Economics Research Paper No. 03-31, UC Berkeley Public Law Research Paper No. 133, *Georgetown Law Journal* 92 (2004): 435, http://papers.ssrn.com/sol3/papers.cfm?abstract_id=426020 (accessed September 10, 2008).

40. Ibid.

41. Microsoft, "Renewed Spirit of Cooperation Between Microsoft and Apple Benefits Mac Customers," January 5, 1999, http://www.microsoft.com/presspass/features/1999/01-05apple.mspx (accessed August 13, 2008).

42. Richard Cauley, "Licensing Competitors: A Knife in Your Rival's Hand or the Monopolist's Best Friend?," posting to *The Art of IP War*, August 17, 2006, http://patent-warrior.blogspot.com/(accessed August 13, 2008).

43. *Star Wars Episode V—The Empire Strikes Back*, Video, directed by Irvin Kershner (20th Century Fox: 1980).

Chapter 4 Decide

1. Lewis Carroll, *Alice's Adventures in Wonderland* (London: Macmillan, 1866).

2. Constance E. Helfat, *The SMS Blackwell Handbook of Organizational Capabilities: Emergence, Development, and Change (Strategic Management Society)* (New York: Wiley-Blackwell, 2003), 417–420.

3. Genrich Altshuller, *40 Principles: TRIZ Keys to Technical Innovation* (Worcester, MA: Technical Innovation Center, Inc., January 1998, original copyright 1974) 27.

4. Morton H. Halperin and David Halperin, "The Key West Key," *Foreign Policy*, no. 53 (Winter 1983-1984).

5. Fred Kaplan, "Chop the Chopper: The Army's Apache Attack-Helicopter Had a Bad War," *Slate*, April 23, 2003, http://www.slate.com/id/2081906 (accessed August 13, 2008).

6. Scot Finnie, "Hands on: A Windows expert tries out Apple's Boot Camp...And likes what he finds," *Computer World*, April 11, 2006, http://www.computerworld.com/softwaretopics/os/macos/story/0,10801,110420 p4,00.html (accessed September 10, 2008).

7. http://www.nationmaster.com/encyclopedia/Not-Invented-Here (accessed July 23, 2008).

8. http://en.wikipedia.org/wiki/List_of_companies_acquired_by_Microsoft_Corporation (accessed July 23, 2008).

9. Matthew Aslett, "Microsoft claims open source infringes 235 patents," *CBRonline*, May 15, 2007, http://www.cbronline.com/article_news.asp?guid=B64949DF-6D27-4B0F-8C1A-D3A1E6F61343 (accessed August 13, 2008).

10. Robert Cantrell, *Art of War: Sun Tzu Strategy Card Deck* (Center for Advantage: 2004).

11. Robert Cantrell, *Understanding Sun Tzu on the Art of War* (Center for Advantage: 2003).

12. Dave Owen, "The Betamax vs VHS Format War," Media College.com, May 1, 2005, http://www.mediacollege.com/video/format/compare/betamax-vhs.html (accessed August 13, 2008).

13. *Polaroid Corp. v. Eastman Kodak Co.*, 16 USPQ2d 1481 (D. Mass. 1990).

14. UnderwaterPhotography.com, "The Nikonos Story," http://www.underwaterphotography.com/Articles/Equipment/Nikon/NikonosStory.asp (accessed July 25, 2008).

15. *eBay Inc. v. MercExchange L.L.C.*, 126 S.Ct. 1837 (2006).

16. Rudyard Kipling, *The Wolf*, Federal Wildlife Officers Association, http://www.fwoa.org/fwoawolf.html (accessed September 29, 2008).

17. Stephen C. Stinson, "Counting on Chiral Drugs," CENEAR 76, no. 38 (September 21, 1998), http://pubs.acs.org/hotartcl/cenear/980921/drugs.html (accessed September 10, 2008).

18. FTI, "Intellectual Property Statistics," http://www.infringementupdates.com/files/intellectual_property_statistics_april_2008.pdf (accessed September 10, 2008).

19. Michael J. Meurer, "Controlling Opportunistic and Anti-Competitive Intellectual Property Litigation," *Boston College Law Review* (2003), http://papers.ssrn.com/sol3/papers.cfm?abstract_id=361760 (accessed August 13, 2008).

20. Luke Timmerman, "All Icos workers losing their jobs," *Seattle Times*, December 12, 2006.

21. Terry Ludlow, "Don't Get Caught With Your Patents Down," ipFrontline.com, August 15, 2006, http://www.ipfrontline.com/depts/article.asp?id=12226&deptid=3 (accessed August 13, 2008).

22. Christensen, 75–76.
23. John Greenwald, "Kodak's Bad Moment," *Time*, June 24, 2001, http://www.time.com/time/magazine/article/0,9171,138360,00.html (accessed August 13, 2008).
24. British Petroleum, "BP Annual Report and Accounts 2007," http://www.bp.com/extendedsectiongenericarticle.do?categoryId=9021605&contentId=7040949 (accessed August 13, 2008).
25. Peter C. Grindley and David J. Teece, "Managing Intellectual Capital: Licensing and Cross-Licensing in Semiconductors and Electronics," *California Management Review*, 39(2) (Winter 1997), 1–34.
26. François Lévêque and Yann Ménière, "Patents and Innovation: Friends or Foes?," CERNA, Centre d'économie industrielle, Ecole Nationale Supérieure des Mines de Paris (December 2006): 73, http://www.cerna.ensmp.fr/Documents/FL-YM-PatentsInnovationJanuary07.pdf (accessed August 13, 2008).
27. Ryan Paul, "IBM, Sony, Novell start Linux patent sharing project," Ars Technica, November 10, 2005, http://arstechnica.com/news.ars/post/20051110-5553.html (accessed September 10, 2008).
28. Alorie Gilbert, "Web services patents fetch $15.5 million," CNET News.com, December 6, 2004, http://news.cnet.com/2100-1038_3-5480341.html (accessed August 13, 2008).
29. David Runk, "Borders Returns to the Web After 7 Year Partnership With Amazon," *The Huffington Post*, May 27, 2008, http://www.huffingtonpost.com/2008/05/27/borders-returns-to-the-we_n_103633.html (accessed August 13, 2008).
30. Ries and Trout, 2–9.
31. Ibid., 44–49.
32. http://www.brainyquote.com/quotes/authors/w/wayne_gretzky.html (accessed July 25, 2008).
33. David Gartman, "Tough Guys and Pretty Boys: The Cultural Antagonisms of Engineering and Aesthetics in Automotive History," *Automobile in American Life and Society*, University of Michigan-Dearborn and Benson Ford Research Center, http://www.autolife.umd.umich.edu/Design/Gartman/D_Casestudy/D_Casestudy7.htm (accessed August 13, 2008).
34. Robert A. Howard, "Interchangeable Parts Reexamined: The Private Sector of the American Arms Industry on the Eve of the Civil War," 19 Technology and Culture, 4 (The Johns Hopkins University Press, October 1978), 633–649.
35. David Gartman.
36. Stan Kaplan, *An Introduction to TRIZ: The Russian Theory of Inventive Problem Solving* (Ideation Int'l, Inc., 1996), 3.
37. Ibid., 5.

38. Bradley Sheard, *Lost Voyages: Two Centuries of Shipwrecks in the Approaches to New York* (Aqua Quest Publications, Inc., 1997), 39-57.

39. Christensen, *The Innovator's Dilemma.*

40. Adrian J. Slywotzky, *Value Migration: How to Think Several Moves Ahead of the Competition* (Boston: Harvard Business School Press, 1996).

41. Laurie J. Flynn, "Profit Rises 25% at Intel on Strong Global Demand," *New York Times*, July 16, 2008, http://www.nytimes.com/2008/07/16/technology/16chip.html (accessed August 13, 2008).

42. Kaplan, 4.

43. Ibid.

44. Ibid.

45. Ibid., 5.

46. Ibid., 4.

47. Semyon D. Savransky, *Engineering of Creativity: Introduction to TRIZ Methodology of Inventive Problem Solving* (Boca Raton, FL.: CRC Press, 2000).

48. Steven Mitchell translator, *Tao Te Ching* (New York: HarperPerennial, 1988), 38.

49. "C-130 Hercules," Military Analysis Network, http://www.fas.org/man/dod-101/sys/ac/c-130.htm (accessed August 13, 2008).

50. Walter J. Boyne, "Fifty Herculean Years: The C-130's Golden Anniversary," Wings Over Kansas, Republication from Journal of the Air Force Association (2004).

51. "NOVA: Dogs and More Dogs," (WGBH Boston, 2004).

52. Megan Scully, "Pentagon punts decision on future F-22, C-17 production," *CongressDaily*, February 6, 2008, http://www.govexec.com/dailyfed/0108/020608cdam1.htm (accessed August 13, 2008).

53. Gina Kolata and Andrew Pollack, "Costly Cancer Drug Offers Hope, but Also a Dilemma," *New York Times*, July 6, 2008, http://www.nytimes.com/2008/07/06/health/06avastin.html?_r=1&oref=slogin (accessed August 13, 2008).

54. Nick Taylor, Laser: *The Inventor, the Nobel Laureate, and the Thirty-Year Patent War*, (New York: Simon & Schuster, 2000).

55. Sheard, 39–57.

56. *MedImmune, Inc. v. Genentech, Inc.*, 549 U.S. 118 (2007).

57. Federal Trade Commission, "Hearings on Global and Innovations Based Competition," Washington, DC, November 29, 1995, http://www.ftc.gov/opp/global/gc120195.pdf (accessed August 13, 2008).

58. Altshuller, 135.

59. *Phillips v. AWH Corp.*, 415 F.3d 1303 (Fed. Cir. 2005).

60. *Nystrom v. Trex Co.*, 424 F.3d 1136 (Fed. Cir. 2005).

61. Ferguson, 36.

62. Ibid., 213.

63. Ibid., 36.

64. Carlene E. Stephens, "Manufacturing Time: Global Competition in the Watch Industry 1795-2000 (review)," *Technology and Culture* 42, no. 4, (October 2001): 791–793.

65. "Combine Against America," *New York Times*, March 24, 1900.

66. Ernest Nagel and James R. Newman, *Gödel's Proof* (New York: NYU Press, 2001).

67. "Murphy's Laws of Combat Operations," http://miljokes.com/murphys. htm (accessed September 18, 2008).

68. *KSR Int'l Co. v. Teleflex Inc.*, 127 S.Ct. 1727 (2007).

69. François Lévêque and Yann Ménière, "Patents and Innovation: Friends or Foes?," CERNA, Centre d'économie industrielle, Ecole Nationale Supérieure des Mines de Paris (December 2006): http://www.cerna.ensmp. fr/Documents/FL-YM-PatentsInnovationJanuary07.pdf (accessed August 13, 2008).

70. Federal Trade Commission, "Hearings on Global and Innovations Based Competition," Washington, DC, November 29, 1995, http://www.ftc.gov/ opp/global/gc120195.pdf (accessed August 13, 2008).

71. Stac Electronics v. Microsoft Corp., No. 93-00413 (C.D. Cal. Jan 23, 1994).

72. Joshua Brockman, "Judge Lets BlackBerry Stay in Play for Now," *New York Times*, February 25, 2006, http://www.nytimes.com/2006/02/ 25/business/25rimm.html (accessed September 11, 2008).

73. Tom Krazit, "Patent Office weakens NTP's Blackberry patent case," *TechWorld*, June 24, 2005, http://www.techworld.com/mobility/news/ index.cfm?newsid=3913 (accessed September 19, 2008).

74. Antone Gonsalves, Elena Malykhina, and Chris Murphy, "RIM NTP Reach $612.5 Million Settlement," *InformationWeek*, March 3, 2006, http://www. informationweek.com/news/mobility/business/showArticle.jhtml?articleID =181500890 (accessed September 11, 2008).

75. *March Networks Corporation, Annual Information Form*, April 23, 2007.

Chapter 5 Act

1. Kathy Rebello, "Inside Microsoft (Part 2)," *BusinessWeek*, July 15, 1996.

2. John Kettice, "Analysis: How Bill Gates discovered the Web," The Register, December 6, 1998, http://www.theregister.co.uk/1998/12/06/ analysis_how_bill_gates_discovered/(accessed September 18, 2008).

3. David Galula, *Counterinsurgency Warfare: Theory and Practice* (Westport, CT: Praeger Security Int'l, 1964) xi.

4. http://www.bp.com/home.do?categoryId=1 (accessed May 1, 2007).

5. Stephen M. Pinkos, "Does China Enact Barriers to Fair Trade?" Committee on Small Business of the House of Representatives (Washington, DC) May 26, 2005, http://www.uspto.gov/smallbusiness/pdfs/USPTOTestimony-Committee_on_Small_Business.pdf (accessed August 13, 2008).

6. "China Dealt With 18,973 Cases of Trademark Infringement in 1st half," *China Industry and Commerce News*, August, 16, 2007, http://English.ipr.gov. cn/ipr/en/info/Article.jsp?a_no=107003&col_no=925&dir=200708 (accessed August 13, 2008).

7. Charles Pillar, "How Piracy Opens Doors for Windows," *Los Angeles Times*, April 9, 2006.

8. Ibid.

9. "Patent Applications Handled by SIPO in the First Half of This Year Increase 30 Percent Year on Year," State Intellectual Property Office of China, July 17, 2008, http://www.sipo.gov.cn/sipo_English/news/official/ 200807/t20080716_411698.htm (accessed August 14, 2008).

10. Grant T. Hammond, *The Mind of War: John Boyd and American Security* (Washington: Smithsonian Institute Press, 2001), 190.

11. Paul Solman and Kim Perry, "Intellectual Property Rights Violations in China," Online NewsHour, October 13, 2005, http://www.pbs.org/ newshour/bb/asia/july-dec05/china_10-13.html (accessed August 14, 2008).

12. Willow Christie, "IBM Contributes 500 U.S. Patents to Open Source in Support of Innovation and Open Standards," January 11, 2005, http:// www-03.ibm.com/press/us/en/pressrelease/7473.wss (accessed August 14, 2008).

13. Irell & Manella LLP, "Trial Team Secures $74 Million Patent Infringe-ment Verdict for DVR Market Leader TiVo," April 20, 2006, http:// www.irell.com/news-1.html (accessed August 14, 2008).

14. Thomas Hawk, "Breaking News: Appeals Court Refuses to Hear Echostar Appeal, TiVo's Patent Victory Stands," Thomas Hawk's Digital Connection, April 11, 2008, http://thomashawk.com/2008/04/breaking-news-appeals-court-refuses-to.html (accessed August 14, 2008).

15. Ibid.

16. http://www.answers.com/topic/rohm-and-haas-company (accessed Sep-tember 30, 2008).

17. Tom Krazit, "Apple settles with Creative for $100 million," CNET News.com, August 23, 2006, http://news.cnet.com/Apple-settles-with-creative-for-100-million/2100-1047_3-6108901.html (accessed August 14, 2008).

18. John Terninko, Alla Zusman, Boris Zlotin, *Systematic Innovation: An Introduc-tion to TRIZ (Theory of Inventive Problem Solving) (APICS Series on Resource Management)*, (Boca Raton: CRC Press) 24-26.

19. Lewis Carroll, *Through the Looking Glass* (London: Macmillan, 1866).

20. *Talladega Nights—The Ballad of Ricky Bobby*, DVD, directed by Adam McKay (Columbia Pictures, 2006).

21. DPhoto Journal, "Konica Minolta Withdraw from Camera & Photo Business," January 19, 2006, http://www.dphotojournal.com/

konica-minolta-withdraw-from-camera-photo-business/(accessed July 29, 2008).

22. Hammond, 160.

23. Robert Coram, *Boyd: The Fighter Pilot Who Changed the Art of War* (Little, Brown and Co.: 2002) 221–313.

24. Sheila Ronis, "Hyperintelligence: Toyota, CIA, NSA, KGB, Mossad and... Sun Tzu," eMotion! Reports.com, July 23, 2002, http://www.emotionreports.com/Hyperintelligence/hyperintelligence.htm (accessed August 14, 2008). The author's personal discussions in Japan provide a second source.

25. Sonshi.com, "Interview with Chet Richards," http://sonshi.com/richards.html (accessed May 29, 2008).

26. Keith Bradsher, "A Nation Challenged: The Treatment; Bayer Halves Price for Cipro, But Rivals Offer Drugs Free," *New York Times*, October 26, 2001, http://query.nytimes.com/gst/fullpage.html?res=9C03EEDB1031F935A15753C1A9679C8B63 (accessed August 14, 2008).

27. *Shaka Zulu— The Complete 10 Part Television Epic*, DVD, directed by William C. Faure (A&E Home Video, 1986).

Chapter 7 Two Imperatives

1. Lévêque and Ménière, "Patents and Innovation: Friends or Foes?"

2. Wikipedia, s.v. "Vince Lombardi."

3. Randy Brown, "How Michael Jordan Killed the Game," NBAce.com: 2005–2008) http://www.nbace.com/2007/03/21/how-michael-jordan-killed-the-game/(accessed September 29, 2008).

Chapter 8 High-Tempo Patent Strategy

1. George S. Patton, Jr., *War As I Knew It* (Boston: Houghton Mifflin Co., 1947).

Chapter 9 Conclusion

1. quotesandpoem.com, http://www.quotesandpoem.com/quotes/listquotes/author/ernest-hemingway (accessed September 19, 2008).

Appendix IP Strategy Boarding and Scenario Play

1. Wikipedia.org, s.v. "Vince Lombardi," http://en.wikipedia.org/wiki/Vince_Lombardi (accessed August 12, 2008). *Note*: One of many sources for information about Vince Lombardi.

2. Wikiquote.org, s.v. "Alexander Suvorov," http://en.wikiquote.org/wiki/Alexander_Vasilyevich_Suvorov (accessed September 30, 2008).

Index

control of technical space, measuring,
     295–301
invention/patent infiltration, 303, 304
Betamax, 117, 118
Bezos, Jeff, 145, 146
Biotechnology and life sciences industry,
     22, 23, 131, 132, 226
Blockbuster patents, 216, 217, 221–228,
     231
Blu-Ray, 13
BMW, 83, 173
Boeing, 20, 25, 159
Bolt the Door Behind the Thief, 312
Bonaparte, Napoleon, 25
Borders, 144–147
BountyQuest.com, 145, 146
Boyd, John, Col., 248, 262–264, 305,
     306
Brainstorming, 279
Brands and branding, 180, 181, 187,
     197–200
British Petroleum, 137, 138, 244
Business Software Alliance, 246
Business strategy and patent strategy, 4

Campbell, Joseph, 61
Canon, 115, 119, 137, 261, 262, 267
Casio, 154
Catch Your Adversary Sleeping, 116
Centers of Excellence
     advancement, 85–88, 166–175
     assess phase of decision cycle, 51,
          84–90, 103
     cooperation and conflict among,
          285
     Federal Express example, 88–90
     innovation, 85–87, 142–165
     leveraging, 106, 141–228, 230
     and need for mastering fundamentals,
          289
     parallel lines of competition, 51, 52,
          90–95, 103, 231
     security, 85–88, 175–228

Change
     equilibrium and disequilibrium,
          106, 131–134, 136, 140, 230, 260
     keeping up with, 68, 147–150, 260,
          265
     and strategy, 25–27, 68
Cheating and illegal activity. See also
          Counterfeiting; Piracy
     counterfeiters and spies, 30, 68, 69
     as method of winning, 30, 31
Chemical industry, 43, 115, 217,
          226
Chess as game of strategy, 127
Chief executive officer (CEO)
     Microsoft example, 287
     patents and patent strategy, importance
          of understanding, 286, 287
     role and responsibilities of,
          283–288
Chief innovation officer (CIO),
          287
Chief intellectual property officer
          (CIPO), 284, 287
China, 245–248
Christensen, Clayton, 14, 136,
          152
Chrysler, 151, 264
Chunghwa Picture Tubes (CPT),
          19
Churchill, Winston S., 72
Cipro, 269, 270
Cisco Systems, 224
Clark, James, 239
Coca-Cola, 95
Commerce One, 141
Competition, generally
     benefits of, 101
     role of, 131, 133
Competitive advantage and patent
          strategy, 1, 2, 261
Competitive equilibrium, 131–141, 230,
          260
Competitive intelligence, 240, 305